SOUTH ASIAN
POLITICAL SYSTEMS

General Editor
RICHARD L. PARK

*The Politics of Nepal: Persistence and
Change in an Asian Monarchy*
by Leo E. Rose *and* Margaret W. Fisher

*The Politics of Pakistan:
A Constitutional Quest*
by Richard S. Wheeler

The Politics of Afghanistan
by Richard S. Newell

*The Politics of Ceylon
(Sri Lanka)*
by Robert N. Kearney

The Politics of Bhutan
by Leo E. Rose

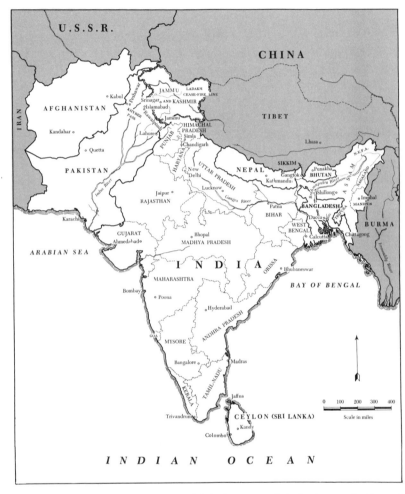

SOUTH ASIA (Jammu and Kashmir areas in dispute)

The Politics of
Bhutan

LEO E. ROSE

Cornell University Press
ITHACA AND LONDON

First published 1977 by Cornell University Press.
Published in the United Kingdom by Cornell University Press Ltd., 2–4 Brook Street, London W1Y 1AA.

International Standard Book Number 0-8014-0909-8
Library of Congress Catalog Card Number 77-4792
Printed in the United States of America by Vail-Ballou Press, Inc.
Librarians: Library of Congress cataloging information appears on the last page of the book.

Foreword

Serious study of modern South Asia is a relatively recent development in the United States. It began shortly after World War II, and was made possible by opportunities for language study and research in the region. Scholarly work on current South Asian themes, however, rests upon older academic traditions that emphasized principally the philosophy, religion, and classical literature of these ancient civilizations. This series, "South Asian Political Systems," is addressed to contemporary political problems, but is presented in the context of institutions and value systems that were centuries in the making.

Over the past quarter century, humanists and social scientists in Asia, Europe, the United States, and elsewhere throughout the world have worked together to study modern South Asian cultures. Their efforts have been encouraged by a recognition of the importance of the rapid rise of nationalism in Asia in the twentieth century, by the decline, hastened by the war, of Western imperial systems, and by the appearance of dozens of independent states since the founding of the United Nations. Scholars were made increasingly aware that the South Asian peoples were not anonymous masses or abstract representatives of distant traditions. They were, like us, concerned with their own political affairs, with raising families, building houses, constructing industries, educating the young, and creating better societies. They were nourished by their heritage, but they also struggled to devise political institutions, economic processes, and social organizations that were responsive to modern needs. And their needs were, and continue to be, great.

It was an awareness of these realities that encouraged private foundations and agencies of government to sponsor intensive field work in South Asia, including firsthand observation of day-to-day life and opportunities to discover and use rare source material. India has received the most attention, in part because of its size and intrinsic importance, in part because scholars have concentrated on teaching Indian languages, and research tends to be done where the languages are understood. More and more the other countries of South Asia—Pakistan, Nepal, Sri Lanka, Bhutan, Afghanistan, and Bangladesh—have begun to attract scholarly attention. Whereas in the late 1940s one was hard pressed to find literature about the region, except in journalistic accounts or in British imperial histories, in the 1970s competent monographs and reliable periodicals are abundantly available. Today one can draw from an impressive bibliography on South Asia, including a commendable list of political works.

It remains true, however, that recent South Asian studies have been largely monographic—books that examine narrow themes in detail and that appeal to a small group of specialists who happen to be concerned with these themes. There are few broad guides to the politics of the countries of South Asia. This series has been designed to fill part of the need.

One of the problems in writing introductory works is that learning about a foreign culture is never a simple process. Experience tells us that each political system is imbedded in a broader social system, which in turn has roots in a particular history and a unique set of values. Language transmits culture, so one way to approach an unfamiliar culture is through the close study of language and literature. Knowledge of history, or of the arts, or of social organization offers another path to understanding.

The focus of this series is on political systems. Each author uses a common organizational framework—brief history, political dynamics, political structure, continuing problems—and weaves in unique factors. For Pakistan, Islamic issues, as well as political and cultural integration, are paramount. The political problems of Sri Lanka intertwine with ethnic, religious, and economic conditions. Bhutan, Nepal, and Afghanistan (which is ruled by a member of the old royal family) represent, in differing ways, monarchical traditions in conflict with pressures to modernize, thus suggesting treatments that give special attention to history. For contemporary evidence in these countries, the authors must rely heavily on interviews with highly placed officials. Used together, the books should provide excellent opportunities for comparison and contrast.

Leo E. Rose of the University of California at Berkeley is a leading scholar on the politics of the Himalayan region and of South Asia generally. He was coauthor with Margaret W. Fisher of the volume in this series on Nepal, and is editor of *Asian Survey.*

His research in the region started in 1956. He has returned regularly ever since and has made several visits to Bhutan since 1972. The royal family and high government officials of Bhutan have granted Professor Rose exceptional access to both interpretations and documentation of this Himalayan country's public life. Although the author's primary interests are addressed to the politics of Bhutan, his inclinations are also historical and humanistic. Very little substantiated scholarly writing on contemporary Bhutan exists. This book presents for the first time an introduction by a field-experienced author to the political culture of a country little known to the outside world.

RICHARD L. PARK

Ann Arbor, Michigan

Preface

My interest in the Buddhist kingdom of Bhutan had been aroused long before 1972, when I was granted permission by the Royal Government to undertake the research program of which this volume is the product. There were several aspects of Bhutan that I considered intriguing and worthy of investigation. It is, for instance, the only surviving Mahayana Buddhist monarchy now that Sikkim has been formally merged into India, and the subtle accommodation of a new and modernizing monarchical polity with the theocratic political culture usually associated with Mahayana Buddhism provides a unique case for examining the relationship between "modernization" and "traditionalism." Until recently, Bhutan had been more successful than other Asian states in isolating itself from modernizing forces—whether Western, Communist, or indigenous Asian in origin. Thus, it is possible in Bhutan to consider the introduction of extraneous and very alien influences into a functioning, viable, and assertively independent political system virtually from the beginning rather than in midstream, as has been the case for most other Asian states.

Geopolitical factors were also of interest, given Bhutan's very vulnerable location between the two antagonistic Asian giants—China and India. On an earlier occasion I had studied the strategies and tactics used by the Hindu Himalayan kingdom of Nepal, a country with pervasive cultural, economic, and political ties to the south, as it struggled to maintain some degree of autonomy in decision-making. In Bhutan, I found the opportunity to do a similar study in a Buddhist society in which the traditional ties, at least until 1960, had been to the north, with Chinese-controlled Tibet. Thus some basis was provided for a comparative analysis of the relative importance of cultural and geopolitical influences on the foreign policies of small buffer states.

Bhutan offers a series of intellectual and pragmatic challenges to anyone interested in social science research, but it poses unusual problems for the researcher. My own work in Bhutan, for instance, was undertaken on the assumption that there might be a significant body of data, published and archival, available somewhere that would provide the empirical basis for a study of contemporary government and politics. While I knew that the existing body of literature on Bhutan in Western languages had not utilized such resources, I believed that such data might exist, particularly since my earlier research in Nepal and Sikkim under similar conditions had uncovered extensive archival and government record collections that had never been used.

My assumption that this would also prove to be the case in Bhutan turned out to be incorrect. There are government records, of course, but these are scarcely adequate for the task I had set for myself. Moreover, the Bhutan authorities have not yet adopted the policy followed in most other countries under which the public is allowed access to public documents after a stipulated time period (for example, after thirty years in India or after twenty years in the United States). Thus, I was able to use the meager record files only on a very selective basis. Bhutan also lacks such published sources as official gazettes, newspapers, and periodicals, which are essential to research because they detail the course of developments and provide some insight into the motives and concepts underlying particular policies and events. The only periodical in Bhutan, the semiofficial *Kuensel,* commenced publication in 1967 and still covers only a few developments. The larger north Indian newspaper may have a correspondent assigned to cover news on Bhutan, but he is not resident in the country, and his infrequent reports on Bhutan are seldom published. There are occasional publications by government departments, but these usually constitute statements of intention rather than substantive reports on operations, achievements, and failures. Bhutan, thus, is about as "data-free" as it is possible for a polity over three hundred years old to be, and lacks the minimal research resources that are standard in even the most backward former colonial societies in Asia and Africa.

This is not meant to be an apology, for I benefited from my experience in Bhutan and found it both challenging and rewarding. Bhutan does, however, pose a novel methodological problem, one for which the usual models adopted by research scholars in the social sciences seemed singularly inappropriate. My work depended almost totally upon personal interviews, not only for interpretations of developments, but even for the most basic facts. Since Bhutan has no nonofficial educated elite of any size or significance, interviews usually were with the government officials who were responsible for the programs and policies under discussion and who were understandably reluctant to elaborate on these subjects any more than necessary. Bhutan stands in striking contrast to all other South Asian societies, in which political gossip (a vital resource for research scholars) is the favorite pastime of virtually everyone. This propensity for extreme discretion in all political discussions in Bhutan was somewhat frustrating for research, but it was rather refreshing otherwise.

The analyses and hypotheses presented here concerning the governmental and political system in Bhutan are highly impressionistic and should be judged accordingly. The most I can claim is that this volume is an introduction to Bhutanese politics, raising several questions for further research but providing at best only tentative answers.

The late King, Druk Gyalpo Jigme Dorji Wangchuck, initially provided me with the opportunity to undertake the research for this book. Unfortunately, he died before my first field trip to Bhutan in the fall of 1972, and I was not able to discuss personally with this remarkable ruler the innovative political and economic development programs introduced during his

twenty-year reign. His successor, Druk Gyalpo Jigme Singye
Wangchuck, adopted an equally positive attitude toward my
work, giving approval for my trips to Bhutan in 1972, 1973,
1974, and 1975, authorizing officials in the Royal Government
to extend their cooperation to the project, and granting me au-
diences in which the political process in Bhutan was discussed
frankly and objectively. Queen Mother H.M. Ashi Kesang
Wangchuck also showed a continuing interest in the research
by commenting at length on various themes that emerged and
by discussing developments in such ways as to help clarify the
complexity of modern Bhutanese political history.

The assistance extended by most high-level government officials was, of course, essential. Their willingness to respond as
frankly and fully as their official positions permitted to a wide
variety of sensitive questions was invaluable. This list is by no
means exhaustive, but I would like to express my appreciation
to the following officials: Home Minister Lyonpo T. Jagar; Finance Minister Lyonpo Chogyal; Foreign Minister Lyonpo
Dawa Tsering; Secretary-General of Development Dr. T.
Tobgyal; Development Secretary Dasho Lam Penjore; the
Commander of the Royal Bhutan Army, Colonel Lam Dorji;
Trade, Industry, and Forestry Secretary Om Pradhan; the Sec-
retary to the King and, until 1975, the Speaker of the National
Assembly, Dasho Shingkar Lam; High Court Justice Paljor
Dorji; royal advisers Dasho Jung Bahadur Chhetri and Dasho
Tsewang Penjor; Bhutan's ambassador to India Lyonpo Sangye
Penjor; Bhutan's ambassador to the United Nations Dago
Tshering; the director of the Bhutan National Library Lopon
Pemala; Lopon Nadu; the four Lopons of the Central Monk
Body in Thimphu/Punakha; and Michael Aris.

The Bhutanese are a most hospitable people who went out of
their way to make a foreign guest feel at home. I would particularly like to extend my thanks to Dophu Tsering, the protocol
officer in the Foreign Affairs Ministry in Thimphu, as well as to
other staff members in the ministry; to Mynak Trulku Rim-
poche, the director of the Bhutan National Museum at Ta
Dzong in Paro; to Lakpa Tsering, the executive engineer in

Phuntsholing, and his wife, Pem Tsering; to Dorji Norbu, the executive engineer in Thimphu; to Tsering Wangdi, the first secretary in Bhutan's mission to the UN; and to Lhendup Dorji.

The cooperation of the Government of India in granting the "Inner Line Permits" required for entry into Bhutan from India and of Indian officials with experience in Bhutan was also important and was generally forthcoming despite the strains in Indo-American relations in the 1970s and the negative attitude assumed by some Indians toward foreign (and particularly American) research in sensitive areas. In this respect, I wish to express my appreciation to Kewal Singh, the former foreign secretary (now ambassador to the United States) in the Ministry of External Affairs, and also to A. K. Gokhale and I. P. Khosla, the two Indian representatives in Bhutan at different periods of my research program; Shankar Bajpai, the Indian political officer in Sikkim until 1974; D. S. Sonam, the Indian adviser to the Bhutan police; and G. N. Mehra, the Indian adviser on economic affairs to the Royal Government of Bhutan. Several Indian scholars and officials who have made significant contributions to the literature on Bhutan are also personal friends whose advice and comments were very helpful to the author. In particular I would like to mention Ram Rahul of the School of International Studies, Jawaharlal Nehru University, New Delhi, India's most learned scholar on the Himalayan region, as well as Nari Rustomji, the chief secretary to the Meghalaya State Government, who has also had extensive experience in Bhutan, Sikkim, and the North-East Frontier Agency (now Arunachal).

Support for my work in Bhutan was obtained from several sources. In 1972 I received a grant from the Center for South/Southeast Asian Studies at the University of California, Berkeley; in 1973 and 1974 I was the recipient of personal grants from the Ford Foundation; and in 1974 and 1975 the Institute of International Studies at the University of California, Berkeley, extended supplementary grants in support of this research. Needless to say, none of the people or organizations mentioned above is responsible for my analysis, comments, and speculation.

LEO E. ROSE

Berkeley, California

Contents

Maps

Tables

Chart

The Politics of Bhutan

1. Historical and Social Heritage

The Himalayan region, dominated by the world's highest mountain ranges and intersected by several of the world's largest river systems, has for nearly two millennia constituted a transitional area between South and Central Asia. The western section from Kashmir to Nepal has long been an intermediate zone in which South and Central Asian cultural and intellectual influences interacted, with the former clearly dominant in most critical respects. The eastern Himalayas, in contrast, were better insulated from political and cultural influences from the south. This allowed the development of Mahayana Buddhist political systems in Bhutan and Sikkim, and enabled them to retain their traditional character intact long after Buddhism had disappeared as a significant force in the plains area to the south. In the twentieth century Sikkim has fallen prey to Indo-Aryan influences, first from a swarm of Hindu Nepali migrants who entered the country in the wake of the extension of British Indian administrative control after 1890, and more recently by its absorption into the Indian Union. Bhutan, however, has so far avoided Sikkim's fate, and thus still constitutes a distinctive cultural and political element in the Himalayas.

There are several reasons why Bhutan has been able to retain its cultural identity while neighboring areas to the south and the north have been undergoing profound and fundamental change. In the historical context, the remarkable degree of diversity and heterogeneity that has characterized the societies of South Asia and the essential tolerance of Hinduism to cultural diversity were of considerable importance. This goes a long way toward explaining why the Buddhist social and politi-

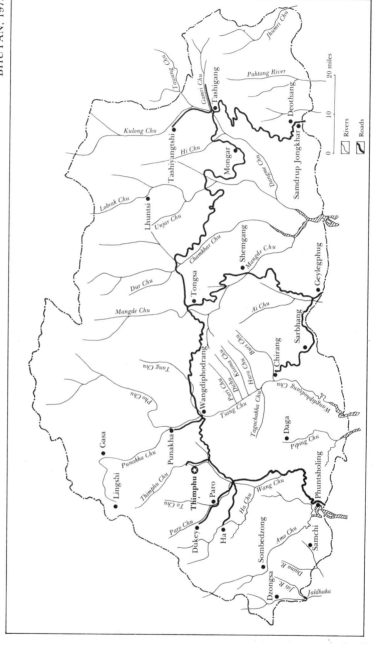

Rivers

Roads

0   10   20 miles

cal system of Bhutan was able to coexist over a long period with the vigorous Hindu culture to the south. But geopolitical factors have also been kind to Bhutan. For one thing, the country's primary and easiest lines of communication were, until recently at least, to the north across the Himalayas with Buddhist Tibet. In and of itself this might not have preserved Bhutan's insulation from the dominant influences to the south if there had not also been more convenient alternative channels of communication between the plains of India and the Central Asian highlands. Thus, neither economic nor strategic considerations made the absorption of Bhutan a compelling necessity for the various powers that have controlled eastern India in the course of the last thousand years. In the first decade of the twentieth century British India gave serious consideration to opening a road to Tibet through Bhutan, and eventually extracted a concession on this matter from a very reluctant Bhutanese government. But the British finally opted for the politically more reliable route through Sikkim, and Bhutan was able to maintain itself in splendid isolation for another half century.

Physical features have also been of importance to Bhutan, whose contemporary borders are well-defined—although not through treaties in all sections. To the south, Bhutan's boundaries with the Indian states of West Bengal and Assam coincide with the point where the foothills meet the plains. To both the east and the west. Bhutan is separated from the Indian hill districts and from Sikkim by rugged mountain ranges. All these borders, except that with Sikkim, have been delimited in international agreements and demarcated on the ground where necessary.

To the northwest, a north-south transverse ridge (the Chomolhari range) forms the border between Bhutan and the Chumbi valley in Tibet, joining the great Himalayan range at Chomolhari peak (23,997 ft.). To the north, the Himalayas separate Bhutan from Tibet. While the range is not quite as high in this sector as it is further to the west, it still constitutes a most imposing barrier, averaging 16,000 to 20,000 feet in height. Thus access into Bhutan from all directions is difficult. The various river systems that cut through the country in a north-south direction are so wild and, in the rainy season, so over-flowing that routes into central Bhutan along the bottom of the deep gorges are not feasible. Roads from the south, therefore, must climb the steep foothills in southern Bhutan by means of numerous hairpin curves and then follow cliff-hanging routes on the transverse ridges that parallel these river valleys. There is one reasonably good pass from Darjeeling district, but this route has not been of much economic or strategic significance since the cession of the Kalimpong area to British India in 1865. On the eastern border, a number of passessconnect Bhutan with Towang and Bomdila subdistricts in Arunachal Pradesh (formerly the North-East Frontier Agency) in India. These are of some importance to local trade but have never ben developed as major channels of communication.

There are several passesson Bhutan's border with Tibet, but only three of any significance. The most important historically are the routes from the Paro and Ha valleys in western Bhutan into the Chumbi valley in Tibet, and the more difficult route across the Lingshi pass that leads down to Punakha, formerly the winter capital of Bhutan and the political center of the country. In eastern Bhutan, the pass that crosses the Himalayas in the vicinity of the Manas river is of great strategic importance since it is usually snow-free during the winter months—which is not the case for other passes in the eastern Himalayas.

A number of transverse north-south ranges run through Bhutan, the most important of which is the Black Mountain range—the traditional dividing line between western and eastern Bhutan. There are also several major river systems in the country, including the Amo Chu (Torsa), Wang Chu (Raidak), Mo Chu (Sankosh), Tongsa Chu, Bumthang, and Dangme Chu (Manas). In the more gently sloping central highland region, some of these rivers have formed fairly broad valleys (4,000 to 9,000 feet) which are intensely cultivated. In southern Bhutan, in the monsoon season, the rivers become raging torrents that debouch onto the plains of India with such force that they are unsuitable for boat traffic for several miles.

For sheer physical beauty, Bhutan is perhaps unmatched, as

the relatively few visitors to the country have attested. But where once it took weeks of difficult travel on foot, pony, and yakback to traverse the country, this can now be done in comparative comfort and safety on the excellent road system constructed with the assistance of the Indian military. These roads run north into western and central Bhutan from the border towns of Phuntsholing and Geylegphug and into eastern Bhutan from Samdrup Jongkhar. A major east-west road across the Pele pass in the Black Mountain range has also been constructed, connecting Ha in the west to Tashigang in the east, intersected along the way by the various north-south roads. The road system has not been extended into northern Bhutan, however, in view of the chronic Sino-Indian confrontation in the Himalayas and the general Indian policy against constructing roads in the vicinity of Chinese-controlled territory. Nevertheless, the main population centers of Bhutan are now only a few hours' drive from India, making them easily accessible for economic, cultural, and security purposes. Thus, the first stage in the reorientation of Bhutan's perspective on its external environment has been accomplished. What this will mean eventually to Bhutan's traditional religious and political culture is still unclear, but it is bound to have a considerable impact.

The Bhutanese Political System

The history of Bhutan as an integrated political system commences only in the first half of the seventeenth century with the establishment of the authority of Ngawang Namgyal, the first Shabdung (Dharma Raja in most non-Bhutanese sources). The early history of the area now comprising Bhutan is murky at best. Indeed, the name Bhutan itself is Indian in origin and has come into general usage in that country only recently. The traditional name for the country is Drukyul (the country of the Drukpas)—which could not predate the establishment of the Shabdung political system, dominated as it was then by the Drukpa sect of Buddhism.[1]

1. Ram Rahul states that "Lho Mon Kha Shi" (four southern lowlands) is the traditional name for Bhutan; but presumably that is Tibetan and not Bhutanese in origin (*Modern Bhutan* [Delhi, 1971], p. 3).

It has been suggested that this section of the eastern Himalayas formed part of the Kamruppa empire that controlled
most of northeastern India to the south of Bhutan until the
seventh century and that subsequently was incorporated into
the Tibetan empire. This would seem reasonable, given the existing political situation in the region between the seventh and
ninth centuries, but the supporting evidence is very flimsy. Neither the Kamruppa nor the Tibetan historical records are at all
specific on this point, nor is there an oral tradition—much less
reliable documentary or archaeological evidence—supportive
of this hypothesis in Bhutan.

In any case, there can be no doubt that since at least the
tenth century no external power has controlled Bhutan, although there have been periods when various of its neighbors
have been able to exert a strong cultural and/or political influence there. From the evidence now available, it would appear
that there were numerous independent principalities in this
area until the seventeenth century, and that no effective centralized authority existed. Presumably, each of the small, relatively inaccessible river valleys in the Bhutan highlands was
controlled by local elite families or, more frequently in western
Bhutan, by the dominant local Buddhist monastic establishment.

The political history of Bhutan, thus, is closely interlinked
with its religious history. It was monastic Buddhism, an import
from Tibet, that provided the institutional dynamism and
foundation for the eventual unification of the country under
the first Shabdung. Moreover, it was the struggle for religious
dominance among the several Buddhist sects that set the para-
meters of the political system as well.

The first of the important Buddhist sects to make its appearance in Bhutan was the Nyingmapa—the "old sect" in Himalayan Buddhism. The period of its introduction is uncertain. In
Bhutanese oral history, it is traced back to the great sage/saint,
Padma Sambhava (who supposedly resided in Bhutan in the
ninth century). In any case, by the twelfth century there were a
number of Nyingmapa centers in Bhutan that competed for
religious and political authority with other Buddhist sects, as

well as with the descendants of a member of the Lhasa royal family who had fled to Bhutan in the tenth century at the time of the overthrow of the centralized monarchy in Tibet.

In the twelfth century, two Kagyupa subsects in Tibet, the Drukpa Kagyupa and the Lhapa Kagyupa, extended their activity into Bhutan and eventually eclipsed the influence of the Nyingmapa. This was a period of virtual anarchy and bitter religious strife in Tibet during which several prestigious Buddhist lamas fled to Bhutan, probably as political refugees. Most of the elite families in Bhutan in subsequent centuries claim descent from these lamas, each of whom achieved a dominant position in local areas in the western Bhutan highlands and, on a more limited scale, in eastern Bhutan as well. From the fourteenth to the seventeenth century, the political history of Bhutan is largely a reflection of the conflict between these various elite families and also between the fortresslike monastic institutions established by the two Kagyupa sects.

The decisive personality and the protagonist of modern Bhutan was the prominent and widely respected Drukpa lama, Ngawang Namgyal, who first came to Bhutan from Tibet in 1616 and stayed to become its first Shabdung. In Tibet, the Gelugpa sect, headed by the Dalai Lama, had finally managed to establish a precarious control over the province in which Lhasa is located. Ralung, the Drukpa monastery which was the residence of Ngawang Namgyal, was temporarily closed by the Gelugpas, forcing this high Drukpa lama to take refuge in Bhutan. Within a few years, Ngawang Namgyal had established his political and religious authority throughout most of western Bhutan and, by the time of his death in 1652, in parts of eastern Bhutan as well.

The conditions in Bhutan that enabled Ngawang Namgyal to unify what had been a highly decentralized political system are unclear in their specific detail, but a general outline of the process can be surmised. It is obvious, for instance, that these events marked the final triumph of the Drukpa sect over all its rivals—both civil and religious. We can assume that the foundations of this victory had been laid in the preceding decades during which the Drukpa monastic institutions had gained a dominant influence over most of the crucial local areas in western Bhutan. All that was required to make the triumph complete was the appearance of a charismatic religiopolitical leader whose authority would be widely accepted by the Drukpa elite, and Ngawang Namgyal filled this requirement magnificently.

Of further importance, in the first Shabdung's campaign to unify Bhutan was the recurrent warfare between the Bhutanese and the Tibetans. For the first time in several centuries, Bhutan had to contend with external aggression. Several times in the first half of the seventeenth century, Tibetan forces invaded western Bhutan, but in each instance they were decisively defeated. The obvious need for a unified response to the Tibetan threat, and the leading role played by Ngawang Namgyal in organizing the resistance, must have contributed significantly to his eventual triumph over both external foes and internal rivals. It was under these conditions that several vital fortified posts—Simtoka in 1630, Wangdiphodrang in 1638, and Tashichhodzong in 1641—were constructed, providing the Drukpa sect with strong religiopolitical centers in western and central Bhutan.

The political system founded by Shabdung Ngawang Namgyal bore a strong resemblance in certain critical respects to the political system headed by the Dalai Lama which emerged in Tibet at approximately the same time. This is not surprising, of course, given the dominant influence of similar religious establishments in both countries in this period. A theocratic political system in which succession to the highest religiopolitical post was determined through the reincarnation process was a predominant feature in both Bhutan and Tibet. Some decades after the death of Ngawang Namgyal in 1652, three trulkus (reincarnations) of the first Shabdung were found—the Ku (body), the Sung (speech), and the Thu (mind) incarnations.

By the mid-eighteenth century the Ku trulku had died out,[2]

2. During his mission to Bhutan in 1773, George Bogle noted that the Ku avatar of the first Shabdung had died twelve years earlier, and that no successor had been found (Clement R. Markham, *Mission of George Bogle to Tibet* [London, 1879], p. 192).

but the Thu and the Sung incarnations continued to reappear into the twentieth century. The traditional practice was to recognize the Thu trulku as the Shabdung,[3] and the seven Shabdungs who held power one after another were all of this incarnation. The system did not always follow the prescribed rules, however. There were occasions in Bhutanese history during which the existence of more than one claimant to the Thu incarnation proved to be a disruptive factor in the political system. Even more critical perhaps was the fact that the Shabdung, under the reincarnation process, was a minor for the first eighteen years of his reign, thus making long and often conflict-ridden regencies necessary. Furthermore, once the Shabdung had reached his majority, he usually found it impossible to assert his authority over the religious and civil officials who had governed in his name for so long. There was a temptation, of course, for these officials to make use of the reincarnation process itself to manipulate the system to their own advantage.

The Shabdungs, consequently, rarely exercised effective authority, yet they continued to play a critical role in the Bhutanese political system as the acknowledged spiritual leaders of the country and as the source of legitimation for both secular and temporal officials. This ceased to be the case after 1907 when the Shabdung system was replaced by an hereditary monarchy. The last Thu trulku recognized as such by the Bhutanese authorities died in 1931,[4] and has not reappeared in Bhutan. Although claimants to the Thu incarnation appeared thereafter in Tibet, they were never accepted as authentic in Bhutan.

The Sung trulku at the time of the establishment of the hereditary monarchy in 1907 died in 1917. His incarnate appeared thereafter in Bhutan but held an ambiguous position in the Drukpa establishment. The last claimant to the Sung trulku

3. "Reports of Ashley Eden," in *Political Missions to Bootan* (Calcutta, 1865), pp. 114–115.
4. According to one Drukpa source, the Thu trulku's brother (who had been to India), sought to contest the accession of Jigme Wangchuck to the throne in 1926. The Shabdung was then "retired" to Talu monastery. His death a few years later, according to rumors, was not by natural causes.

status who resided in Bhutan died in the late 1940s. A nephew, claiming to be his reincarnate, lived for some time near the prestigious Gelugpa monastery at Towang [5] in the Indian district bordering on Bhutan in the east, but was never recognized as such in Bhutan. Thus, both the Thu and Sung reincarnations of the first Shabdung have disappeared in Bhutan, at least for the time being. Under the reincarnation system, however, trulkus can always be rediscovered long after the death of the last manifestation, so it should not be assumed that claimants to the Shabdung status have necessarily disappeared permanently in Bhutan. The existence of claimants to both incarnations, living beyond the borders of Bhutan yet susceptible to exploitation by either domestic dissident forces or external powers, has been a matter of continuing concern to the Bhutanese authorities. The reincarnation principle, in the words of one observer, "is still deeply engrained in Bhutanese culture."

Civil and Religious Officials. The administrative structure in Bhutan was until recently largely the work of the first Shabdung. Toward the end of his reign in the mid-seventeenth century, Ngawang Namgyal appointed two of his followers, both Drukpa lamas from Ralung monastery who had accompanied him to Bhutan, as his chief assistants in the religious and civil administration. The first was made Je Khempo (Lord Abbot) and was entrusted with the supervision of the religious establishment throughout Bhutan. By tradition, the Je Khempo also served as regent during the long minorities of the Shabdung, a position of considerable political importance, at least potentially, since it held ultimate authority for approving the appointment of both civil and religious officials during such periods.

5. This claimant to the Sung status resided at Towang monastery until the Sino-Indian border war in late 1962 forced his evacuation. A high Indian official was sent to Towang to effect his rescue at the very last minute, as the Indian government did not want an incarnation of the Shabdung to fall into Chinese hands. Since then, he has lived in Indian territory in the western Himalayas, some distance from Bhutan, but still available if needed. While the Indian authorities have never extended any form of official recognition to the claims of the Sung trulku, they are certainly aware of his potential usefulness in any political crisis in Bhutan that might involve the present royal dynasty.

After the establishment of the hereditary monarchy in 1907, the Je Khempo was retained as the head of the Buddhist establishment. Today the Je Khempo is the only official in Bhutan other than the Druk Gyalpo (King) entitled to wear the saffron-colored scarf, a symbol of the former's spiritual authority and the latter's temporal authority,[6] and an indication of the importance of the office.

The second companion of Shabdung Ngawang Namgyal was placed in charge of the civil administration in 1651 with the title of Druk Desi (or Deb Raja as he is usually designated in Western-language sources). Thereafter, the Shabdungs were deliberately kept isolated from temporal affairs even after they had reached their majority. It became the practice for the Druk Desi to run the administration under the Shabdung's ultimate, but usually nominal, sovereignty, thus gaining for himself the same status in the temporal sphere that the Je Khempo held over religious affairs.

For some time after the appointment of the first Druk Desi, this position was held by monks. Laymen and monks later shared the post, with the appointment of a layman becoming the more common occurrence. By the nineteenth century, the Druk Desi was usually a lay official,[7] and even when a monk held this office he was more often than not a pawn of one of the more powerful civil officials in the country rather than a representative of the religious establishment.

This careful division of authority did not succeed in deterring rivalry between the Shabdung and the Druk Desi or, as was more typical in the eighteenth and nineteenth centuries, between the lay and religious officials upon whom they de-

6. The color of the scarf worn by all Bhutanese officials provides an easy guide to their status and rank. The king and Je Khempo wear saffron scarfs, ministers orange scarfs, people's representatives blue scarfs, high civil and religious officials and High Court judges red scarfs, lower officials white scarfs, and village headmen red and white scarfs.

7. According to an early nineteenth century source, the Druk Desi was selected from the ranks of the Pönlops, Zimpöns, and Dzongpöns (all usually lay officials by this time) who composed the State Council. If the Council could not agree upon one of their own number, they would then try to find a suitable candidate among the leading monastic officials ("Account of Babu Kishen Kant Bose," in *Political Missions to Bootan*, p. 146).

pended for support. George Bogle, who headed a British mission to Bhutan in 1773, reported on an almost classic case of civil strife. The family of the Shabdung, who was then a young boy, had raised a rebellion against the ruling Druk Desi with the support of a number of provincial and local officials. The Druk Desi fled to Tibet, and a close follower of the Shabdung's family was appointed in his place. The Panchen Lama in Tibet, who continued to recognize the former Druk Desi, countered these maneuvers by recognizing another young boy as the "true" Thu trulku of Ngawang Namgyal and thus the rightful claimant to the office of the Shabdung. This countermove failed, however, when the rebellion in Bhutan that followed was suppressed and both the Shabdung and the newly appointed Druk Desi managed to retain their positions.

The term of office of the Druk Desi, traditionally, was three years. A glance at a list of Druk Desis and their years in office, however, demonstrates that a majority of the fifty-five holders of this office between 1651 and 1907 did not last out a full term, while several of the more powerful or strongly supported served successive terms. In the nineteenth century, few of the Druk Desis lasted the full three years, indicative of the extensive civil strife and decentralization of political authority that characterized that period in Bhutan.

There would also appear to have been a change in the system of selecting the Druk Desi. In 1773, at the time of Bogle's visit to Bhutan, a council consisting of high monastic officials was given the authority to select the Druk Desi. But later British visitors (Pemberton, 1839; Eden, 1865) reported that the State Council (Lhungye Tsok) elected the Druk Desi and assisted him in the governance of the country. The Council at that time was composed largely of civil officials, including the Dzongpöns (district officers) of the three main military posts at Punakha, Thimphu, and Wangdiphodrang, the Pönlops (governors) of Paro, Daga, and Tongsa provinces, the Zimpöns (chamberlains) of the Shabdung and the Druk Desi, and the Shung Kalön (chief minister).

The secularization of the administrative apparatus was thus far advanced by the nineteenth century and apparently oc-

had come to institutionalize his family's political authority by abolishing the Shabdung system and establishing an hereditary monarchy. The British, who were interested in encouraging political stability in the buffer areas between India and Tibet, raised no objections and, indeed, appear to have encouraged the Tongsa Pönlop's ambitions. On December 17, 1907, Ugyen Wangchuck was unanimously acclaimed by most of the important civil and monastic officials as the first Druk Gyalpo of Bhutan. Subsequently, he was succeeded on the throne by his son, Jigme Wangchuck, in August 1926; by Jigme Dorji Wangchuck in March 1952; and by Jigme Singye Wangchuck in July 1972.

Kazi Ugyen Dorji had been associated with Ugyen Wangchuck since about 1890, when the two men had first met and discovered that they were related to each other through their respective paternal grandfathers.[13] They became close friends, and indeed Kazi Dorji soon was the most trusted supporter of the Tongsa Pönlop. In the ensuing years he was assigned broad administrative responsibilities and also served as an influential adviser and consultant on political matters, in particular on relations with British India. In 1898, for instance, the Kazi was given full administrative authority over the whole of southern Bhutan, including the right to settle Nepali immigrants in what was then a virtually uninhabited section of the country. A few years later he was made district officer of Ha district, a strategic area of western Bhutan then under the (nominal) jurisdiction of the Paro Pönlop. Both of these appointments, moreover, were made hereditary in the Dorji family as long as the incumbent served the Bhutan government (that is, the Tongsa Pönlop) "faithfully."

The services rendered by Kazi Dorji to Ugyen Wangchuck during the 1903–1905 Younghusband Expedition that sought to make Tibet a British sphere of influence also further strengthened the ties between the two men. Virtually the entire civil and religious establishment in Bhutan warned the Tongsa

13. For information on the evolving relationship between the Wangchuck and Dorji families and for the translation of various documents in which ranks and powers were conferred upon Kazi Ugyen Dorji I am grateful to Lopon Pemala, the national librarian of the government of Bhutan.

Pönlop of dire consequences if he assisted the British in any way. Kazi Dorji, on the other hand, strongly urged Ugyen Wangchuck to assume the role of a mediator between the British and Tibetans, arguing that any other policy would be identified as unfriendly by the British authorities and could result in the absorption of Bhutan into their Indian empire. Ugyen Wangchuck acted on this advice, with very tangible consequences: both he and Kazu Dorji received titles from the British for their services in Tibet. It was these events that set the stage for the introduction of a monarchical system in Bhutan.

As a further token of his appreciation, the Tongsa Pönlop appointed Kazi Dorji as Gongzim (chief chamberlain) in 1908, the highest post in the Bhutan government at that time. In this instance the Gongzim was not made hereditary within the Dorji family—not explicitly at least—but in the document of conferment Ugyen Wangchuck did express the wish "that from this date your descendants will also be given this rank." And indeed these various titles and positions were held on an hereditary basis thereafter by the Dorji family, with the higher title of Lonchen (prime minister) replacing that of Gongzim in 1958. Following the assassination of Prime Minister Jigme Dorji in 1964, however, the hereditary system was distorted by the appointment of Jigme Dorji's youngest brother, Lhendup, as acting prime minister, rather than his eldest son, causing some dissension within the Dorji family. The following year the hereditary principle was terminated when Lhendup Dorji surrendered all titles and powers on seeking political asylum in Nepal due to the strain in his relationship with the king.

Thus, the close collaboration between the Wangchuck and Dorji family, extending over a 75-year period, was temporarily interrupted in the mid-1960s, with potentially dangerous consequences for the stability of the political system in Bhutan. This familial alliance had provided the foundation for the creation of a stable, centralized monarchical polity after 1907. The disaffection that characterized the relationship between various factions in the two families in the 1965–1972 period, however, did not constitute a total disruption of this familial alliance system. Even while Lhendup Dorji and his sister Tashi were in exile—between 1965 and 1974—the children of the late Prime Minister Jigme Dorji resided in Bhutan, holding government posts and benefiting from lucrative trading commissions. Moreover, the Queen of Bhutan, Ashi Kesang Wangchuck, was a member of the Dorji family (the sister of the late prime minister). Thus the present ruler, Druk Gyalpo Jigme Singye Wangchuck, belongs to both families. In any case, by 1975 there had been a broad reconciliation between the various factions of the Wangchucks and Dorjis, and all members of both families were once again resident in Bhutan. What the future role of the Dorjis will be in Bhutan is still a matter of conjecture, but it is widely assumed that they will play an increasingly influential role (although probably not on the same terms as prior to 1964), either as informal advisers to the young Druk Gyalpo or in high official positions.

With the exception of the novel role created for the Dorji family, the establishment of an hereditary monarchical system does not appear to have resulted in fundamental structural changes in the Bhutan administration during the reign of the first two Wangchuck rulers. As Druk Gyalpos, the Wangchucks introduced a strong centralization trend and carefully moved to concentrate full powers in their own hands. The Shabdung and Druk Desi titles and positions were eventually abolished, but in any case their participation in the governance of the country had long since been reduced to a mere formality. More important was the elimination of the office of Pönlop, except as an honorary title, during the reign of the second Druk Gyalpo. Otherwise, the basic pattern under which Bhutan was divided into Dzongs (district headquarters), administered by Dzongpöns, was retained. At this point, however, it was the Druk Gyalpo rather than the Pönlops who exercised full authority over civil appointments. At the center, the Druk Gyalpo was assisted by a consultative body consisting of the Thimphu and Punakha Dzongpöns, and the Shung Kalön and Shung Drönyer, all of whom were given the title of Lhengyel (minister). But this was an advisory body, which retained little of the power and influence of the old Lhungye Tsok, in either the members' collective or individual capacities.

In *real politik* terms, probably the most important development administratively was the organization of a Palace Secretariat modeled after traditional monastic practices. Young boys, some from poor, nonelite families, were brought into the palace at an early age, trained in a wide variety of tasks and, if they proved competent, were appointed to high posts either in the palace or in the provincial and district administration. This provided the Druk Gyalpo with a cadre of administrators that were both technically competent and politically dependable. It also served to weaken the position of the local elite families that had previously provided most of the recruits for the administration, a custom that had contributed to the further centralization of the Bhutanese political and administrative system.

The third Druk Gyalpo, Jigme Dorji Wangchuck, was the great innovator in Bhutan, and between his accession to the throne in 1952 and his death two decades later, the entire political and administrative system was restructured. A popular assembly and the nucleus of a cabinet system of government was introduced; the administrative machinery was modernized; and an economic development program was inaugurated with specialized economic departments established for the purpose. In twenty years Bhutan was transformed from a society marked by almost total political, economic, and intellectual isolation from the rest of the world to one in which an intensive effort is being made to relate the country to modernization processes introduced in most other developing societies. Not everyone in Bhutan is ecstatic about these changes, of course, but there is a broad consensus that they are inevitable and necessary if Bhutan is to survive.

But the fairly rapid transformation of society now underway in Bhutan has not yet limited the significance of the country's historical and cultural heritage. Most Bhutanese, even the young educated elite, are still the products of a traditional social system with a well-defined set of values and a particularistic world-view. The importance of preserving this heritage if Bhutan is to retain its cultural and national identity is fully accepted by those responsible for introducing and implementing the changes. There is a determination that these innovations will be

fitted into the existing pattern as far as possible and that traumatic and destructive changes should be avoided. Whether this
will prove possible is another matter, but there is no doubt that
the innovative elite in Bhutan is fully aware of the harmful as
well as the beneficial effects of the process called modernization.

Bhutan's Society and Economy
   Any discussion of contemporary Bhutan should commence
with the acknowledgment that virtually no data on its society or
economy of even minimal levels of reliability are available to
the foreign scholar—nor, possibly, to the government of Bhutan. No anthropologist, sociologist, or even a student of Buddhist social institutions has yet been able to undertake the field
work that is essential to an understanding of the cultural and
social values that underlie the interrelationship between the
various ethnic and religious communities in Bhutan. A few
economists have been able to work in Bhutan, but under the
aegis of the Indian aid mission. They have concentrated their
attention upon the various aid programs and only supplemen-
tally upon the Bhutanese economy. Statistics of any kind—
demographic or economic—are most notable by their absence
or, where they do exist, by their vagueness. The few that are
available (other than those detailing the input of Indian economic and technical assistance) would appear to be of doubtful
accuracy, at least according to the appraisal of Bhutanese officials themselves who are only too aware of their inadequacy.
   A beginning has been made to correct this serious deficiency
in a country that has set out on a program of planned economic development. A Statistics Department has been set up,
and the laborious task of collecting reliable and relevant data
has commenced. But if the experience of other countries is any
guide, it will be at least a decade before sufficient data will be
available to allow even a modest degree of sophistication in
projections on such complex questions as economic- and popu-
lation-growth rates, alternative approaches to the utilization of
national resources, or even the technical and education
requirements of the kingdom. Meanwhile, "planned" develop-

ment will continue on an essentially short-term but pragmatic basis, dependent for the most part on the intimate knowledge most Bhutanese officials have acquired about their people through serving in a variety of posts in various parts of the country.

This latter point deserves further elaboration. At this stage in Bhutan's development the Bhutanese official elite is not yet a separate and distinct element in the population—not yet, that is, detached from the conditions under which the people subsist, nor unsympathetic to their needs and opportunities. No doubt field studies by competent and experienced scholars in the various social sciences would provide some new insights and perhaps even suggest some different approaches to the solution of Bhutan's problems, but the need for such research has not impressed itself on most Bhutanese officials. For a foreigner such as this author, then, it will be quite some time before anything more than an impressionistic, second-hand knowledge of Bhutanese social and economic systems is possible. The few generalizations tentatively offered in this section of the study, therefore, will by necessity provide only a glimpse into the dynamics of a fascinatingly complex and eclectic society.

The Population. Until 1969, when the first census of Bhutan was taken, the estimates of population ranged from 300,000 to 800,000. The 1969 census (which would hardly have been classified as scientific by demographers, conducted as it was on a rather haphazard basis by Bhutanese language teachers and students) gave the total population of Bhutan as 930,614.[14] A breakdown by districts provides figures for the distribution of the population by region and shows that a majority of the

14. The original count placed the population at over one million, a figure which the Bhutan government delightedly announced to the world, but a district-by-district recount of the data indicated that errors had been made and that the correct figure is the one cited in the text. It is not clear, however, whether the many temporary residents of Bhutan, mostly Nepalese working on the roads or on other construction projects, were included in the census. This seems improbable, as presumably only permanent residents of Bhutan were counted, but if the laborers were counted, perhaps the actual population of the country at the time the census was taken did exceed one million.

Table 1. Population by region and district

Region	District *		Population
Eastern Bhutan	Tashigang		234,708
	Mongar		121,252
	Ja		37,816
	Lhuntsi		45,651
	Chotse		46,316
	Shemgang		53,136
		Total:	538,879
Western Bhutan	Wangdzong		61,338
	Dar		16,908
	Pangdzong		21,212
	Gardzong		10,344
	Thimphu		60,027
	Rinpung (Paro)		63,032
	Ha		21,356
		Total:	254,217
Southern Bhutan	Samchi		57,161
	Chirang		80,357
		Total:	137,518
		Grand Total:	930,614

Source: Census Report, 1969, Ministry of Development, Government of Bhutan, Thimphu.

* The list of districts and the spelling of district names in the census does not correspond to the district lists in other official sources of the same period. No explanation for this was provided by officials, but I was assured that the breakdown by region —eastern Bhutan, western Bhutan, southern Bhutan—is accurate.

population (538,879 or approximately 57%) live in eastern Bhutan, that another 254,217 (28%) live in western Bhutan, and that 137,518 (15%) reside in the southern region of the country (see Table 1).

The census report set forth figures for "cultivated areas" and "total number of animals"—which is useful economic data—but it provides no demographic information on such important questions as the population breakdown in terms of ethnic origin, religion, or language of the household. That the bulk of the population is concentrated in the eastern Bhutan hill areas merely confirms available impressionistic accounts which have usually described this region as the most densely populated and central and western Bhutan as underpopulated.

More surprising are the relatively low figures for southern Bhutan, which is separated from mid-montane Bhutan by a 25-mile-wide forest belt. The several duars and the foothills had been described by some casual observers as relatively heavily populated, and one would have expected to find a larger proportion of Bhutan's total population in this area. The inconsistency between the census results and these sources may be due to certain geographic features in southern Bhutan. The foothills generally rise very precipitously from the Indian plains and thus are extremely difficult to cultivate. The several pass areas through which Bhutan's river systems debouch onto the Indian plans, on the other hand, provide more gentle slopes, and the population of southern Bhutan is heavily concentrated in such areas. Since these are the sections of southern Bhutan which the foreign traveler would have seen, an unrealistic basis may have been used for estimating population density for the region as a whole.

Language Structure. The official language of Bhutan is Dzongkha (literally "language of the Dzong"), which is a dialect of Tibetan that has developed certain distinct characteristics of its own over the past few centuries.[15] It is the language of administration, and the *lingua franca* of the country—at least to the extent there is one. It is also the language used (along with Tibetan) within the Drukpa religious establishment, which makes it a medium of communication on a limited but important scale throughout most of the country. Finally, it is the language of the home in western Bhutan, where even the small non-Tibetan communities, such as the Doyas and Lepchas, which reside in this region and have tribal languages of their own, also usually speak Dzongkha.

The linguistic structure in eastern Bhutan, where a number of dialects of non-Tibetan origin are spoken, is far more complex. Dzongkha is generally understood only by those people who live in the vicinity of the Dzong itself; it has been reported that government officials from outside usually require an interpreter to communicate with the people in their area of juris-

15. Spoken Dzongkha is not easily understood by someone who knows Lhasa Tibetan, but the two written languages bear more similarities.

diction. According to an official Bhutanese source, there are eleven different dialects spoken in eastern Bhutan.[16] Most of these, however, fall into two broad linguistic categories—the Bumthang or the Tashigang dialect. In addition, there are three or four dialects that cannot be identified with any other local languages, though it may turn out that these are related to dialects spoken to the eastward in the Assam Himalayas once the basic linguistic research has been completed. But the main point to note here is that not only do eastern Bhutanese have problems in communicating with their fellow-countrymen from other regions but often even with people from neighboring villages.

The Nepali Bhutanese who make up the vast majority of the population in southern Bhutan come from a wide variety of communities in Nepal, most of which have their own language or dialect. In Bhutan, as in Sikkim, however, Nepali has come to be used as the language of the home as well as the medium of communication within this disparate migrant population. By and large, Dzongkha would be known only by those Nepali Bhutanese who hold government posts or who need to communicate with the central authorities on a regular basis. Thus, southern Bhutan is another distinct linguistic region, with no easy medium with which to communicate with Bhutanese from other areas of the country.

The Bhutan government would not seem to have any well-defined language policy aimed at facilitating communication between Bhutanese from different regions. Traditionally, the elite families were small in number, Tibetan in origin, and spoke Dzongkha wherever they happened to reside. Communication between different regions was confined largely to this elite, and the wide variety of languages spoken in Bhutan did not constitute a major problem. Political modernization, economic development, and construction of an extensive road system has changed this situation dramatically since 1960, and

16. These are: (1) Bumthang-Pai-Kha; (2) Mangdeg-Pai-Kha; (3) Tashigang-Pai-Kha; (4) Kurtey-Khome-Kha; (5) Kheng-Gung-Dupai-Kha; (6) Merogsa-teng-Kha; (7) Durdog-Gi-Kha; (8) Laya-Lingshi-Kha; (9) Tsa-Mang-Pai-Kha; (10) Mon; and (11) Tagbop-Damteng-Pai-Kha (*Kuensel,* 6:9 [Jan. 2, 1972], 7).

the localism so typical of the past is beginning to break down. So far, the government has resisted the temptation to try and impose Dzongkha on the majority of the population that does not speak the language, rejecting the "national language" policies adopted by the neighboring states of Nepal and, formally at least, India. Dzongkha is taught in the schools, but English has been made the medium of instruction. As many of the younger civil servants from various parts of Bhutan are now products of this educational system, English has become the effective language of communication within the administration as well. Since English is not associated with any particular group or region, and use of this language is considered to be non-discriminatory, no vocal opposition to this policy has yet emerged. Nor is there a Dzongkha irredentist movement in Bhutan, similar to the Hindi movement in India, except to a limited extent within the religious establishment. The linguistic diversity of Bhutan will continue to be a major problem for the Bhutan government, but probably not as dangerously divisive as in neighboring states—at least for some time to come.

Ethnic and Communal Divisions in Bhutan. For analytic purposes, the population of Bhutan can be divided into four broad, but not necessarily mutually exclusive, categories. The first is composed of several groups of people of Tibetan (Bhotia) origin, some of whom may have migrated to Bhutan as early as the ninth century and others as recently as 1959–1960. Second, there are a number of distinct but related communities in eastern Bhutan which, according to some observers, are related to similar Indo-Mongoloid groups in the Assam Himalayas and which presumably migrated to Bhutan from that area in the past millennium. A third element in Bhutan's population consists of a number of small tribal groups such as the Drokpas, Lepchas, and Doyas, which are sometimes described as the aboriginal or indigenous inhabitants of the country, to which can be added the families of the ex-slaves, often from similar tribal communities in the areas of India adjacent to Bhutan. This latter group tends to be concentrated around the Dzongs where they once constituted the labor force for the government offices. Finally, there are the Nepali Bhutanese, most of whom have been resident in Bhutan for only three or four generations, representing a new, still somewhat alien, element in the population structure.

The Bhutanese of Tibetan origin, as already noted, provide most of the social and political elite throughout Bhutan, but probably are only a plurality in the population of the country as a whole.[17] They are concentrated in western Bhutan, where they form a large majority, and along the northern border areas from west to east. But according to several sources, in the more populous eastern Bhutan area the Bhotias are heavily outnumbered by the Indo-Mongoloids of non-Tibetan origin [18] and in the southern region, constitute only a minute proportion of the population—being almost exclusively officials, landowners, or traders.[19]

The most prestigious of the Bhotia families trace their area of origin to central Tibet, but much of the northern border area of Bhutan is reportedly inhabited by migrants from eastern Tibet (Kham). There are also approximately 4,000 recent Tibetan migrants, most of them refugees who fled to Bhutan following the abortive 1959 uprising against Chinese rule in Tibet. Many of these have now been settled on uncultivated agricultural lands in the mid-montane area, but they also provide much of the small-scale entrepreneurial activity in Bhutan.

If the literature on Bhutan's people is reliable, virtually all of the eastern Bhutanese of Indo-Mongoloid origin have been thoroughly assimilated into the Buddhist-derived culture of Bhutan's traditional Bhotia elite and thus do not constitute a

17. Since the census does not provide a breakdown of the population on any social-structure basis, there is no reliable way to estimate the size of these various communities. The very imprecise estimates cited here are based on available published sources as well as on information obtained in interviews with Bhutanese, mostly in government service, who have resided in the various sections of the country.

18. See, for instance, Ram Rahul, *Modern Bhutan*, pp. 7–8.

19. Bhutanese highlanders prefer to avoid the lower altitudes and the duars, and have traditionally refused to settle in such areas. This was due in part to the hot, humid climate which they find oppressive, and to the various tropical diseases, such as malaria, to which they are particularly susceptible. One result has been to open southern Bhutan to settlement by a few small tribal communities and by Nepalese immigrants who are better able to adjust themselves both to the climate and the terrain.

serious potential disintegrative force in the country. While they speak dialects of non-Tibetan origin and have some distinctive dress and food habits as well as local traditions and festivals, these qualities are comparatively incidental to the broader over-riding Drukpa Buddhist cultural patterns that are common throughout the Bhutan hills and which provide a viable basis for a sense of *national* identity.

Far more complex and serious for the Bhutanese political and social system are the problems posed by the large commu-nity of Nepalese origin in southern Bhutan. The size of this community is a subject of some controversy: some Nepalese claim that it constitutes 25 to 30 percent of the total population of Bhutan, but the Bhutanese official estimates generally run much lower. Virtually all of the Nepali Bhutanese are concen-trated in the southern region except for a few government ser-vants assigned to central Bhutan or Nepalese laborers who work in the hill areas on a restrictive contractual basis. If the census figures for Samchi and Chirang subdivisions (in south-ern Bhutan) are correct (138,000 in 1969), then *permanent* Ne-pali residents do not constitute more than 15 percent of the population. But reportedly there are large numbers of Nepa-lese illegally resident in southern Bhutan (presumably not counted in the census). When these are added to the 15,000–20,000 Nepalese on labor contracts who do not have residential status, this community may number about 200,000 (approximately 20%) of the total population of Bhutan.

The Nepali Bhutanese constitute a problem for the Bhutan government for several reasons. They are relatively recent im-migrants, stemming from the very difference (and in some re-spects antagonistic) Hindu cultural and values system, and are generally resistant to integration into Bhutan's traditional so-cial, community, and political culture. Many of them retain close familial and caste relations with Nepal, Sikkim, or India (or all three), and their more natural lines of association run south and west rather than north. Moreover, a few of the Ne-pali Bhutanese have been socialized in Indian political values—democratic, Marxist, and Hindu orthodox—either before migration to Bhutan or as part of their education across the border in India where they have attended school. The political traditions of Bhutan, including perhaps those surrounding the monarchy, are not deeply engrained in the Nepali Bhutanese, and their loyalty to the system is sometimes questioned. Nor is there an integrating process at work that might change their political and social environment to one more congruent with the rest of Bhutan. The Nepali Bhutanese are concentrated in an area where they constitute the overwhelming majority of the population. Most of them reside in villages which are as classically Nepali Hindu as any in Nepal, harboring at least some sense of alienation from the broader society in which they live and the government which rules over them.

The "Nepalese problem" has long perplexed the Bhutanese authorities, and their responses to this perceived challenge to the dominant culture in Bhutan have varied over the decades. Their initial policy was to isolate the Nepali Bhutanese as completely as possible from the rest of Bhutan's society by restricting them to southern Bhutan. This had the desired social and political effect, as there was little interaction. But this also had negative consequences. For one thing, it populated the area of Bhutan most susceptible to rapid economic development and to ideological penetration from India with a community that had not been integrated, either socially or politically, into the broader Bhutanese society.

More recently, there have been some subtle changes in Bhutan's policy toward the Nepali Bhutanese in the direction of liberalization. Intermarriage between communities is being officially encouraged. Nepali Bhutanese are now being absorbed into the administration at a much higher rate than in the past, and now are posted occasionally in the central highlands. More liberal policies with respect to land ownership and taxation in southern Bhutan have also been introduced, modifying the discriminatory system that had sometimes led Nepali Bhutanese to describe themselves as second-class citizens. Even the policy, introduced in the early 1950s at the time of the organization of the Bhutan State Congress (a Nepali Bhutanese political party), has been liberalized enough to allow the few leaders of this organization who had been in exile in India for two decades to return to Bhutan at their own request.

But there are limitations, of course, upon what the Bhutanese authorities are prepared to do to meet the demands of the Nepali Bhutanese. The restrictions on permanent immigration into Bhutan have been tightened to prevent the country from becoming "another Sikkim" in which the "sons of the soil" (Bhutanese Buddhists) are overwhelmed by a flood of Nepalese Hindu immigrants. The events in Sikkim in 1973–1975 that led to revolutionary changes in the political system there are likely to strengthen Bhutanese apprehensions on this score. Moreover, the discouragement of Nepali Bhutanese settlement outside of the southern region has been retained, and it is unlikely that this policy will be modified despite the fact that there is land available for cultivation in some of the highland river valleys.[20]

The general impression given both by outside observers and by most Bhutanese is that the Nepali Bhutanese community is politically quiescent at this time. Moreover, it should be remembered that the Nepali Bhutanese community has its own economic stake in the government's policy restricting immigration, for any new residents would eventually compete for what is becoming an increasingly scarcer commodity in the south—cultivable land.

20. A number of Nepali Bhutanese have been allowed to purchase land in the highland areas in recent years, but reportedly these are all government servants or traders who do not have agriculture as their primary occupation. Whether ordinary Nepali Bhutanese farmers would also be allowed to acquire land outside of southern Bhutan seems more doubtful, for this would raise the prospect of the country becoming "another Sikkim" in the eyes of the highlanders.

One other recent change of some significance concerns the regulation under which all residents of southern Bhutan (i.e., Nepali Bhutanese) have to carry identity papers, a system which has been used as one form of control over their movement within Bhutan. In the Fall 1975 session of the National Assembly, legislation was enacted requiring all Bhutanese to carry such identity papers (*Kuensel* [Nov. 2, 1975], 3). While this eliminates the discriminatory aspect of the policy toward the Nepali Bhutanese community, it would not appear to be the objective of the legislation to remove the restrictions on their migration to areas of the country other than southern Bhutan.

Nevertheless, the Bhutan government would appear to be operating on the assumption that the present political stability in southern Bhutan may prove to be a temporary phenomenon, and that this region is likely to pose serious problems in the future. Proximity to India means that it will be the Nepali Bhutanese who will be the first to be politicized in the democratic and Marxist political idioms so rampant just across the border in Bengal and Assam. The example of Sikkim, where involvement in agitational politics has seemingly brought the Nepali Sikkimese community tangible economic and political gains, is likely to prove attractive to some Nepali Bhutanese as well. The liberalization of the Bhutanese political system and the expansion of the political elite to include elements from all of Bhutan's major communities in the last two decades may also prove to be an important factor in the future political role of the Nepali Bhutanese community. What this has done is provide the leadership of this community with a privilege they lacked previously—the capacity to participate in the decision-making process both in their own locality and at the center.

With respect to the demands posed by various elements of Bhutan's population in recent years, the Royal Government has another distinct advantage over its immediate neighbors because of its still relatively low ratio of population to land. It is able to devise and experiment with alternative social, political, and economic development strategies free from the stultifying pressures of massive overpopulation that often tend to intimidate and immobilize the governments of India, Bangladesh, and Nepal. There is, thus, a sound pragmatic basis for the optimism with which the Bhutanese elite approach the solution of their political and economic problems and the confidence with which they view such potentially dangerous problems as the integration of minority communities—that is, the Nepali Bhutanese—into the national culture. Whether this will in fact prove to be the history of Bhutanese politics in subsequent decades is still uncertain, but in any case the Royal Government does have many more things working for it in this respect than most of the beleaguered governments of other South Asian states.

The Bhutanese Economy. Comparative economic data on such factors as gross national product, per capital income, labor mobility, and so on, would seem to indicate that Bhutan is an extremely poor country with a population living in abject poverty. One does not have to be in Bhutan long, however, to realize that such statistics can be very misleading. The Bhutanese may lack many of the material indices of prosperity of developed societies, but it is apparent that they are not hunger-ridden or poverty-stricken. Indeed, in comparative Asian terms, the Bhutanese appear to be reasonably well-off, certainly much more so than most of their neighbors either to the south or north.

The explanation for the divergence between the hard economic data and reality is, of course, the nonapplicability of such concepts as gross national product and per capita income to subsistence agrarian economies. The significant criteria in such societies are the ratio of population to cultivable land and the terms upon which this land is distributed—that is, whether distribution is on an equitable enough basis to assure most people a reasonably satisfactory standard of living. It is these criteria that will concern us in this highly impressionistic (there is little data available) survey of the Bhutanese economy.

With respect to the availability of land, the situation is clear and hopeful, for Bhutan is the only country in all of South Asia with an overall favorable landpopulation ratio. The rich river valleys in the highlands, particularly in western and central Bhutan, are still underdeveloped and underutilized when compared to similar hill areas in India, Nepal, and Sikkim. Some districts in eastern and southern Bhutan face more severe population pressure on the land, but the problem is still of manageable proportions. It has been estimated that the introduction of simple changes in production techniques, involving no new resource inputs, would enable enough new land to be brought under cultivation to service Bhutan's population at its present level. Such modest inputs as more modern irrigation facilities (quite feasible now with the development of power resources) and fertilizers would increase both agricultural production and area under cultivation sufficiently to assure self-sufficiency for the remainder of the twentieth century.

Whether the land distribution system is "equitable enough" is a more difficult question to answer on the basis of available information. The traditional landholding system in Bhutan was feudal, at least in the larger valley areas, and thus essentially inequitable. Major changes have taken place in this system in the last few decades, but some holdover effects still persist. Tenancy, which was the norm earlier in most of Bhutan, has been much reduced in scope, but it has by no means disappeared. But what is more important perhaps is that the character of the tenancy system has changed. More often than not now it is families that are already landholders in their own right who sublet additional land for cultivation from the old elite landowning families. The dependent and subordinate psychology that typified relations between tenants and landowners under the traditional system is now largely a relic of the past. The old local elite families may still command respect and homage, but this is attributable more to their high social status based on prestigious ancestry than to their dominance of the economic system.

There is no question that the size of landholdings still varies considerably from family to family, and the government's feeble efforts to redistribute land on a more equitable basis have had little effect to date. Nevertheless, if verbal reports are correct, most families in most sections of the country (southern Bhutan may be an exception) have about as much land at their disposal as they can cultivate using traditional production methods that employ limited labor power. Indeed, in many villages the local authorities still have land available for distribution to any family that is prepared to bring it under cultivation (much of the land legislation in Bhutan regulates the conditions under which such land is distributed, with various incentives to cultivation emphasized). This is not the kind of land-distribution situation that is likely to lead to extensive agrarian unrest.

Traditionally, Bhutan has been virtually self-sufficient in agricultural products, with salt and wool from Tibet (the former now coming from India) as the only imports that might fall under the category of essential commodities. Today, the range of imports is much wider due to the extensive road system connecting Bhutan with India, but most of these imports constitute luxury items in the perspective of the average Bhutanese. The Royal Government does find it necessary to import some food products—including rice, which was a surplus commodity not long ago. But this statement is somewhat deceptive, for most of these imports are used to provide food grains for the large Nepali labor gangs working on projects in Bhutan on a temporary basis, or for the Indian advisers and technicians, as well as for the growing corps of government servants in the Secretariat at Thimphu. Most Bhutanese families are still basically self-sufficient. They may have acquired a taste for the Indian luxuries that are now available on the market, but removal would not engender any great strain on their living style.

As noted earlier, although land availability is not yet a critical issue in Bhutan's economy, there is a growing problem with respect to the distribution of population throughout the country. Some districts are beginning to suffer from overpopulation while others still have unutilized land available in some abundance. Until recently, the government had made no effort to facilitate migration from land-deficit to land-surplus areas, preferring instead to provide alternative forms of employment to agriculture in the districts where this seemed necessary. This change was accomplished in the 1960s largely through major road construction projects that required all the excess labor available in the country—and then some.

By 1975 most of these large-scale construction programs requiring a massive input of labor (by Bhutan's standards) had been completed. New policies have had to be devised to handle the underemployment that is an intrinsic aspect of the traditional agricultural system. Some attention is now being given to resettlement programs. Under the Chhukha hydel (hydroelectric) project, for instance, it is planned to resettle some 4,000 to 5,000 people from the more overpopulated areas of eastern Bhutan to western Bhutan. Once the hydel project has been completed, the newly unemployed will be eligible to obtain land for cultivation.

The development of a modern communication system has

made it possible for Bhutanese to move about their country relatively easily. No longer is it a major enterprise to travel from one's home valley to the next valley. Nor does the movement of the place of residence across the country now mean a total disruption of familial ties as it once did. Thus, the capacity for much greater mobility is there, but it is still unclear whether many Bhutanese will respond to new opportunities. The Bhutanese psychology still appears to be highly parochial, localist, family-oriented and not very adventurist. There is little evidence as yet (except among the educated young) of a propensity toward mobility when the price to be paid is a disruption of established familial ties.[21] The family system, moreover, absorbs and even welcomes some degree of underemployment among its members, for this provides surplus labor at critical points in the cultivation system. Custom thus tends to mitigate pressure upon the underemployed to migrate to areas where the land and jobs may be available.

In any case, some Bhutanese doubt that population pressure will make large-scale in-country migration necessary for some time to come. They point to the considerable potential for the development of industries other than agriculture—in particular the lumber industry. Most of the more densely populated areas of Bhutan are situated close to immense forest reserves that have never been exploited on an organized basis. The construction of several north-south highways in various areas of Bhutan has made the development of a lumber industry feasible for the first time. If this should be undertaken on a modest scale, according to estimates, virtually all presently underemployed labor could be gainfully employed in such enterprises without the workers having to leave their familial home areas.

There are also several hydroelectric-power projects either underway or on the drawing board that will require labor in large quantities during the construction period. Once com-

21. In 1975, however, it appeared to the author that most of the laborers on the Chhukha hydel project were Nepalis brought in on labor contracts. It may well be that this program, directed toward facilitating the resettlement of eastern Bhutanese in land-surplus areas in western Bhutan, has not yet met with much response.

pleted, these facilities should earn badly needed foreign capital from the sale of power to energy-short areas of northeastern India and Bangladesh. This, at least, is the expectation in official circles in Bhutan, and it is one of the reasons for the Royal Government's confidence that it will be able to handle economic development problems successfully in the future with only a minimal disruption of the existing agricultural system—which will, as planned, continue to provide the foundation for the country's economy. In the process, intense pressure upon Bhutan's social and political system will also be avoided. All this sounds rather Utopian, particularly when placed in the context of the rapid and revolutionary changes taking place in all of the societies surrounding Bhutan. Nevertheless, Bhutan is the one area of South Asia where the potential for controlled economic development at a rate sufficient to meet public requirements without concomitant political and social changes still seems feasible. What is also required, however, is the cooperation of Bhutan's external environment in allowing the country to develop and change at its own pace. This is by no means assured.

2. Foreign Relations: Neutralizing the External Environment

Bhutan's vulnerable geopolitical location between vastly larger, richer, stronger, and occasionally antagonistic neighbors has made external relations crucial not only to its survival as an independent state, but also to its internal politics. Like other buffer-area societies, the Bhutanese have often sought security by a withdrawal from the surrounding world—when this was both possible and necessary. And, indeed, the debate over foreign policy in modern Bhutan has usually focused on this issue, in the 1770s as well as two centuries later. It is useful, therefore, to commence this study of the contemporary Bhutanese political system with an analysis of the ways in which external factors have impinged upon the country and the responses devised by Bhutan to meet these challenges.

The Historical Perspective

Isolationism had been the fundamental principle upon which Bhutan based its foreign policy for so much of the modern period that it came to be viewed as an immutable, unchanging factor by Bhutanese and foreigners alike. Yet it is apparent from our limited knowledge of Bhutan's history that isolationism was, in fact, a relatively recent phenomenon, dating back only to the late eighteenth century when pressure from the Tibetans (supported by the Chinese) to the north and from the British to the south appeared to make a diminution in relations in both directions essential to the survival of Bhutan as an independent political entity. Too close a relationship with either neighbor came to be viewed as threatening, in part because excessive friendship with one was viewed with suspicion and concern by the other.

What happened in the mid-eighteenth century that convinced the Bhutanese authorities of the need to isolate the country from the outside world? The Bhutanese historical tradition does not shed much light on what must have been a deliberate policy decision, but the following conjecture may not be too far off the mark. While Tibet had long constituted a threat to Bhutan's independence, the relationship between the two countries had been managed successfully in the past and was probably considered to be manageable in the future. The insertion of a dominant Chinese influence (control is probably not an accurate descriptive term) at Lhasa in the latter half of the eighteenth century was a far more serious matter, however. In particular, Bhutan must have been disturbed by the joint Chinese/Tibetan invasion of Nepal in 1792–1793, even though this was not a completely triumphant venture for Chinese arms. Lhasa, backed by limited Chinese military support, posed a quite different problem for Bhutan than a Tibet tenuously united under the political authority of the Dalai Lama.

Bhutan's geopolitical situation was made even more precarious by the coincidence between the timing of the expansion of Chinese influence in Tibet and the intrusion of British rule in northeastern India. Earlier, the Moghul dynasty had to contend with a still-vigorous Ahom kingdom in the Brahmaputra valley and had only occasionally been able to divert its attention to Bhutan and other areas of the eastern Himalayas. The first half of the eighteenth century marked the decline of both the Moghul and Ahom empires. This presented Bhutan with an unprecedented opportunity to expand into the plains area to the south, which it proceeded to do with some vigor. In northern Bengal, the principality of Kuch Bihar had to accept what might best be described as Bhutan's "paramountcy," conceding to the Bhutanese the right to intervene in Kuch Bihari politics on a formalized basis. In northwestern Assam also, Bhutan forced a succession of weak Ahom rulers to make a series of concessions: ceding some territory outright; granting the Bhutanese the right to certain revenue sources in other areas; and even establishing a curious form of joint administration under which certain districts were governed by the Ahoms for several months and by the Bhutanese for the remainder of the year. Obviously, a system of administration based upon such complex principles implied some degree of coordination between the two governments.

In the latter half of the eighteenth century, certain complications set in that had a great impact on Bhutan. By 1775 the British East India Company had established its authority throughout northern Bengal, and approximately fifty years later it replaced the Ahoms as the rulers of Assam. These developments alarmed the Bhutanese, as they placed into jeopardy the various forms of influence and control that Bhutan exerted in the plains to the south of the hills. The Bhutanese elite were forced to make a major psychological adjustment to sublimate their exuberant expansionist and interventionist instincts on their southern borders and assumed a basically defensive posture. This was finally accomplished, though not without several costly conflicts with the British that spelled out the facts of life in increasingly clear terms. The isolation policy eventually adopted by the Bhutanese elite was a natural outcome of this change in status. It was rigorously adhered to for more than a century, until the reinsertion of a strong Chinese presence in Tibet in the 1950s and the dynamism of the democratic political system in post-1947 India forced Bhutan to once again reconsider and eventually revise its entire approach to external relations.

Bhutan and Tibet. One of the more prevalent themes in the Western literature on Bhutan focuses on the Tibetan origin of Bhutan's traditional elite and its theocratic political system, symbolized by the strong cultural and political ties between the two countries. Since at least the twelfth century, virtually all Bhutanese civil and ecclesiastical officials can trace their ancestry to migrants from Tibet, and intermarriage between the elites of the two countries has continued on a limited scale up to the present time. The intimate ties between their respective lamaistic Buddhist systems and religiopolitical institutions are also readily apparent. It is quite correct, therefore, to conclude that

Tibetan influence had been of great importance in Bhutan for several centuries and had been a critical factor in the evolution of its political and social institutions.

But perhaps too much has been made of the relationship between the two countries' common northern Mahayana Buddhist culture, and not enough attention paid to the subtle but significant differences between the functioning of institutions bearing the same name in the two societies.[1] From the Bhutanese point of view, in any case, one of the most persistent and insidious assumptions is that the traditional Tibet-Bhutan relationship should be interpreted in terms of a superior/inferior syndrome, supposedly involving some form of Bhutanese vassalage to a Tibetan ruler, or that institutions bearing the same name were necessarily Tibetan rather than Bhutanese in origin.[2]

In fact, the relationship between Tibet and Bhutan (at least up to 1910) defies facile analysis in modern Western concepts of international relations. The political elite of Bhutan may have been largely Tibetan in origin, but it is far more important in this respect that virtually all of their ancestors came to Bhutan as political refugees, that is, as the enemies of the existing political authorities in various parts of Tibet rather than as their feudatories. There are no known cases in Bhutanese history in which Tibetan migrant communities in Bhutan recognized and accepted political obligations and allegiance to Ti-

1. The undue emphasis may be blamed on Westerners who were primarily interested in Bhutan's Tibetan Buddhist culture. They were, in other words, displaced Tibetologists, seeking to study in Bhutan what was not accessible to them in Tibet. More recently several Indian authors have sought to counter this unintentional bias in the literature by citing evidence (rather flimsy in my view) to Indian cultural influence in Bhutan, from which they have derived comforting conclusions about what they believe to be Bhutan's "natural" lines of association.

2. In discussing the Tshogdu (National Assembly) with one Bhutanese official, for instance, I assumed that Bhutan had borrowed the name and the institution from Tibet which also had a traditional institution bearing this name. He insisted, however, that both the name and the institution were Bhutanese in origin and that Tibet might have borrowed it from Bhutan. Whatever the facts may be in this particular instance, the point was well taken, for influences did run in various directions in the lamaistic Buddhist world and not just from Lhasa outwards.

betan civil rulers. Tibetan migration to Bhutan, thus, did not constitute colonization similar to, for instance, British migration to North America and Australia. Nor did it constitute an extension of Tibetan political authority into new lands south of the Himalayan range. Indeed, the relationship between Bhutan and Tibet in much of this early period was marked by intermittent hostilities. There were several Tibetan invasions of Bhutan in the seventeenth and eighteenth centuries, aimed usually at the assertion of Tibetan authority or influence. All failed, and the Tibetan forces never managed to operate for more than a few months in Bhutanese territory (Bhutan's Dzongs and monasteries are still filled with Tibetan weapons and armor captured in these various invasions). While there were several instances in this same period in which Tibetan Buddhist leaders in Shigatse or Lhasa exerted an active influence in Bhutan's politics, this was always either in the role of a mediator (not an arbitrator) between contending Bhutanese forces or, more often, as a supporter of a particular faction in the frequent Bhutanese civil strifes. Indeed, these attempts by Tibetan officials to intervene in Bhutanese politics are quite instructive in one sense, for only on one occasion in recorded history did the Tibetan-supported factions emerge triumphant.

While the formal political relationship between the two countries, then, is properly identified as one of complete independence, there is more ambiguity concerning the political implications of their religiocultural relationship. Both states had what were in theory—and for a long period in essence—theocratic political systems, and these constituted a form of interdependence that went deeper, in some respects at least, than their diplomatic relationship. The question remains, however, whether Bhutan's religious subordination to Tibet's Buddhist establishment on certain levels also constituted a form of political dependency.

The relationship between the Dalai Lama, head of both the civil and religious systems in Tibet, and the Bhutanese authorities is one key factor, in particular after 1642 when all of central Tibet was unified under his authority. The Dalai Lama was (and is), the most prestigious of Buddhist reincarnates to whom the greatest degree of deference and respect was due. Since the reign of the seventh Dalai Lama (1708–1750), for instance, it was customary for the Shabdung of Bhutan to send gifts to the Dalai Lama periodically, and to receive gifts in return. Confusion about the political significance of this exchange was compounded, because on several occasions the Dalai Lama or his religious (but politically subordinate) co-equal, the Panchen Lama, wrote to the British in India in terms that implied Bhutanese vassalage, and especially because these documents became part of the very limited Western-language literature on Bhutan.[3]

The Bhutanese, on the other hand, insist that the gifts to the Dalai Lama were just that—gifts, not tribute—and that furthermore they were presented to him in his religious rather than his political capacity in Tibet. Whatever pretensions the Tibetans may have projected to the British, it is apparent from the course of events that the most the Dalai Lama or Panchen Lama could do was advise the Bhutanese, not command them. But perhaps the most conclusive evidence of the limitations of Tibetan government influence in Bhutan is that *no* monastic institutions of the Dalai Lama's Gelugpa (yellow hat) sect were ever allowed in Bhutan. It was the normal practice of the Gelugpa-dominated political system in Tibet to establish Gelugpa monasteries wherever its political writ extended, using these as the principal instrument for effectuating Lhasa's authority in areas in which its principal political rivals, the "red hat" sects, had long been dominant. The first Shabdung apparently introduced a policy banning the Gelugpa sect from Bhutan after Lhasa's conquest ot Tsang province in 1642, and this policy was strictly adhered to by the Bhutan government from that time on. This should be considered conclusive evidence that Lhasa never exercised political authority over Bhutan.

3. See, for instance, the correspondence between the Panchen Lama and the East India Company officials in Calcutta in 1772–1773, in the contest of the first Anglo-Bhutanese War and the first British (Bogle) mission to Tibet (Markham, p. 237). But even here the Panchen Lama, while inferring Bhutan's vassalage, was careful not to assume any responsibility for Bhutanese actions or to make any guarantees about their future behavior.

Somewhat more complicated in its political significance are the relations between the dominant Drukpa sect in Bhutan and its "mother" monastery in Tibet—Ralung. There is an implicit superior/inferior status in their traditional relationship, for there are recorded cases in which Ralung (or its subordinate monasteries in Tibet) provided high-level monastic officials to Bhutan, men who were on occasion also appointed to top civil posts in the Bhutan government.

What was the political significance of this relationship? If the red hat sects had been the dominant political authority in Tibet, the nature of their relationship with Drukpa institutions might have provided a rationale of sorts for a Tibetan claim to Bhutan. But in fact the red hats were a subordinate sect in a Gelugpa-dominated political system in Tibet, on occasion even allying themselves with red-hat institutions beyond Tibet's borders as one form of protection against Gelugpa domination. To a certain extent, then, both the Tibetan red hats and the Bhutanese Drukpas had a common opponent in the Gelugpas—at least in the seventeenth and eighteenth centuries.

Another question that has recently assumed some importance concerns the nature of the relationship existing today between Bhutan and China. The Ch'ing dynasty had established a substantial presence in Tibet after 1720, and some contemporary specialists on the Himalayan area—George Patterson, for instance [4]—have stated that China, as a consequence of the early connections has a residual claim upon Bhutan which it can and probably will reassert at the appropriate moment.[5] The Chinese Communist regime, however, has been cautious and circumspect (in its public statements at least). There is no

4. George Patterson, *Peking versus Delhi* (New York: Praeger, 1964), p. 207.
5. In the 1910–1912 period, Peking asserted its suzerainty over Bhutan in correspondence with the British (Secret Dept., May 21, 1910 [India Office Library, London], Prince Ch'ing to British Minister, April 18, 1910). But this was with reference to the Chinese invasion of Tibet in 1910 when, for a brief period just before the demise of the Ch'ing dynasty, Peking for the first time established firm control over Tibet. After the collapse of the Ch'ings and the formation of the Republic, the Chinese allowed their claim to Bhutan to lapse, and have never reasserted it in public, nor does any further reference appear, in records in the public domain, of correspondence between China and the British or Indian governments.

hard evidence that Peking considers Bhutan to be part of the great Chinese motherland still to be liberated from imperialist domination, although this is not a totally implausible scenario for the future.

The first point to be made is that any Chinese claim to Bhutan is totally dependent upon the Tibetan claim, for it is only through Peking's alleged historical sovereignty over Tibet that any assertions of rights could be extended to Bhutan. Direct relations between Bhutan and China did not exist prior to the establishment of the Chinese Ambans (residents) in Lhasa in the eighteenth century.[6] Even thereafter, there were no Bhutanese missions to Peking similar to those sent periodically by Nepal which the Chinese (but not the Nepalese) records described as "tributary" in character. The Bhutanese missions went only to the Dalai Lamas, and while they usually called on the Chinese Ambans in Lhasa, no letters or gifts were forwarded to the emperor at Peking, not, at least, as a regular, prescribed practice.

There were a few instances in the eighteenth and nineteenth centuries when Chinese emperors bestowed "patents of office" upon various Bhutanese officials. If one reads the Chinese records, the implication is that this was the act of a superior to an inferior and that some grant of authority went along with the titles. Again, it is clear that this was not the case. In the first place, only a few Bhutanese officials ever received such titles, and these usually were granted only some time *after* they had assumed office. There was, thus, no relationship between exercising the authority of an office and receiving a Chinese title— and indeed most Bhutanese officials were never the recipients of such patents. The titles were prestigious, and may have helped strengthen the political position of the recipient, but they were of no more political significance in terms of legitimacy in office than the titles bestowed on Bhutanese officials by

6. During the 1792–1793 Nepal-China war, the Chinese commander, Fu Kang-an, instructed the Bhutanese to assist him in his war against Nepal. The Bhutanese refused to cooperate and were denounced to the emperor, but no action was taken against Bhutan. Obviously, Fu Kang-an was looking for support from allies, not vassals (*Chin-Ting K'uo-er-k'a* [*Account of the War against the Gurkhas*], Peking, 1795, chuan 14–22, pp. 10a–12a).

the British "Emperor of India" in the nineteenth and twentieth centuries.

Relations between Bhutan and Tibet were not smooth in the period following the establishment of the Shabdung system; later, in the seventeenth and eighteenth centuries, warfare was the normal condition between the two countries, as the Gelugpa-dominated political system in Tibet sought to establish its authority over the whole of the lamaistic Buddhist world and the various red-hat principalities, including Bhutan, resisted. But by the early decades of the nineteenth century a *modus vivendi* had been achieved between Tibet and Bhutan. This was in part a consequence of their mutually perceived concern with the British threat from India, which both Lhasa and Punakha agreed required some degree of cooperation if their independence was to be preserved. This lasted, however, only as long as British efforts to open Tibet were not pushed with any vigor or force. By the first decade of the twentieth century, Bhutan had concluded that it had no alternative but to side with the far more powerful British. The Tibetans resented what they called a betrayal by the Bhutanese but were in no position to retaliate. In any case, from 1904 to 1947, relations between Bhutan and Tibet were conducted within the context of British "paramountcy" over this buffer area. Trade and religiocultural relations continued, but it was the British that provided a quietly restrained but effective political influence at both Lhasa and Punakha until their withdrawal from the subcontinent in 1947.

Bhutan and British India. The advent of the British East India Company on Bhutan's southern borders in the mid-eighteenth century posed some new questions for Punakha. The British could not be identified as enemies of the Buddhist religion as had been the Muslim Moghuls and the Hindu Ahoms, for the Company was assertively neutral in religious matters in this period. The Bhutanese were not even sure, initially at least, whether the Company was a political institution, with all this implied, or primarily a commercial institution that had been forced by circumstances to assume some of the political functions of the rapidly disintegrating Moghul empire. If the former, then the British were potentially dangerous foes; if the latter, then they were a likely source of economic prosperity with which mutually advantageous commercial relations could be developed.

The situation was finally clarified by the 1772–1773 Anglo-Bhutan war over Kuch Bihar in which the British East India Company demonstrated conclusively that it was not prepared to concede to Bhutan a sphere of influence in the plains area between the Bhutan hills and the Brahmaputra-Gangetic river system. Even more disturbing, perhaps, was the apparent disinclination of the British to make anything more than minimal concessions to Bhutanese participation in the India-Tibet commerce via the Bhutan trade channel. In the process, the Company dealt a disastrous blow to the revenue sources of virtually the entire Bhutanese elite which had become heavily dependent upon the income derived from the exploitation of the plains as well as the trade with Tibet.

Under the circumstances prevailing in 1772—that is, the threat of a British invasion of central Bhutan—Punakha was forced to offer a temporary submission while seeking to devise new policies to meet the threat. Treaties were signed with the British which, in effect, conceded Kuch Bihar to the Company and also opened Bhutan as a trade channel to Tibet on terms that were less favorable than under the traditional trade system prior to these events. The first British mission, led by Lt. George Bogle, was received in Punakha, and the Bhutanese authorities were forced—reluctantly—to help arrange Bogle's visit to the Panchen Lama at Shigatse, a visit they correctly perceived as promoting relationships which were potentially disadvantageous to Bhutan.

The first real opportunity to correct the imbalance that ensued came with the death of the Panchen Lama in 1780, after which the trade treaty between Bhutan and the Company lost its force. Meanwhile, having been expelled from northern Bengal, the Bhutanese directed their expansionist programs at the still-independent but rapidly weakening Ahom kingdom in Assam, seizing some areas in northwestern Assam before the British themselves decided to move in that direction.

With the British conquest of Assam in 1826, Bhutanese con-

trol over these former Ahom districts also came into dispute.
British policy along the whole of the Himalayas was based upon
the general principle that all independent hill principalities
should be deprived of whatever plains areas they controlled at
the foot of the hills. This was in part a reflection of the British
view that the foothills constituted the natural boundary between India and the hill principalities, and that all plains areas
belonged by right to whomever ruled northern India. It was
also realized, of course, that such plains areas were important
sources of revenue for the hill rulers who would be seriously
weakened by their loss or, even better, made dependent upon
the British. Keeping the plains areas usually involved the payment of a nominal tribute to the Company.

The disputes that soon developed between the British and
the Bhutanese over the privileges that the latter had enjoyed in
the Bengal and Assamese plains areas was to plague relations
between the two countries for much of the nineteenth century.
Some powerful regional officials in Bhutan, and in particular
the Tongsa Pönlop, were very reluctant to surrender their re-
munerative privileges. This led to constant dissension between
the two powers and, finally, to the Second Anglo-Bhutan War
of 1865. In the treaty that ended the war, Bhutan had to cede
what remained of the plains areas it held in the Bengal and
Assam duars, as well as the hill area to the east of Darjeeling
(Kalimpong) and the small Dewangiri hill areas in southern
Bhutan.[7] As compensation for the revenues lost, Bhutan was
granted an annual subsidy of Rs. 50,000 (increased to Rs.

7. Up until this time, the Bhutanese had on occasion attempted to use the
Tibetans and Chinese as counterbalance to the British. Prior to 1865, the
Tongsa Pönlop had been the most ardent advocate of such a policy, and had
even provoked conflict with the British on the assumption that substantial support would be forthcoming from the north. The failure of the Tibetans and
Chinese to do anything to aid the Bhutanese in the 1865 war and the obvious
disparity between British and Tibetan-Chinese strength exposed this policy as
obsolete. From this time on, the Tongsa Pönlop accepted as an absolute necessity the need to reach terms with the British if Bhutan was to survive—and if
his family was to prosper. There were occasions subsequently when Tibetan
and/or Chinese officials came to Bhutan to urge the Bhutanese to reject British
efforts to open communication with Tibet via Bhutan. By and large, the officials were treated with scant respect by the Bhutanese who were not inclined
to endanger Bhutan's relations with the British for Tibet's protection.

100,000 in 1910), but this constituted a form of blackmail for Bhutan's "good behavior" as well as a constant source of conflict among the Bhutanese elite.[8]

But there was one source of consolation for the Bhutanese in all these otherwise disastrous developments. The British never pressed hard for any form of permanent representation in Bhutan, and thus were rarely in a position to intervene effectively in internal Bhutanese politics. Moreover, the British were quite prepared to accept Bhutan's isolation policy which indeed fitted well into the British concept of the proper role of a buffer area. For what the British wanted in buffer zones were autonomous political entities to which they owed only limited responsibility as far as internal order was concerned but over which they exercised substantial influence with respect to external relations. This objective provided the rationale for the 1910 Treaty between the British and the newly established monarchy in Bhutan in which the latter's internal independence was recognized in exchange for Ugyen Wangchuck's agreement to accept British guidance on foreign-policy matters. By this time, then, mutually satisfactory relations had been established between the authorities in both countries.

There were occasions thereafter during which the exact nature of the relationship between Bhutan and British India was pondered by British officials, Did, for instance, the paramountcy of the British Crown extend to Bhutan as it did to the numerous Indian "princely states" and, according to some officials, to Sikkim? The most explicit British statement on this question was made by the Secretary of State for India in 1924 in which he defined Bhutan as under the suzerainty of the Brit-

8. A 1943 British report noted that the Rs. 100,000 subsidy was still "paid away to various interests which it was considered necessary to conciliate." In addition to the subsidy, another Rs. 100,000 had been paid to Bhutan after 1917 as compensation for Bhutan's agreement to ban liquor shops from within ten miles of the Indian border. In 1942, the Indian government added another Rs. 100,000 to the amount paid to the Bhutan king, ostensibly because his cash revenues were so limited, but one suspects in reality to strengthen his loyalty to the British at a time when the Japanese were threatening to invade eastern India (Political [External] Department, Collection 44/5 [India Office Library, London] a report by B. J. Gould on his visit to Bhutan in February 1943).

ish Crown but on a different basis from the Indian princely states: "Bhutan then is not at present a part of India; the frontier of India runs along the foothills and not as in Sikkim on the main Himalayan range; but Bhutan's foreign relations, and consequently its defense, are, unlike those of Nepal, formally guaranteed by the Government of India, and the State is really a Protectorate in close treaty relations with His Majesty's Government." [9]

This was all rather academic in any case, as the British never made any effort to add substance to their claims of suzerainty in Bhutan, and it is doubtful if the Bhutanese even knew about these gratuitous assertions of rights. If they did, they ignored them, and there is no question that Bhutan considered itself a fully independent country throughout the British period—and thereafter. Even the clause of the 1910 Treaty concerning the acceptance of British guidance of Bhutan's foreign relations was interpreted differently by the Bhutanese as not inhibiting in any way diplomatic relations with Tibet or deterring Bhutan from establishing relations with China if the opportunity should arise—that is, if the Chinese were to re-establish a significant presence in Tibet. Far more important, after independence, the Indian government never used these ambiguous assertions of British suzerainty as the basis for any kinds of claims that might have limited Bhutan's independence in the same way as occurred in Sikkim. Bhutan emerged from the British period in India with the broadest degree of independence in *de facto,* if not necessarily in *de jure,* terms of all the Himalayan border states, and was less inhibited by formal and informal qualifications on their relations with India than either Nepal or Sikkim.

Bhutan and Other Foreign Powers. For obvious geopolitical and

9. External Department, Collection 38/4 (India Office Library, London), a note on "The Mongolian Fringe" by Olaf Caroe, Foreign Secretary, Government of India, quoting from the 1924 statement by the Secretary of State for India. In a 1939 statement, an Indian government official again stated that "Bhutan is under His Majesty's suzerainty, though *not yet* included in India" (italics mine) (Political [External] Department, Collection 44/5 [India Office Library, London], GOI External to Secretary of State, 24 Nov., 1939).

economic reasons, Bhutan's world view has been focused almost exclusively upon its more intrusive neighbors—central Tibet, China, and the ruling power or powers in northeastern India. There have been certain periods, however, when Bhutan's relations with other Himalayan area principalities or regions have assumed some importance. Nepal, Sikkim, Ladakh (until its absorption into Kashmir in 1839), Kham (eastern Tibet), and the Buddhist areas directly to the east of Bhutan in what is now Arunachal Pradesh (formerly the North-East Frontier Agency of India) have all had a role to play in Bhutan's international relations. Initially, this was because all of these but Nepal were red-hat areas, religiously and politically,[10] with a common sense of identity in their separate but related struggles against the Gelugpas. By the late eighteenth century, the need for cooperation was supplemented by Britain's forward policy, which was directed at bringing buffer states on India's northern frontier under British influence. This seemed to make some kind of common response essential to the more perceptive rulers in these different areas of the Himalayas.

The need for cooperation and the capacity to cooperate, however, were two very different things, and it was only under specific sets of circumstances that cooperation was possible. More frequently, pressure from the larger neighboring states, which usually preferred to discourage interrelationships between the various societies, forced the latter to adopt divisive policies. While there have been tacit alliances formed on occasion—Bhutan and Ladakh against Lhasa in the 1680s and Bhutan and Nepal against the British in the early 1770s—these were the exception. More typical was Sikkim's support of both the Chinese (1792–1793) and the British (1814–1816) in their respective wars with Nepal, or Nepal's offer of assistance to the Tibetans in their war with Ladakh and Kashmir in the 1840s. In such cases, dimly perceived common regional interests were

10. Nepal's political hierarchy was largely Hindu, but the substantial Buddhist component in its population was red hat. As elsewhere in the Himalayan area, Gelugpa monastic institutions had not been able to penetrate the Nepali Buddhist communities.

generally sublimated to more readily apparent private and local interests.

One would have expected, for instance, a better record of co-operation between Sikkim and Bhutan than has in fact existed. Both emerged as political entities at approximately the same time in the first half of the seventeenth century, and as red-hat strongholds against the Gelugpa menace. But it would appear that cooperation between the two countries was the exception rather than the rule. In the 1770s and 1780s, for instance, when Sikkim was fighting for its survival against a rapidly expanding Nepal, Bhutan took advantage of the situation to seize the area of southern Sikkim to the east of the Tista river.[11] It was the Tibetans and the Chinese, and later the British, who guaranteed Sikkim's survival as a separate political entity with at least limited autonomy.

The record of the relationship between Bhutan and Nepal is somewhat better but nevertheless still spotty. In the seventeenth and eighteenth centuries, Ram Shah, a ruler of Gorkha, and Prithvi Narayan Shah, a scion of the same dynasty and the father of modern Nepal, both recognized the importance of Bhutan to Nepal, as had several of the Malla dynasty rulers in Kathmandu valley. To encourage friendly relations and to provide what in those days was a normal form of diplomatic relations, the Shabdung of Bhutan was given control over Swayambhunath, the most prestigious Buddhist shrine in Nepal, as well as several other Buddhist establishments. These were all seized by the Nepal government in the aftermath of the 1854–1856 Nepal-Tibet war, however, because of Kathmandu's suspicion (probably unjustified) that Bhutan had aided the Tibetans in these hostilities. This ended the special relationship between the two countries. While the representatives of both governments did what they could to assist the Younghusband Expedition to Tibet in 1903–1905, their sup-

---

11. It is probable in this case, however, that Bhutan assumed that Sikkim's case was lost and that it was preferable for both Nepal and Bhutan to share control of the important channel of communication between India and Tibet through Sikkim. In other words, this may have been a case of Nepal-Bhutan cooperation—at Sikkim's expense.

port was not due to any agreement on their part but rather to the fact that by this time both were heavily dependent on British goodwill for their own survival.

In the seventeenth century, there is some evidence of a close relationship, perhaps even a formal alliance, between Bhutan and the independent Buddhist kingdom of Ladakh. Indeed, one of the Tibetan invasions of Bhutan in the 1680s was justified by Lhasa on the ground that Bhutan had assisted Ladakh in the Tibet-Ladakh war of 1684–1685. There would seem to be some basis for this allegation, as earlier the Ladakhi ruler had granted Bhutan several enclaves in western Tibet (which was then controlled by Ladakh) for its assistance in earlier conflicts with Tibet. These enclaves remained under Bhutan's control even after western Tibet had come under the rule of the Dalai Lama's government in Lhasa, but presumably their significance as a channel of communication and a point of contact between Bhutan and Ladakh was greatly diminished. These enclaves have usually been explained in Ladakhi and Bhutanese historical traditions in religious terms—that is, sister monasteries of the same Buddhist sect—but it is probable that both political and trade factors were of at least equal importance at the time of their establishment.

For Bhutan, probably one of the most sensitive neighboring areas lies directly to the east in what is now the Kameng district of Arunachal Pradesh in India. Part of the population in Kameng is Buddhist, closely related to various Drukpa communities in eastern Bhutan.[12] Traditionally, however, the principal religiopolitical center is the Gelugpa monastery at Towang in northwestern Kameng, which was the only significant Gelugpa center south of the Himalayas prior to the flood of refugees

12. In the Simla Convention of 1914 between Tibet and British India, the McMahon line (i.e., the boundary) was generally drawn at the crest of the Himalayas. One exception was made on the border between Siang district and Tibet in an area called Pemako, which was granted to Tibet on the grounds that its inhabitants were Tibetans, even though it lies south of the Himalayan crest. In fact, most of the inhabitants of Pemako are Bhutanese who migrated there in the early nineteenth century, although they paid their taxes to one of the local rulers (Pome) in eastern Tibet (Leo E. Rose and Margaret W. Fisher, *The North-East Frontier Agency of India* [U.S. Department of State, Publication 8288, 1967], p. 12).

who left Tibet after the crushing of the 1959 revolt by the Chinese. In the past, Bhutan apparently had been distressed with this Gelugpa projection south of the Himalayas, and Towang was a source of contention and conflict between the two governments for at least two centuries. A compromise would seem to have been reached eventually under which Towang continued as a Gelugpa institution but was autonomous from either Lhasa's or Punakha's direct political authority.

At the time the British withdrew from India in 1947, then, Bhutan had formal if rather distant relations with British India, more informal but in some respects more intimate relations with the Dalai Lama's government in Lhasa, and no contacts of any formal kind with China, Nepal, or Sikkim. Bhutan's isolation policy was generally judged to have been a success, even though the country had probably paid a high price economically because of it. In 1947, there seemed to be no reason to change courses, but events in the 1950s soon made existing policy obsolete and raised anew the question of Bhutan's alignment in the complex politics of the Himalayan area. The response that eventually emerged was the consequence of a number of factors, but the world view that has grown out of Bhutan's experience with its various neighbors is one very important ingredient. Contemporary Bhutan's foreign policy should not be interpreted directly in terms of the country's history, but it is certainly heavily influenced by the past.

The Adjustment with India: 1947–1952

The British formally handed over authority to the governments of India and Pakistan in August 1947. For Bhutan and the other Himalayan border states, it was the India government that assumed the role of successor to the British, and it was with New Delhi that an agreement had to be reached. For Nepal, Sikkim, and Tibet this was accomplished on a temporary basis by the signing of "standstill agreements" under which relations with India were continued on the same basis as before until new treaties could be negotiated. Bhutan and India did not sign a standstill agreement as such, but both governments

operated as if they had. The Bhutan agent in India continued
to function in his previous capacities, and the Indian political
officer in Sikkim was still accredited to Bhutan as well.

There were several high-placed officials in Bhutan who advocated retention of the 1910 Treaty, reflecting uncertainty
within the Royal Government concerning the terms India
might impose in the negotiation of a new treaty. In Bhutan, as
in Nepal and Sikkim, there was some apprehension in the immediate postindependence period that India would prove less
accommodating than the British. The skillful way in which Indian Home Minister Sardar Patel coerced the numerous Indian
princely states into accession to the Indian Union led to fears
that the Himalayan border states might be handled in a similar
fashion. This nearly happened in Sikkim in the spring of 1949,
for India took this small principality under direct administrative control when a popular movement against the ruling dynasty seemed on the verge of getting out of control.[13]

The negotiation of a new Indo-Bhutanese treaty commenced
in the summer of 1949. Bhutan's objectives were comparatively
simple and straightforward: New Delhi's recognition of its independence and the restoration of the Dewangiri hill strip on
the frontier with India. It came as a pleasant surprise to the
Royal Government when the Indians proved to be receptive on
both issues. New Delhi indicated its willingness to sign an
agreement that incorporated the essential provisions of the
1910 Treaty and also conceded Bhutan's territorial claims. The
Bhutanese delegation accepted the Indian proposal with little
debate—indeed, with an audible sign of relief.[14] The treaty
signed on August 8, 1949, specifically recognized Bhutan's independence but also included the clause of the 1910 Treaty
under which the Royal Government agreed to accept Indian
guidance on foreign policy. In other clauses of the 1949

13. India intervened at the request of the Sikkim ruler, but at the time some
Nepalese and Bhutanese suspected that the intervention had been maneuvered
by New Delhi and was the first stage in a contrived accession of Sikkim to the
Indian Union.
14. In a letter to Prime Minister Jigme Dorji, King Jigme Wangchuck described the 1949 Treaty as "very good," and an improvement over the 1910
Treaty (unpublished manuscript, Bhutan National Library, Thimphu).

Treaty, the Dewangiri strip was restored to Bhutan, and the annual Indian subsidy to the Royal Government was increased to Rs 500,000.

Viewed in retrospect, Bhutan was probably fortunate to have concluded the agreement with India in 1949, for New Delhi's terms might have been somewhat stiffer if the negotiations had taken place even a few months later. In the Fall of 1949 India did not perceive any serious threat to its northeastern border with Tibet, and thus saw no reason to redefine its relationship with Bhutan. In contrast, when New Delhi was negotiating new treaty relations with both Nepal and Sikkim in 1950 the Indians were acutely disturbed by the expressed determination of the new Communist regime in China to reunite Tibet with the Chinese motherland. India's heightened concern over the vulnerability of its Himalayan bulwark was reflected in the secret letters attached to the 1950 Treaty of Peace and Friendship with Nepal, and with the retention of Sikkim as a protectorate in the 1951 Treaty with that state.

The threatened Chinese offensive against independent Tibet was launched on the eastern frontier in October 1950. Another Chinese force moved into western Tibet from Sinkiang that winter—crossing territory claimed by India in the process. This convinced Prime Minister Nehru of the need to state India's defense policy on the northern frontier in the clearest terms possible. In a statement to Parliament on December 6, 1950, he declared: "From time immemorial the Himalayas have provided us with magnificent frontiers. . . . We cannot allow that barrier to be penetrated because it is also the principal barrier to India. Therefore, much as we appreciate the independence of Nepal, we cannot allow anything to go wrong in Nepal or permit that barrier to be crossed or weakened, because that would be a risk to our own security." [15]

The specific reference in Nehru's statement was to Nepal, which was then in the throes of a revolution that threatened to result in political chaos. But by implication, at least, Bhutan too was a vital part of India's frontier security system if security was

15. *Jawaharlal Nehru Speeches, 1949–1953* (Publications Division, Government of India, 3rd cl., 1963), p. 252.

to be based upon the inviolability of the Himalayan barrier. In some ways, because of the Buddhist cultural background it shared with Tibet, Bhutan may have seemed to be even more vulnerable to subversion than Nepal.

While the Royal Government did not comment publicly upon Nehru's policy statement, its significance for Bhutan's own northern border was recognized. By and large, the Bhutanese shared the Indian prime minister's concern over the strategic and security implications of a Chinese-controlled Tibet. The Royal Government was reluctant to formally and publicly align itself with India in any overt way at this time, but its confidence was considerably enhanced by the implicit guarantee of Indian support in the event problems should arise with the Chinese on Bhutan's border with Tibet.

By 1954, both Indian and Bhutanese apprehensions over the Chinese conquest of Tibet had subsided. The Sino-Tibetan Treaty signed in May 1951 guaranteed a limited autonomy for the Dalai Lama's government and also theoretically restricted the Chinese presence in Tibet. Relations between China and India improved further in 1952 with the conclusion of an agreement that allowed New Delhi to maintain a consul-general in Lhasa, and even more dramatically in May 1954 with the signing of a treaty based upon the "five principles" of "peaceful coexistence." Bhutan, like New Delhi, seems to have concluded that China had limited ambitions on the Himalayan frontier and that, therefore, no fundamental changes in the Royal Government's foreign and defense policies were required. Bhutan's representative at Lhasa continued to function in a near-normal fashion, and the trade and political relationship between the Bhutanese and the Dalai Lama's governments was not seriously impaired by the Chinese. But this was not to last.

The Re-emergence of China: 1952–1962

The amity, amounting to a limited alliance on some issues, that characterized Sino-Indian relations after 1954 proved to have a short survival capacity. Developments both in Tibet and along the lengthy Himalayan border placed ever-increasing strains on the relationship. Persistent Chinese violations of the

1951 Sino-Tibetan agreement, once Chinese military forces had moved into Tibet in some strength, made it evident that Nehru's hope that the Dalai Lama's government would be able to maintain an autonomous status had been unrealistic. The outbreak of a full-scale revolt against the Chinese in eastern Tibet (Kham) in 1954–1955 contributed to the deterioration in Sino-Indian relations. Peking reportedly suspected that support for the rebels in the form of arms and supplies was being channeled through northeastern India, presumably with the connivance of officials in New Delhi. The rebellion in Kham also intersected China's vital communication system to central Tibet intermittently. This led Peking to decide on the construction of a road from Sinkiang to western Tibet that cut across territory claimed by India. A direct confrontation on this issue was postponed for several years but finally erupted in 1959. By that time, Sino-Indian amity had been replaced by ever-deepening enmity in which Bhutan inevitably became enmeshed.

By 1958, the stronghold of the Khampa rebellion had shifted from eastern to central Tibet. The rebels had also established a stronghold in the area around Tsona, a short distance directly to the north of the Bhutan border. It was at this time that Nehru decided to make a personal visit to Bhutan—his first— in the Fall of 1958 to discuss with the Druk Gyalpo the policies to be pursued by their respective governments. Nehru strongly urged the Royal Government to modify its isolation policy, at least to the extent of accepting Indian economic aid. New Delhi was particularly interested in the construction of a road connecting India with central and western Bhutan which would have obvious strategic and economic significance. Bhutan's immediate response was noncommittal despite its own increasing concern over developments to the north. The Royal Government still hoped to avoid any direct role in the big-power confrontation then emerging, since involvement was perceived as holding grave dangers for Bhutan.[16]

Bhutan's hopes to preserve its isolation policy intact, how-

16. When Nehru was asked how Bhutan had reacted to India's offer of aid, he replied: "You will be surprised to learn how reluctant the Maharaja [Druk

ever, dissipated with the course of developments in 1959 that seemed to make inescapable a much closer relationship with India. In March, a massive popular uprising against the Chinese in Lhasa was finally suppressed after several days of hard fighting, but by this time virtually all of central Tibet was in revolt. The Dalai Lama, taking advantage of the confusion in Lhasa, made his escape to India through the Kameng district of the North-East Frontier Agency directly adjacent to Bhutan on the east. The crisis in Tibet coincided with the first public announcement by the Indian authorities that a border dispute on the Ladakh-western Tibet border had led to several small-scale encounters between Chinese and Indian military forces in the disputed area. By the end of 1959, New Delhi and Peking were exchanging acrimonious allegations against each other, and the principle of peaceful coexistence had come back to haunt the creator of the concept, Prime Minister Nehru.

The Bhutan government's response to the rapidly deteriorating situation in the Himalayan region was initially characterized by vacillation and uncertainty,[17] but a basic policy decision obviously could not be long delayed. Tibetan refugees, including a few with marital ties to prominent Bhutanese families, were pouring into Bhutan in numbers quite beyond the capacity of the Royal Government to handle. Their stories of Chinese atrocities against both the Tibetan people and religious institutions had a strong impact on the Bhutanese, most of whom

---

Gyalpo] is. He is not at all happy. He could have had aid the last two or three years if he had asked for it" (*The Hindustan Times*, Oct. 3, 1958).

17. According to one Tibetan source, the Bhutanese border guards at first tried to prevent the refugees from entering Bhutan (see Mary Taring, *Daughter of Tibet*). A short time before the uprising in Lhasa, Prime Minister Jigme Dorji noted that the Tibetan rebels had moved close to the Bhutan border and said, "If they try to transgress our territory and trouble our people, we will resist them with all our strength." Asked if Bhutan would allow entry to Tibetan refugees, he replied, "We will not be in a position to grant them asylum nor would we encourage their settlement on our soil" (*Asian Recorder*, 5:11 [March 14–20, 1959], 2559). The Bhutan government finally decided to permit entry to Tibetan refugees, most of whom were funneled down to India as quickly as possible. New Delhi was not too happy with this, and it was only after some discussion that India finally agreed to accept the refugees. One of the reasons why Bhutan closed its borders with Tibet in 1960 was to stem the flow of refugees into the country.

were devout Buddhists deeply attached to the culture and religion which they shared with Tibet.[18]

The Chinese offensive against the Tibetan rebels made slow progress, but by late 1959 key centers in southern Tibet were brought under control. The following spring the offensive was extended to Tsona district, directly to the north of Bhutan. By the end of 1960 all the major passes were patrolled by Chinese border guards. A number of minor incidents occurred in this period, usually involving small-scale Chinese incursions into Bhutanese territory. While these were probably attributable to uncertainty on the part of the Chinese—and the Bhutanese—as to the actual location of the border, the Bhutanese, alert to any indications of hostile intentions on the part of China, were not certain that these incidents were of only local significance.

Enhancing the Royal Government's sensitivity on relations with China was the publication in 1961 of a new map depicting Peking's version of the border along the entire Himalayan frontier. While the map was primarily intended to support Chinese territorial claims against India, it also contained several minor divergences from previous Chinese maps concerning the border with Bhutan. Considerable publicity in both the Indian and Western press was given at this time to alleged Chinese historical claims to the Himalayan border states of Bhutan, Sikkim, and Nepal. While the claims were never substantiated by citation to specific Chinese statements, there were enough wholesale irredentist claims in print by Mao Tse-tung and other Chinese leaders, based for the most part upon exaggerated assumptions about the extent of imperial China's frontiers, to make such allegations seem plausible to the Bhutanese authorities.

The publicity concerning new claims coincided with increasing pressure from New Delhi directed toward the opening up of Bhutan and the establishment of a substantial Indian presence in the country. In New Delhi, Bhutan appeared to be one of the most vulnerable points in the Indian security system,

18. For instance, Prime Minister Jigme Dorji's father-in-law, the Tsarong Shape, was arrested and subjected to such indignities by the Chinese that he committed suicide (*The Hindustan Times*, Sept. 7, 1959).

since it was the only area on the Himalayan frontier that was not under direct Indian administration and at the same time the only area with which India did not have some form of security arrangement. This weak point in the Indian defense system, in New Delhi's view, had to be rectified quickly if the Himalayan barrier was to be maintained intact.

Given the Bhutanese interpretation of the course of events in the Himalayan region in 1959–1960 and the political orientation of the dominant elites in the Royal Government, the decision to accept a broad-scale alignment with India was not surprising. In any event, there do not appear to have been serious differences within the government on this issue at the time the decision was taken. The disagreements came later.

Bhutan's alignment with India took a number of forms. In 1959–1960, several economic-aid agreements, including a major road project linking central Bhutan with India, were concluded between the two governments. In 1961, the training of the Royal Bhutan Army was formally entrusted to the Indian Army, by implication at least bringing Bhutan within the Indian security and defense system. Prime Minister Nehru specifically declared in 1959 that an attack on Nepal or Bhutan would be interpreted as an attack on Indian territory, thus extending the Indian security system to the entire sub-Himalayan region. While the Nepal government expressed some reservations on Nehru's statement in its public comments (although in private it welcomed the assurances of Indian support), Bhutan raised no objections, either publicly or privately, implicitly accepting India's defense guarantee.[19]

Indeed, Bhutan occasionally moved slightly ahead of India on certain aspects of its China policy. In 1960, for instance, the Royal Government imposed a total ban on trade with Tibet [20]

19. Indeed, Prime Minister Jigme Dorji stated in Calcutta that Bhutan welcomed Nehru's assurance of support in the event of Chinese aggression, but added that "it is nevertheless eager to make its sovereign status clear" (*Asian Recorder*, 5:36 [Sept. 5–11, 1959], 2868).
20. According to Prime Minister Jigme Dorji, the ban was first imposed "as a defensive measure," as Bhutanese traders in Tibet were systematically subjected to "anti-Bhutanese" propaganda by the Chinese (*Asian Recorder*, 6:26 [June 27–July 1, 1960], 3402–3403).

several months before New Delhi declared its own embargo on trade across the Himalayas. The ban was a severe blow to the Bhutanese economy which had long depended upon the Tibetan market for the disposal of its substantial rice surplus (and in 1959–1960 the Chinese were paying premium prices for food grains and other essential commodities). India was neither a feasible alternative market nor a source of supply for those goods that Bhutan had imported from Tibet. Thus, until the road to India was opened in 1963, Bhutan paid a high price for its trade policy. The Royal Government, however, was not disposed to seek economic advantages for itself by helping to sustain the Chinese military forces in what was interpreted in Bhutan as a war against the Tibetan people.

Peking's policy toward Bhutan in this period varied from occasional blustering denunciations seemingly aimed at intimidating the Royal Government to conciliatory gestures presumably intended to convince the Bhutanese that they had nothing to fear from China. There have been reports, later substantiated by authoritative Bhutanese sources, that the Chinese offered economic assistance to Bhutan. Chou En-lai also reassured the Royal Government on several occasions that China had no aggressive intentions against Bhutan and that Peking was prepared to settle all outstanding disputes through direct negotiations.

This raised a delicate procedural problem for the Bhutan government, since under the 1949 Indo-Bhutanese Treaty it had agreed to accept the guidance of the Indian government on its external relations. New Delhi interpreted this to mean that Bhutan could not have direct relations with a third power except with India's concurrence, and this the Indian authorities were not prepared to concede with respect to Sino-Bhutanese negotiations in the context of its own confrontation with China. Bhutan's interpretation of the relevant Treaty clause differed from that of India, the Bhutanese contending that the Royal Government was obligated only to consult with New Delhi on external relations questions but not necessarily to accept the advice received.

In the context of the situation pertaining in the 1960–1962

period, however, this was an academic question, as Bhutan was not disposed to press its own interpretation of the treaty clause too avidly. Indeed, the Royal Government requested the Indian government to raise the various issues in dispute between Bhutan and China in the series of Sino-Indian border talks held in 1961.[21] Peking categorically refused to discuss the subject with the Indian delegation, in effect rejecting New Delhi's right to speak for Bhutan even when authorized to do so by the Royal Government. Chou En-lai was careful to state that China would respect the "proper relations" between Bhutan and India, implying among other things that Bhutan should be allowed to conduct its own negotiations with third states. New Delhi, on the other hand, insisted that its special relationship with Bhutan, derived from the guidance clause in the 1949 Treaty, should be recognized by other powers.[22]

Because of this difference in their respective viewpoints, Bhutan was never considered a subject for discussion in the 1961 Sino-Indian talks, although India did insert a statement supportive of Bhutan's position on the border with Tibet in its own report on these negotiations. This situation has remained unchanged subsequently, and there has not yet been an international forum of any kind in which the comparatively minor differences between Bhutan and China might have been resolved or even discussed by the parties to the dispute. This has been an irritant to the Royal Government, although not a serious problem in any real sense.

The 1962 Sino-Indian Border War and Bhutan

The long-smoldering dispute between India and China finally erupted into a border war in October 1962. The hostili-

21. One of the issues in dispute between Bhutan and China concerned the eight enclaves in western Tibet that had been administered by Bhutan since the seventeenth century. These enclaves were seized by the Chinese in 1959, and the Bhutanese officials were expelled. New Delhi has sought on several occasions to raise this point with Peking at the request of the Bhutan government, but the Chinese have always refused to discuss the matter through an Indian intermediary.

22. In a press conference in New Delhi during his April 1961 visit, Chou En-lai inadvertently referred to India's "special relations" with Sikkim and Bhutan, but this was changed to "proper relations" in the official Chinese news release on the prime minister's comments.

ties, however, were limited to the eastern and western extremities of the long Himalayan frontier–the North-East Frontier Agency (NEFA) and Ladakh, respectively. Kameng district in NEFA, bordering on eastern Bhutan, was the scene of the largest and most decisive battles in this brief border war.

After some preliminary skirmishes in September 1962, mostly for control of a few strategic frontier posts, the Chinese launched an offensive so massive in scale for this difficult mountainous region that it must have been at least several months in preparation. The badly outnumbered Indian forces in Kameng district were quickly overwhelmed. The Chinese forces then outflanked the main Indian defense line at Se La, forcing the trapped Indian units to retreat through Bhutan—with the assistance of the Bhutanese authorities in the Tashigang area. At this point China announced a unilateral ceasefire and a withdrawal of its forces north of the main Himalayan crest, thus virtually restoring the situation to what had existed prior to the war.

The response of the Bhutan government to this unprecedented crisis was marked by uncertainty as to China's ultimate objectives and to India's capacity to assist Bhutan if it should inadvertently become involved in the conflict. The Royal Government sought to maintain strict neutrality, at least formally, but it was only too aware that its close alignment with India made Bhutan a vulnerable target if the Chinese were disposed to move against it.

One important factor in the Royal Government's calculation was the realization that the Himalayan pass most critical to the support of Chinese operations in the Kameng district of NEFA is situated on the Bhutan-Tibet border. This pass is formed by a trans-Himalayan tributary of the Manas river and is the only pass in the eastern Himalayas that is usually snow-free during the winter season. If the Chinese had intended to continue military operations in NEFA, they would have had to use this pass for logistical support purposes. This would have brought Bhutan into the war. Peking's unilateral withdrawal decision, therefore, was welcomed in Thimphu.

The sudden and drastic changes in the power balance in the Himalayas in the immediate post-1962 war period led inevitably to a re-evaluation of certain aspects of Bhutan's foreign policy. For the first time, some support was expressed in Bhutanese elite circles for emulation of the Nepali foreign-policy model based upon equal friendship with India and China combined with a balance-of-power strategy. The Nepali approach to foreign policy has several features appealing to the Bhutanese, and indeed the debate on this issue has by no means subsided a decade later.

The Royal Government, however, eventually rejected the Nepali foreign-policy model as inappropriate for Bhutan and opted instead for an expansion of relations with India. One reason was the basically different Bhutanese and Nepali perception of Chinese policy in Tibet. The Nepali political elite had little real empathy for the Buddhist political and cultural system in Tibet and demonstrated only minimal sympathy for the fate suffered by Tibet at the hands of a much larger and more powerful neighbor. Most Bhutanese, on the other hand, were appalled at the wanton and deliberate destruction of an ancient culture that had so much in common with their own.

Moreover, the justification advanced by the Chinese for their aggressive policy in Tibet, based largely upon historical claims (which the Bhutanese consider spurious), raised questions in the minds of the Royal Government as to whether their own country might not at some point share the same fate as their Tibetan neighbor. In other words, there were much stronger doubts about China's *bona fides* and ultimate objectives in Thimphu than there were in Kathmandu.

Significant differences in Nepal's and Bhutan's treaty relations with India also were of some importance. Under their respective treaties with India, Kathmandu is merely required to consult with New Delhi on matters of common concern, while Thimphu is obligated to seek the guidance of India on its external relations. If Bhutan had decided to adopt a foreign policy based on the Nepali model, it would have had to gain New Delhi's agreement to the amendment of the 1949 Treaty. The Indian government, which at that time was striving to preserve what remained of its northern-border security system, was not at all disposed to consider revision of the treaty, and Bhutan lacked the capacity to pressure New Delhi into unwanted concessions.

But perhaps the key factor in the Royal Government's decision against embarking on any novel foreign policy adventures in the post-1962 period were its reservations about the long-run viability of the Nepali model for Bhutan.[23] There was a strong impression in Thimphu that Kathmandu had often sacrificed long-range interests in its relationship with India for short-term gains that were primarily intended to pander to the nationalistic sentiments of the articulate Nepali public. Nepal had succeeded in creating a more positive international image abroad and had seemingly gained greater autonomy in policy-making on some foreign policy issues. But much of this was a mirage, as later developments demonstrated, and the price paid, both politically and economically, was frequently very high. Moreover, in the process Nepal was transformed into an arena of big-power competition and, potentially, confrontation. The Bhutanese decision-makers believed that they could attain as positive results, if in a more gradual and less dramatic fashion, by a different approach that posed fewer dangers to the existing political and social culture in the country.

The Bhutanese foreign-policy strategy was based upon the assumption that New Delhi would not obstruct the gradual expansion of Bhutan's relations with the outside world if this could be accomplished without undermining India's regional and security interests. In 1961, it was noted, India had sponsored Bhutan's membership in the Colombo Plan when requested to do so by the Royal Government, the first occasion upon which Bhutan had sought and obtained membership in an international organization. It was expected that India would prove just as accommodating if Bhutan should decide to expand its international relations in other directions as well. The Royal Government felt no great urgency on these matters in the early 1960s, and indeed proceeded with the utmost caution—and not only because of Indian sensitivity on such ques-

23. One relevant fact is that Nepal is twelve times the size of Bhutan in population and has more substantial internal resources. Thus, what might be a viable foreign policy for Nepal is not necessarily the case for Bhutan.

tions. Thimphu did not generally perceive New Delhi as an in-transigent obstacle to Bhutan's foreign-policy objectives but rather as the most plausible channel for their fulfillment *if* the Royal Government played its cards carefully and with some evident concern for India's interests as well.[24]

Closer Ties with New Delhi

There were several indications in 1963 that the Royal Government had decided that the critical situation in the Himalayas required an even closer relationship with India. One of the most significant perhaps was its agreement to the deputation of an Indian adviser to assist Prime Minister Jigme Dorji. Nari Rustomji, an officer in the Indian Frontier Service with extensive experience in Sikkim and NEFA,[25] was selected for this post by New Delhi on the recommendation of his good friend, Prime Minister Jigme Dorji. His duties and responsibilities were left undefined, but he served both as a consultant to the prime minister on policy matters and as a channel of communication between the two governments. The latter function assumed increasing importance with the rapid expansion of political and economic relations between the two countries.

Jigme Dorji had been given the rank of Lonchen in 1958 at the time of the Druk Gyalpo's first heart attack and had been granted extensive powers in the internal administration of Bhutan. The Druk Gyalpo's second attack in 1963 was more severe, and this time Jigme Dorji was appointed regent during the king's absence abroad for medical treatment.[26]

The timing of Rustomji's assumption of his duties in Thimphu with the Druk Gyalpo's second heart attack added considerably to the importance of the adviser's role. For several

---

24. That Bhutan did not seek to take advantage of India's temporary embarrassment in the aftermath of the 1962 border war was appreciated in New Delhi and partly explains the subsequent responsiveness of the Indian government to requests from Bhutan.
25. Rustomji had served as chief minister (Dewan) of Sikkim and as adviser to the governor of Assam on NEFA, both critical frontier administrative positions.
26. It was in these circumstances that Jigme Dorji requested the Indian government to depute his good friend, Nari Rustomji, to Bhutan as his adviser.

months, the Druk Gyalpo was virtually incapacitated in Switzerland where he was recuperating from the heart attack. The Royal Government, so long dependent upon a firm guiding hand from the palace, faced a severe leadership crisis, for this was a period of ferment and indecision within Bhutanese governmental circles on both foreign and domestic policy issues. Prime Minister Jigme Dorji sought to fill the leadership gap in the administration, but he faced strong opposition within both the Royal Government and the Bhutan Army.

In April 1964 the assassination of Prime Minister Jigme Dorji led to a crisis of major proportions within the government that for a time threatened to erupt into open civil war. The Druk Gyalpo rushed back from Switzerland to resume his position of leadership, but his ill-health did not permit him to operate on a full-time basis. He depended heavily upon his younger half-brother, Namgyal Wangchuck, and also provided some continuity in the administration through the appointment of Lhendup Dorji, the late prime minister's younger brother, as acting prime minister. The political elite was still in a state of turmoil, however, and rumors of conspiracies and counterconspiracies filled the air, compounded by what was described as an abortive assassination attempt on the Druk Gyalpo himself in July 1965. Lhendup Dorji, fearing that his own life was in jeopardy, fled to Nepal shortly thereafter, followed by his sister, Tashi, several members of his political faction, and two high-ranking army officers.

The role of Indian officials posted to Bhutan in this period has been a subject for controversy ever since. Statements originating in Kathmandu—eagerly reported by the anti-Indian elements in the Nepalese press—alleged that the Indian government officials had master-minded both Jigme Dorji's assassination and the conspiracy against Lhendup Dorji that had forced him to flee from Bhutan.[27] India was motivated, supposedly, by the determination of the Dorji brothers to revise

27. There were allegations in Bhutan that the commander of IMTRAT (the Indian Military Training Team in Bhutan) was behind the conspiracy. Rustomji's name was also brought into the plot on a couple of occasions, but no specific charges were directed against him.

Bhutan's foreign policy in the direction of a more nonaligned position between India and China.

While all the details about these events in 1964–1965 have still not been disclosed, the evidence available casts doubts upon the reliability of the press reports from Kathmandu. Prime Minister Jigme Dorji had long been one of the principal supporters of the alignment policy with India, and no substantive evidence has yet been presented to indicate that he had changed his position before he was assassinated.[28] Lhendup Dorji was a more mercurial figure, as he was not as experienced in the palace-based politics of Bhutan and thus was in no position to dominate the government as his brother had done during the illnesses of the Druk Gyalpo.

Whatever the facts may be, the Druk Gyalpo went out of his way to reassure New Delhi that his government's policy on relations with India had not been affected by the dramatic series of events. He undertook a state visit to India in May 1966 and told the Indian public that "I am deeply touched by the sympathy and understanding with which the Government of India views our problems. The help and advice furnished by the Government of India are of great value to us and are appreciated by my Government and my people." [29] He added substance to this reaffirmation of Bhutan's alignment policy by agreeing to a considerable expansion of the Indian aid program, including military aid, during India's Second Five Year Plan period.

The role of the Indian adviser, however, continued to be an irritant to Bhutanese political circles. The Tshogdu (National Assembly), in particular, expressed concern with what some of its members perceived as direct Indian involvement in Bhutan's decision-making process. On Rustomji's appointment to an-

28. The author had an interview with Jigme Dorji in Calcutta in February 1964, approximately two months before his assassination. On that occasion, he strongly supported continuance of the alignment with India. Moreover, it was Jigme Dorji who, for the first time, invited an Indian adviser to Bhutan, thus expanding Indian influence in domestic politics. It seems unlikely that he would have done this if a more balanced relationship with India and China was his objective.

29. V. H. Coelho, *Sikkim and Bhutan* (Delhi: 1971), p. 73.

other position in the Indian Frontier Service in 1966, therefore, it was mutually agreed that no successor should be appointed, and the post of adviser was, in effect, eliminated.
This raised some problems with respect to the formal lines of
communication between the two governments. The post of
Bhutan agent in India had been abolished some time after
Jigme Dorji's assassination, closing what had been the established channel. There was a Bhutan State Trading Corpora-
tion office in Calcutta, headed by an Indian businessman, but
its location, leadership, and restriction to strictly commercial
operations made it an inappropriate agency to represent Bhutan in India. The Indian political officer in Gangtok was still officially accredited to Bhutan, but in fact rarely functioned in
this capacity. There were numerous other Indian officials in
the various aid programs in Bhutan, but they were specifically
forbidden by mutual agreement from assuming any role in the
political relations between the two countries. The Bhutanese
were particularly sensitive on this latter point, for they were determined to prevent India's economic-aid programs from becoming instruments for Indian intervention in Bhutan's decision-making process.

There was recognition in both Thimphu and New Delhi that
some form of *de facto* diplomatic relationship was essential, particularly as the Royal Government was slowly and cautiously expanding its international contacts. In 1966, Thimphu asked the
Indian government to sponsor Bhutan's membership in the
Universal Postal Union. New Delhi agreed, and in 1969 Bhutan
became a member of a second international organization, the
Colombo Plan being its first venture. In the 1966 and 1967 sessions of the Tshogdu, widespread support was voiced for Bhutan's participation in the United Nations. Obviously this would
require detailed and continuous negotiations between Bhutan
and India, for UN membership would constitute a most significant expansion of Bhutan's external relations.

Periodic exchanges of visits between leading officials of the
two governments were no longer sufficient to serve the new
relationship, and some new institutional arrangement seemed
necessary to both sides. In 1967, therefore, New Delhi pro-

posed the appointment of an officer of its External Affairs Ministry on full-time deputation to Thimphu. The Royal Government was reportedly disposed to accept the Indian proposal until the plan received a very hostile reception in the Tshogdu. When submitted for consideration, some members of the Tshogdu expressed concern that the Indian representative would be able to exert undue influence within the Bhutan government, and would in the process raise further doubts abroad about the country's sovereignty. It was also argued that the Indian proposal was inequitable in that it did not provide for the establishment of a Bhutanese mission in New Delhi.

The Indian government expressed surprise over the adverse response to its proposal, but also indicated its willingness to go some distance to accommodate the criticism. In late 1968, Bhutan permitted the Indian government to depute an official with the title of "special officer" to Thimphu, on the condition that his activities would be restricted to normal diplomatic functions—primarily he would serve as a channel of communication between the two governments. Bhutan at that time was not interested in establishing its own mission in New Delhi, but the Royal Government's position on this subject changed with Bhutan's admission to the UN in the Fall of 1971, since it was considered necessary to have missions in both New York and New Delhi if complications in Bhutan's relationship with India were to be avoided. Accordingly, an agreement was reached in 1972 under which missions were exchanged between India and Bhutan, headed by officials designated as "representatives." [30]

The Trend of Developments

The 1960s were difficult and dangerous years for Bhutan, both internally and externally. At times the survival of the monarchical polity, and indeed the country itself, seemed to be in jeopardy. But by the end of the decade the most serious problems had been effectively handled, if not necessarily resolved, by the third Druk Gyalpo and the corps of experienced administrators upon whom he had come to depend.

30. Later, however, their respective representatives had the titles "Ambassador and Plenipotentiary Extraordinary" used in their letters of credential.

Prospects for the 1970s, thus, appear much brighter. Even the death of Druk Gyalpo Jigme Dorji Wangchuck in mid-1972, and the succession of the 17-year-old crown prince to the throne, did not result in a major political crisis as would almost certainly have been the case a few years earlier. While the gradual institutionalization of a more broadly inclusive political system was primarily responsible for the smooth succession, recent successes in Bhutan's external relations also served to enhance the confidence with which the political elite perceive the future. *United Nations Membership.* Wider recognition abroad of Bhutan's sovereign national identity had become a high priority in the government's foreign policy in the latter half of the 1960s. Most of the discussion on this subject focused on Bhutan's admission to the United Nations, for it was generally assumed that the UN was the most suitable institution through which to project a more positive image of Bhutan's national identity. While a few Bhutanese continued to question the wisdom of abandoning the country's traditional isolation policy, there was a broad censensus within governmental circles on the UN membership issue.

There was also, of course, the delicate task of eliciting New Delhi's cooperation in this endeavor, for without such aid the project would have been infeasible. While India had sponsored Bhutan's membership in two other international organizations, these had been of comparatively minor significance to the political relations between the two countries. Participation in the United Nations was a very different proposition, with much broader implications for both Bhutan and India. New Delhi had been disturbed by the precedent set by Nepal in the 1950s when Kathmandu had combined admission to the UN with foreign-policy innovations that sought to replace Nepal's special relationship with India by a policy of equal friendship with India and China. Obviously, extensive negotiations between Thimphu and New Delhi were required if the UN membership issue was not to place a heavy strain on relations between the two governments.

In the 1967–1969 period, several discussions were held on this question between various levels of Indian and Bhutanese officialdom before a mutually satisfactory meeting of the minds was finally achieved.[31] Thereafter, in the 1970 session of the UN, India proposed Bhutan's admission to the international organization, and a resolution to this effect was quickly approved without opposition from any source. Bhutan's formal admission as a full member occurred at the 1971 Fall session of the UN. This was universally welcomed in Bhutan as one of the proudest achievements of the country's foreign policy, and India's cooperative attitude and support on this issue were lauded in subsequent public statements.

The opening of a permanent mission to the United Nations in New York in 1972 had several immediate consequences. For one thing, it provided Bhutan with an alternative channel of communication to the outside world, and one that is in some respects of more importance than the mission in New Delhi where the mission has to function in an Indian environment. Both missions are of course in normal contact with other foreign delegations, including those of China, Pakistan, Nepal, and other neighboring Asian states with which Bhutan does not yet have direct bilateral relations. Bhutan's dependence upon India as its intermediary with the outside world has thus been substantially reduced.[32] While the provisions of the 1949 Indo-Bhutanese Treaty still apply, the manner in which guidance is provided by New Delhi has undergone modification. According to Bhutanese sources, India has now accepted Thimphu's interpretation of the treaty—namely, that Bhutan is obligated to seek India's advice on foreign-policy questions but is not necessarily obliged to accept it. New Delhi has never publicly acknowledged this but appears to operate on this basis as a general practice.

31. Observers had been sent to UN sessions in 1968 and 1969 in order to familiarize themselves with UN procedures and operations and, more discreetly, to lobby for Bhutan's admission to the international organization.
32. It was a regular practice for the New Delhi embassies of several countries to send delegations to Bhutan for brief visits. While useful, these were not adequate substitutes for more regularized contacts, at least not to the Bhutanese. Moreover, such important embassies in New Delhi as the Chinese and Pakistani had never been included among the list of visitors to Bhutan until 1974 when the Chinese charge d'affaires in New Delhi attended the coronation of Druk Gyalpo Jigme Singye Wangchuck.

The establishment of two missions abroad and the need to maintain contacts with a growing number of foreign countries on a regularized basis have had another significant consequence—the formation of a Foreign Affairs Department in 1970 and then a Ministry of Foreign Affairs in 1972. For the first time there is a government institution in Bhutan whose primary responsibility is the formulation and implementation of foreign policy, a task that had been managed previously on an *ad hoc,* nonprofessional basis. The new ministry faces a formidable task, for there are several questions of fundamental importance to Bhutan with which it will have to deal in the 1970s.

Diversification of Economic Aid. In 1961, the Royal Government in effect handed over primary responsibility for the economic development of Bhutan to India, so much so indeed that the Development Secretariat in Bhutan was virtually established as a Government of India enterprise. Within the Development Ministry "Bhutanization" has been a very gradual process. By the mid-1970s most of the highest executive positions were held by Bhutanese, but a high proportion of subordinate and technical posts in the development departments were still staffed by Indians.

This situation has led to a long-term dialogue within the Bhutanese political elite on alternative strategies to lessen Bhutan's dependence upon a single source of economic and technical assistance. There have already been small aid inputs from Australia, Great Britain, New Zealand, Canada, Singapore, and Japan through the Colombo Plan and some bilateral aid from Switzerland. But these contributions have been so minute as to be insignificant in the total development program. Something more is required if diversification of aid sources is to be achieved. The discussion continues, focused, first, on whether Bhutan should seek further diversification and, second, on how best to diversify.

One factor that has inhibited Bhutan's search for alternative aid sources is the comparative liberality of the Indian aid program. The Royal Government has few legitimate complaints with respect to the quantity of aid, which has been generous, or to the way in which it is given. The practice has been for New Delhi to grant a sum of money, and to leave it to the sole discretion of the Bhutanese authorities to decide on the allocation of funds to the various development programs. This contrasts with the policy followed by virtually all economic-aid programs elsewhere (including the Indian aid program in Nepal) in which the donor country insists upon the right to select the projects which it will assist.

The procedure followed by India in this respect has mitigated to some extent the usual strains between donor and recipient countries. But some Bhutanese foresee new problems and requirements arising in the future that India may be hard pressed to meet. It is becoming increasingly difficult, for instance, for New Delhi to reserve a sufficient number of seats for Bhutanese students in Indian educational and technical institutions because of the heavy pressure for admittance within India itself. Bhutan, thus, may have to look elsewhere if it is to provide advanced educational opportunities for Bhutanese on the scale the country requires. As Bhutan develops, there is also the probability that certain types of aid will not be readily available from India (as, for example, in the large-scale exploitation of Bhutan's vast forest reserves, a project which may prove to be beyond India's capacity).

The Royal Government, therefore, has devised a developmental policy based upon limited diversification of aid sources, a policy which will nonetheless provide funds sufficient to meet its very minimal immediate requirements. In this respect the United Nations has been perceived as the most plausible, noncontroversial source of aid—in part because New Delhi tends to respond much less sensitively to international than to bilateral aid programs coming into its area of hegemony. Discussions with the United Nations Development Program (UNDP) culminated in a 1973 agreement under which $3.3 U.S. million in aid was promised over a three-year period, while another $6 million has been obtained from UNICEF, the World Food Program, and other UN agencies. The small-scale aid that Bhutan receives under the Colombo Plan has also been slightly expanded, though again on projects peripheral to the developmental enterprise.

This constitutes only very limited diversification, but it may well be the most Bhutan is prepared to permit for some time. The Royal Government appears to be disinclined to consider aid from either of the superpowers or from countries closely associated with them, or from other sources—for example, China—which might complicate Bhutan's political policies. The decision with respect to Japanese aid may prove to be more difficult, for Japan may be both interested in and capable of providing substantial economic assistance at a relatively low political price. But Bhutan's own reservations over a close aid relationship with Japan are reinforced by India's obvious lack of enthusiasm for any expansion of Japanese economic involvement in South Asia.

The Royal Government's attitude toward private foreign investment—from any source—is also essentially negative, if to a certain extent somewhat ambivalent, and extends not only to third-power private investment but even more directly to Indian sources. The regulations barring private Indian investment are very strict indeed, and even "disguised" Indian investments through indigenous "fronts"—so common in Nepal—have been effectively discouraged. The Royal Government is determined to prevent Indian private interests, and in particular the ubiquitous Marwari community's commercial enterprises that dominate credit and trade facilities throughout most of the Himalayas, from establishing themselves in Bhutan. No modification of this policy is projected, although the government's stance may well prove futile and result in counterproductive economic consequences over the long run.

There is the possibility that at some point third-power private investors would be permitted access if this could be accomplished to Bhutan's advantage economically and with minimal political consequences. But for the foreseeable future it is government sources that will continue to provide most of the foreign-aid input into Bhutan. And, despite the projected diversification of aid sources, it is India that will continue to provide the bulk of such aid.

China Policy. The spirit of détente in the early 1970s, battered though it may be, has to some extent imbued Bhutan's approach to relations with China. While the Royal Government's abhorrence of Chinese behavior and policy in Tibet has by no means disappeared, the government has reluctantly accepted the inevitability of having to accommodate itself to Peking's dominance of the area beyond the Himalayas. Relations with China, thus, are a most sensitive issue with which Bhutan's Ministry of Foreign Affairs will have to deal.

The immediate problem facing the two governments is the formal delimitation and on-the-spot demarcation of their 200-mile border. The boundary has never been demarcated in the past, and it is only in the more important pass areas through which the trade with Tibet once passed that there is any very precise understanding of where the limit of authority of one government ends and that of the other begins. Along most of the rest of the frontier there was apparently no felt need for the delimitation of jurisdiction prior to 1959, and this is where some problems arise. Most of the minor disputes since 1960 concern high-altitude pasture lands on the frontier that were, by tradition, used by both Bhutanese and Tibetan herdsmen. Several of the Chinese incursions into Bhutan in the past decade have involved such pasture lands, since Peking's policy along the entire Himalayan frontier region has been to claim such areas on the basis of usage by Tibetans.

The Chinese government has indicated its interest in a boundary settlement with Bhutan on several occasions since 1960, but has always insisted that agreement be accomplished through direct *bilateral* negotiations. The Royal Government has no inherent objection to such an approach, but its treaty commitments to India have made this infeasible—at least until very recently. It is understood in Thimphu that bilateral negotiations with China are possible at this time only in the context of some form of normalization of Sino-Indian relations—that is, if Bhutan's relations with India are not to be seriously affected. Meanwhile, the Royal Government is conducting surveys on its northern border and collecting whatever relevant documentary material is available in preparation for the day when Bhutanese and Chinese officials will face each other across the table to resolve their disagreements over borders and related issues.

Another aspect of Bhutan's China policy that may before too long lead to divisiveness in the Royal Government concerns the resumption of trade with Tibet. The Bhutanese economy, particularly in the barren northern border areas where resources are very limited, was adversely affected by the 1960 ban on trade with the Chinese in Tibet. The blockade was a unilateral imposition by Bhutan and presumably could be removed in the same way. The problem is not that simple, however, as Bhutan's relations with India are also intimately involved. As long as India retains its own embargo on trade with Tibet, Thimphu will be under strong pressure to follow suit. Here also, a rapprochement between India and China would seem to be a *sina qua non* for any liberalization of Bhutan's trade policy.

But even if the blockade should be lifted, it seems unlikely that the old Bhutan-Tibet trade pattern will re-emerge. Chinese policy toward trans-Himalayan trade has changed in some important respects since 1960. Commodities (such as wool) which formerly constituted a large proportion of Tibet's exports to Bhutan are now directed toward the vast market in China proper. Nor is Bhutan any longer in a position to provide the goods—rice in particular—that were exported to Tibet prior to the imposition of the embargo. The Royal Government would probably be interested in developing Paro as an entrepôt for trans-Himalayan trade if Sino-Indian relations should improve, but both Gangtok and Kathmandu are probably better situated for this kind of role.

Moreover, it is probable that Tibet would prove to be as much of a disappointment to Bhutan as it has been to Nepal as an alternative source for commodities presently imported from India. A whole new Bhutanese trade pattern has emerged since 1960, based upon ready access to India as both a market and a source of supply, and any changes in this trade structure would be highly disruptive to Bhutan's economy. The removal of the trade embargo with Tibet, therefore, would have at best a limited impact on Bhutan's trade system, except possibly in the sparsely populated but highly strategic northern border areas. Unlike Kathmandu in the early 1960s, Thimphu is still disinclined to pay a potentially high political price in its relations with India for the minimal economic gains that might accrue from a renewal of trade with Tibet.

In any case, it is readily apparent that Bhutan's policy toward China has very limited objectives at this time and does not project any substantial expansion of the relationship with that country. Apprehension over the ultimate objectives of Chinese policy in the Himalayan region has not disappeared, and the Royal Government's primary concern is with the settlement of those issues which have the potential of causing tension on its northern border. Any form of direct diplomatic relations with Peking is generally considered to be a long-term prospect at best.

There are, of course, a few Bhutanese who argue in official councils that Bhutan should emulate Nepal by cultivating China as a counterbalance to India's "neocolonial" political and economic presence in the country. Such arguments, however, have had little impact as yet. For one thing, the early 1970s are not like the early 1960s when a serious imbalance in Sino-Indian military capacity in the Himalayan region provided Nepal with an opportunity to play the delicate balancing games that the current strategic environment no longer permits. Nor is it considered plausible at this late date to attempt to redirect Bhutan's heavy economic dependence on India, or much optimism that China could be of any real assistance in programs with that as the objective. Kathmandu's failure to achieve economic diversification after two decades of intensive effort is a case in point, and Thimphu sees no reason to assume that it would be any more successful. To the Royal Government, then, Nepal is as much an example of how *not* to manage a country's external relations as it is an object for emulation. No doubt the Royal Government wants China as a friendly (or at least nonthreatening) neighbor, but one with whom relations are correct rather than intimate.

Diversification of Diplomatic Relations. Bhutan introduced a carefully contrived policy directed at expanding its external relations beyond India in the mid-1960s.[33] The decision to join

33. However, as early as 1959 the Legal Adviser to the Bhutan government, D. K. Sen (an Indian citizen), had announced that Bhutan was considering es-

the United Nations was, of course, a major step forward, but this was qualitatively different from the establishment of diplomatic relations with other governments on a bilateral basis. It was only in 1973, therefore, with the exchange of diplomatic representation with Bangladesh, that the Royal Government introduced a new facet to its foreign policy. But even this innovation was limited by the provision in the agreement under which the heads of the Bhutan and Bangladesh missions in New Delhi were each accredited to the other government. For the time being, there is no intention on either side to establish permanent missions in Thimphu and Dacca. It was considered significant, however, that the heads of the two missions were designated as "ambassadors" rather than as "representatives" as was the case with India and Bhutan.

Several factors made Bangladesh an attractive choice as the second country with which to establish bilateral relations. Proximity was of some importance, of course, although that was not the decisive consideration (China, after all, is more proximate to Bhutan than Bangladesh). There had also been strong sympathy in Bhutan for Bangladesh during its war of independence in 1971. That Bhutan had been the second government to recognize Bangladesh [34] had been greatly appreciated in Dacca, and made it responsive to the proposal for an exchange of ambassadors.

Economic calculations also played an important role in Bhutan's decision, since there are some expectations for development of trade relations with Bangladesh. While trade will have to be on a modest scale initially, the potential for rapid expansion is assumed to exist. Bangladesh provides Bhutan with an

tablishing diplomatic relations with third countries, including the U.S.S.R., the United States, Great Britain, and a few Buddhist neighbors (*Asian Recorder*, 5:36 [Sept. 5–11, 1959], 2686). After consultations with Prime Minister Jigme Dorji in New Delhi, Nehru wrote the Bhutan government that "it would be inadvisable for Bhutan to establish direct contacts with foreign powers" as this would involve it in big-power confrontations. His advice was accepted (*The Hindustan Times*, June 3, 1960).

34. It was generally assumed abroad that Bhutan was merely following India's lead on this issue. According to authoritative Bhutanese sources, however, the Royal Government acted on its own initiative and without any prodding from New Delhi in recognizing Bangladesh.

alternative, easily accessible market and source of supply, as well as another outlet to the rest of the world through its two major seaports. To a landlocked country such as Bhutan, this is important—psychologically at this time and possibly economically and politically in the future.[35]

Finally, Bangladesh in 1973 may have been the only additional country with which Bhutan could establish diplomatic relations without complicating its relations with New Delhi. Since India, after the 1971 Indo-Pakistani War, had been encouraging other governments to establish relations with one another, it could not reasonably refuse Bhutan the same privilege. Bangladesh was, thus, the logical choice as the second government with which Bhutan might establish bilateral relations. Further choices, however, are likely to prove much more difficult as the political environment cannot be expected to be as favorable and clearcut as it was in the case of Bangladesh.

Nepal is another neighbor that has indicated interest in the development of diplomatic relations with Bhutan, but substantial problems intrude. For one thing, there is some suspicion in Thimphu that what Kathmandu wants is an Himalayan ally that will follow its lead on foreign-policy issues. There are serious reservations in the Royal Government over any form of association with Nepali initiatives in regional or international organization politics. While the idea of an "Himalayan Federation" may be a figment of some journalist's imagination (it certainly has little appeal to Bhutan) the Royal Government is not inclined to ignore New Delhi's evident sensitivity on this subject.

The large Nepali Bhutanese community in Bhutan, which is still a potential source of dissension within the country, further complicates the question of diplomatic relations with Nepal. There is some apprehension that closer relations might raise expectations of support from Kathmandu for a political move-

35. Political developments in Bangladesh since the assassination of President Mujibur Rahman in August 1975, and the subsequent deterioration in Indo-Bangladeshi relations, cannot help but have an adverse impact on Thimphu's relations with Dacca. The idea of using Chittagong harbor in Bangladesh as an alternate access to the sea (to Calcutta), for instance, is not feasible under such adverse conditions.

ment in southern Bhutan, and the sensationalist, highly exaggerated reports on Bhutan that appear on occasion in the "guided" Nepali press do not relieve Bhutanese anxieties on this point. There are, thus, several good reasons for the Royal Government to welcome diplomatic relations with Nepal, but at least for the immediate future the arguments against such a venture will probably prove to be more persuasive.

Nor are the prospects for diplomatic relations with the other South Asian states—Pakistan and Sri Lanka—any brighter. Neither country is of any economic importance to Bhutan now, nor likely to be in the future. India's perennially strained relations with Pakistan are likely to discourage the Bhutan government from seriously considering diplomatic relations with the latter country until a regional settlement acceptable to New Delhi has been achieved—still an unlikely proposition. Sri Lanka, as another Buddhist country, may have some appeal to the Bhutan government, but diplomatic relations with this country would be devoid of much political or economic significance.

It is possible, therefore, that Bhutan's next venture in bilateral diplomatic relations will be with states outside the southern Asia region. Switzerland is the Western country with which the Bhutan royal family has had particularly intimate contacts, and a diplomatic initiative in this direction might appear both safe and attractive. Australia and New Zealand are two other countries with which Bhutan has limited economic relations that might be expanded into the diplomatic sphere. The exchange of diplomatic representation with these three states would have the added attraction of raising only minor complications in Bhutan's relations with India. Japan is yet another country which might respond favorably to overtures from Bhutan, but in this instance the political obstacles are more formidable.

Neither the United States nor the Soviet Union have as yet demonstrated much public interest in Bhutan, and this diffidence is more than matched by Thimphu's reservations about its relationship with the superpowers. It would be a simple matter for Bhutan to accredit its ambassador to the United Nations in New York to Washington as well, as Nepal did in the 1950s.

But diplomatic relations with the United States and not with the Soviet Union is not a viable policy for the Royal Government, particularly in view of New Delhi's close alignment with Moscow and its continuing antagonism toward Washington. The basic principle of Bhutan's foreign policy in the 1970s is to gain international recognition of its status as a sovereign component of the comity of nations without, however, at the same time becoming entangled in international politics—beyond South Asia, that is. Relations with the major actors on the world-politics stage—the United States, Soviet Union, Japan, China, and the larger Western European states—could compromise Bhutan's noninvolvement (not nonalignment) policy, and are thus best avoided at this stage.

Yet another factor that would seriously inhibit Bhutan's involvement in international politics is the requirement that diplomatic missions be established abroad, as Bhutan's stringent financial limitations (particularly the lack of foreign exchange) make this infeasible. Under the normal rules of international protocol, if Bhutan does not establish missions abroad, any of the countries—other than India—with which Bhutan may develop bilateral diplomatic relations will not establish missions in Thimphu. Thus, any diversification in Bhutan's bilateral relations with other countries in the 1970s is likely to be of limited significance. No doubt New Delhi and New York will continue to serve as Bhutan's principal windows on the outside world.

The Emerging Relationship with India. While no fundamental change in Bhutan's close alignment with India has occurred as yet, there have been several minor modifications, as the preceding discussion has indicated. But there are too many ties, political and economic, binding the two countries together to make substantive adjustments by either side a simple proposition. Barring an internal political upheaval that threatens the unity of India or a renewal of Sino-Indian hostilities on terms drastically unfavorable to New Delhi—both unlikely prospects—the political environment in South Asia will not be conducive to wholesale experimentation in the foreign policies of the Himalayan states.

The relationship between Thimphu and New Delhi, moreover, continues on an even keel, with the key elements among the political elite in both countries reasonably satisfied with the present pattern of interaction. Among the educated youth there are, to be sure, occasional signs of a growing resentment against India's dominant presence; and there are still some reservations about the degree to which Bhutan has been "opened" to the Indians among what is left of the more traditional courtier class. But these groups are of limited significance in the total Bhutanese polity, and the inherent pragmatism and sense of discipline of most Bhutanese would seem to incline them toward making the best possible adjustment to the situation. Today, government jobs are readily available for most educated Bhutanese, advancement in the service is comparatively rapid, and Bhutanization of the administration is proceeding at a rate commensurate with the availability of qualified personnel. As long as this situation prevails, there may be occasional tension in the relationship between the Bhutanese and Indians, but no real crisis.

There are, however, several aspects of Indo-Bhutanese relations that disturb even those Bhutanese who welcome the alignment with India. The increasingly coordinated economics of the two countries, for instance, makes Bhutan vulnerable to fluctuations and crises in the Indian economy: a high inflationary rate in India has immediate repercussions in Bhutan, indeed in somewhat exaggerated forms.

Furthermore, dependence on India for virtually all imported commodities tends to enhance the vulnerability of the Bhutanese economy to external pressures. In this respect Bhutan is in the same position as Nepal, which, as another landlocked country in the Himalayas, conducts approximately 95 percent of its foreign trade with India. Developments in Indo-Nepali trade, thus, are closely watched in Thimphu as possible indicators of future Indian policy toward Bhutan. When in 1975 New Delhi suddenly informed Kathmandu that Nepali purchases on the Indian market of such commodities as coal and cement would now be charged at international prices rather than the lower Indian market prices, there was some concern in Thimphu that this new Indian policy would be extended to Bhutan eventually—and at considerable cost to the Bhutanese economy.

While the economic relationship with India has both its positive and negative side, there is a realization in Bhutan that there is little the Royal Government can do about it. To revert to the pre-1960 isolated subsistence economy would require a major change in all aspects of Bhutan's policy of economic and political development, a virtual impossibility under existing conditions. In the view of most Bhutanese officials, the best available strategy is to exploit whatever advantages are forthcoming from the economic relationship with India rather than to maneuver endlessly—and almost inevitably unsuccessfully— to circumvent the limitations imposed by the situation.

India has some reservations of its own about the economic relationship with Bhutan. So far, the diversion of scarce Indian financial and technical resources to Bhutan has been justified by New Delhi on strategic grounds in the context of the Sino-Indian competition for hegemony in the Himalayan region. A détente on this issue between India and China, even if limited in scope, could well reduce India's enthusiasm for aid programs in the northern border area. This possibility, while still reasonably remote, cannot be ignored by the Royal Government, for Bhutan's entire development program is dependent upon the long-term availability of substantial Indian aid. This is another reason why at least a limited diversification of aid sources has become attractive to the Bhutanese.

Political relations between India and Bhutan have been stable and generally resistent to aggravation in recent years. A new border agreement was signed in 1973, and there are no outstanding problems on this issue.[36] While there is some irredentist sentiment in Bhutan that occasionally calls for the restoration of territories "stolen" by the British in the eighteenth and

36. According to one report, as early as 1961 the Druk Gyalpo had discussed with the Indian government—at the Tshogdu's request—the failure of Indian map makers to depict the Indo-Bhutani border as an international boundary on official Indian maps (Murarka Dev, "Isolated Bhutan," *Eastern World*, 15:5 [May 1961], 14). This agitated Bhutanese national sentiments, of course, but it was only several years and several discussions later that the Indian government finally changed its policy on this question.

nineteenth centuries, its relevance in contemporary Bhutan is very limited.

More disturbing to most Bhutanese has been the fate of Sikkim, its neighbor to the west which also had a monarchical system based upon Mahayana Buddhist traditions. The series of events in 1973–1975 that led to the abolition of the monarchy and to Sikkim's merger into the Indian Union did not sit well with the Bhutanese elite. While there was the impression in Bhutan that the Chogyal (Sikkim's king) had made a number of serious and unnecessary mistakes in his approach to both internal politics and relations with India, there was also considerable sympathy for him as well as deep concern over Sikkim's fate. The important question for Thimphu, of course, is what does this mean for Bhutan? Was this some kind of precedent which, under conditions of internal discord and disruption, might also apply to Bhutan at some point in the future? More immediately perhaps, would it encourage the small number of politically conscious Nepali Bhutanese to follow the example of the Nepali Sikkimese who provided much of the leadership and most of the support for the political movement in Sikkim? For it was the Nepali Sikkimese who sought Indian support for the introduction of a new political system, and it was they who pressed for the novel relationship with the Indian Union.

The official response to these questions in Thimphu is that the Sikkim and Bhutan situations are qualitatively different, both in legal terms and in objective political terms. Bhutan was never a part of the British Indian Raj as was Sikkim prior to 1947, and thus there is no basis for Indian claims to a special relationship with the former state. Nor is Bhutan a protectorate of India as was Sikkim. Indeed, the relationship between Thimphu and New Delhi is based upon a treaty in which the former's independence is specifically recognized. Bhutan is also a member of the United Nations and thus of the international comity of nations, a status the Chogyal aspired to for Sikkim but never achieved. The Nepali Bhutanese, moreover, are a small minority restricted for the most part to a fringe area of the country. They are not, as in Sikkim, the majority community throughout most of the country. While they may prove to be a disruptive element in the Bhutanese polity in the future, they can never be the dominant force in the country—as their leaders fully recognize.

In Thimphu's view, therefore, Sikkim does not provide a precedent that at some future point might be applied to Bhutan. Nor have the developments in Sikkim been denounced in Bhutan as evidence of Indian expansionist ambitions as they have been by much of the political public in the neighboring Himalayan kingdom of Nepal and, more obliquely, by the Nepal government.[37] But the restraint used by Bhutanese officials in both their public and private statements on Sikkim should not be interpreted as indicative of a lack of concern over these events. The Bhutanese perspective on their external environment in general and on their relationship with India in particular cannot help but be affected, for it raises once again in dramatic form the basic principle of the country's foreign policy—the across-the-board alignment with India. It would still seem, however, that a viable alternative policy is not readily available. About all that can be expected is that Bhutan will continue to exert a maximum effort to preserve its decision-making process from excessive external intervention. In this respect, it is possible that India's interest in reassuring Bhutan about its regional objectives in the light of the Sikkim denouement may work to Thimphu's advantage, at least in the short run.

Probably the aspect of Indo-Bhutanese relations that is least susceptible to management is the multifarious sources of Indian political and ideological influence in Bhutan. Most of the Bhutanese who have been educated to an advanced level have attended Indian universities where they were exposed to a wide variety of contemporary political philosophies. So, also, are the Indian press, cinema, and radio a constant source of new ideas,

37. It is a curious anomaly that Nepali critics of Indian policy in Sikkim have generally tended to express concern for its implications with respect to Bhutan rather than with their own country, expressing the fear that Bhutan might go the way of Sikkim before too long. Such solicitude from this source is not particularly appreciated in Thimphu, for it is thought to reflect basic misunderstandings in Kathmandu about Bhutan's status as a sovereign state.

especially the radio now that transistors are found throughout Bhutan. What this means is that Indians and Bhutanese are now interacting on a scale unimaginable even a decade ago; the frequent contact is bound to have an impact on both countries. Any attempt to immunize Bhutan from these widely divergent sources of Indian political penetration would be an exercise in futility, and the interaction is bound to contribute substantially to the evolution of Bhutan's political, social, and economic institutions.

Nevertheless, despite the obvious challenges posed by the relationship with India at a number of levels, the Bhutanese political elite appear to view the future with a broad degree of confidence. This may be attributable in part to the intrinsic differences between the culture, the psychology, and the value systems of the two countries. Buddhist Bhutan does not feel nearly as oppressed by the dynamism of India's society as do the Nepalis who share a basic Hindu culture with the Indians. Nor do the Bhutanese share the difficulties faced by the Nepalis in defining a separate and distinct national identity from India. Bhutanese take pride in their national institutions and culture and feel indeed that they have a unique contribution to make to a world community in which diversity and complexity are respected and encouraged.

3. Politics and Public Policy

The politics of Bhutan defy description and analysis, at least in such terms as are normally used in comparative studies of developing societies. There is, to my knowledge, no other political system presently extant with which the Bhutanese polity is broadly comparable in either its "traditional" polity or its process of political development. Indeed, I have been asked on occasion whether there *are* politics in Bhutan. The question is facetious. Politics are abundant in Bhutan, even if they may not always be easily identified as such by the casual outside observer.

What might be more germane to ask is whether anything in Bhutan can be classified as a political *process,* as that concept is widely understood in contemporary social science—that is, as political behavior patterns that are not reducible to familial, kinship, or feudal relationships. In other words, are there political forces and factions in Bhutan that can be defined in more modern terms, such as ideological affinity, economic, communal, or regional interests, or even a nationalistic outlook that incorporates some notion of the public good and is not merely a xenophobic response to an outside world that is perceived to be hostile and threatening?

Can Bhutanese forms of participation in politics, then, be analyzed in process terms? There is a problem in this respect, for political behavior patterns in Bhutan are difficult to relate either to a traditional/feudal or to a modern/secular framework as defined in most of the literature on developing countries. Nor does Bhutan appear to be in a clear transitional period from one to the other stage. This does not mean that change is not occurring in Bhutan, for it is, and fairly rapidly. But the tradition/modernity concepts and models so popular with social scientists working on non-Western societies do not seem to be readily applicable to Bhutan, where traditional institutions, and particularly the monarchy, have been the primary domestic agents of modernization and change in ways unique even for monarchical systems. The problem is further complicated by the apparent lack of a dominant political ideology, even a monarchical ideology. In Bhutan, monarchical institutions emerged only in the early twentieth century from a Mahayana Buddhist theocratic tradition that provided little ideological support for a system of hereditary kingship. The monarchy came first; the theoretical rationalizations for the system have been appended—rather haphazardly and with some antithetical concessions to the theocratic tradition—only thereafter. This may well have been the case for most other monarchies, past and present. The difference is that this occurred elsewhere centuries or even millenniums ago; in Bhutan it is a contemporary phenomenon.

Historically, there have been few happy marriages between Buddhism and absolute monarchies—which may explain why ruling dynasties in Buddhist societies have often brought in Brahman preceptors, for Hindu political philosophy does specifically legitimize monarchical institutions. In present-day Bhutan, supporters of the existing political system generally use utilitarian rather than value-loaded arguments. Bhutan, it is pointed out, was in terrible shape prior to the establishment of the monarchy in 1907 and would probably relapse into a similar condition if this vital unifying institution should be abolished or emasculated. Indeed, the very existence of Bhutan as an autonomous culture and a sovereign state would be endangered by both disintegrative and external influences if this should occur.

This argument is persuasive to most politically articulate Bhutanese, but it does little to enhance the legitimacy of the monarchical system. As a result, the Wangchuck dynasty lacks the traditional ideological legitimation that has been crucial so far to the survival of monarchies in such neighboring countries as Nepal and Thailand. The kings of Bhutan will be judged primarily upon their performance record. In the Bhutanese context, this has been rated good, to date, but it is likely to be subjected to much closer and more critical scrutiny in the future.

This study obviously cannot provide an ideology for the political system in Bhutan nor even a developmental model appropriate to its distinctive politics. We have two limited objectives in this chapter: first, to exemplify the "modern" and "traditional" forms of politics, as these terms should be applied in Bhutan, through two case studies. One of these will focus on the efforts in the early 1950s to organize a political party along lines then prevalent in neighboring countries; the other will analyze the functioning of the traditional palace-centered establishment in the crisis caused by the assassination of Prime Minister Jigme Dorji in 1964. Second, through an analysis of some of the more crucial public-policy decisions in the period since 1950, we will examine the substantive output of the existing political system and its underlying, if still incipient, ideological proclivities. Such an analysis may provide some basis for a prognosis on the direction in which Bhutan is moving institutionally and politically, and what can be expected in the future. It will also provide limited but useful insight into both minority community and elitist politics in Bhutan.

Political Developments and Political Forces

When the British withdrew from the subcontinent in 1947, Bhutan had been virtually unaffected either by the British imperial experience or by the change-oriented political concepts that dominated nationalist political movements in India and were beginning to create problems for the ruling authorities in the two other Himalayan kingdoms—Nepal and Sikkim. There were reasons for Bhutan's comparative immunity to demands for modernization. Bhutan was the most effectively isolated of the Himalayan border states. Contact with even the neighboring outside world was largely limited to a few members of the Wangchuck and Dorji families, several traders who had commercial ties with both Tibet and India, and the Nepali Bhutanese community concentrated in the Bhutan-India border area. There was as yet no substantial new, young elite educated in Western-style schools in Western ideas. Even visitors from outside were rare, and were in any case never permitted more than a short sojourn in the country. It was not that most Bhutanese were resistant to modern political concepts; they had never heard of them.

Moreover, most of the small number of Bhutanese from privileged backgrounds who had had a limited exposure to political currents in India were not favorably impressed with what they had seen and heard. Strong Bhutanese nationalists themselves, they were nevertheless rather unenthusiastic about Indian nationalism, which they perceived as potentially a greater challenge to the existing political and social system in Bhutan than an India ruled by the British. The ideologies of democracy and socialism which impelled some sections of the Indian nationalist movement held little attraction for them, and modernization, with all it implied, seemed of doubtful utility to Bhutan's quiet polity and self-sufficient subsistence economy. At the most, the Bhutanese were determined to be very selective about those facets of modernization that would be introduced into Bhutan. Such totally alien institutions as political parties were, of course, anathema.

One potentially dangerous exception to the "quiet polity" was the Nepali Bhutanese minority in southern Bhutan which by 1948 had had a limited exposure to the radical political process thriving across the border in India. There were, also, other Nepali migrant communities with which the Nepali Bhutanese maintained some contacts. The Nepali community in India, for instance, had been organized since the 1920s for both political and social purposes by the Gorkha League. The character of this movement had undergone substantial change with the formation of the Nepali National Congress in Calcutta in 1947. The new party was assertively modernistic in ideology and had as its primary objective the overthrow of the autocratic Rana family regime in Nepal. So too, in neighboring Sikkim, several local Nepali Sikkimese political organizations had been formed in 1946, most of which were absorbed into the antiroyalist Sikkim State Congress on its formation in 1948.

India's independence in August 1947 had a catalytic effect upon Nepali communities throughout the Himalayas. No one was sure what the policy of the new Indian government would be toward its small northern neighbors, but Indian nationalist rhetoric about democracy and the right of the people to organize politically was no doubt encouraging to Nepali political activists. It was in these circumstances that political agitation aimed at popular mobilization—in this instance of a minority community—was for the first time introduced into Bhutan. The movement had its origin in the Dagenpala area of southern Bhutan. Its greatest appeal was to some recent Nepali migrants who had illegally cleared reserved forest lands for cultivation. When the Bhutan government moved to enforce the forest regulations barring the cultivation of such lands, a confrontation occurred, and some of the Nepali settlers fled across the border into India. In 1950, further Nepali migration into Bhutan was strictly regulated and an effort was made by the authorities to control access across what had been a *de facto* open border previously.

The Bhutan State Congress. This small "refugee" Nepali Bhutanese community settled down on a temporary basis in districts of Assam and West Bengal bordering on Bhutan. Their political leaders met at Patgaon in Assam in November 1952 and formed the Bhutan State Congress under the leadership of D. B. Gurung, D. B. Chhetri, and G. P. Sharma. Initially, at least, the primary objective was "the redress of the grievances of those people now living as refugees in Goalpara and Jalpaiguri,"[1] but this was soon expanded to include demands for more broad-based political reforms internally in Bhutan and a closer association with India externally.[2] The new party also an-

1. Resolution adopted at the Patgaon meeting of the Bhutan State Congress (*The Statesman* [Calcutta], Nov. 18, 1952).
2. The General Secretary of the Bhutan State Congress told an Indian correspondent in 1953 that events taking place in Bhutan were "fraught with danger for the Indian Union" and that the 1949 Indo-Bhutanese Treaty was inadequate since Bhutan borders Tibet where "vast changes are taking place" (*Times of India,* May 27, 1953). In this respect, the Bhutan Congress would seem to

nounced its intention to launch a non-violent mass movement (*satyagraha*) in Bhutan to achieve its objectives.

The program of the Bhutan State Congress, as stated in the party's political manifesto, was scarcely radical, except possibly in the Bhutanese context.[3] The primary goal was the elimination of governmental policies that were allegedly discriminatory against the Nepali Bhutanese community vis-à-vis other communities in Bhutan. It was alleged that the Nepali Bhutanese had most of the obligations associated with subjectship but few of the privileges of citizenship.[4] For example, their right to own and cultivate land was strictly regulated, not only in the Bhutan highlands which were to all extent and purposes closed to them, but in southern Bhutan as well. Even their residence in Bhutan was on a tenuous basis, making them easy objects of exploitation by the local Bhutanese officials and their Nepali Bhutanese agents.

Organizational activities among the Nepali Bhutanese resident in the areas of India bordering on Bhutan absorbed the attention of the Bhutan Congress until 1953, and it was only in early 1954 that an effort was made to extend the party's operations into Bhutan itself. On March 22, approximately 100 Bhutan Congress "volunteers" marched across the border to launch a *satyagraha* campaign at Sarbhang, the center of the largest concentration of Nepali Bhutanese in southern Bhutan. The Bhutan government, forewarned by the numerous public statements issued by the party leaders in their efforts to attract support from a variety of sources in India, had mobilized the national militia and dispatched it to the Sarbhang area to

---

have been following the example of the Sikkim State Congress which sought to obtain Indian support in its struggle against the palace in Sikkim by demanding the State's accession into the Indian Union. The Bhutan Congress also adopted a party flag that was identical to that of the Indian Congress Party, with the addition of a "dorji"—a traditional Bhutanese Buddhist symbol (*Hindustan Times*, Jan. 21, 1953).

3. D. B. Gurung, "Political Problems of Bhutan," *United Asia*, 12:4 (1960), 368–369, and his "Bhutan's Woes," *Mankind*, 4:7 (Feb. 1960), 43–45.

4. On the other hand, some of the discriminatory policies actually favored the Nepali Bhutanese. For instance, they paid lower land tax rates than most other Bhutanese and were also exempt from some forms of *chunidom* (involuntary labor) and from service in the militia.

maintain order. When the Bhutan Congress workers refused to obey the order to disperse and to return to India, repressive action was taken against them. The *satyagraha* campaign collapsed before it even got started, with the party leaders fleeing back to India where they remained in exile for another fifteen years. The failure of the movement, however, was due less to the Bhutan government's repressive action than to the inability of the Bhutan Congress to engender broad-based support among the Nepali Bhutanese community. The capability of the Bhutan government to mobilize and sustain repressive activity in southern Bhutan over an extended period in the early 1950s was very limited. With strong and continuing support from the local populace, the Bhutan Congress could have posed a grave threat to the regime's authority in the south, particularly as unofficial support from some Indian and Nepali sources would probably have been forthcoming. But, in fact, the party represented only an insignificant section of the Nepali Bhutanese community. Its appeal was very limited, since most members of the community had acquired land to cultivate and were not inclined to support political activities that might endanger their rights to the land. Nor was the prospect of large-scale Nepali migration into southern Bhutan—what the Bhutan Congress was really trying to arrange—attractive to many Nepali Bhutanese. This would have the dual disadvantage of increasing pressure upon limited land resources in southern Bhutan as well as arousing the Bhutan government's apprehensions over the size of the alien Nepali minority in Bhutan's population.

The social divisions based on caste and tribe that were characteristic of Nepali society had been carried over into Bhutan, and the likelihood of cooperation between various Nepali ethnic groups was very remote.[5] A unified response on the part of the Nepali Bhutanese community might have become possible if the Bhutan government had proved unwilling to alleviate at

5. The Pradhan family of Newari extraction from Kathmandu valley served for many years as principal agent for the Dorji family in its various concessions in southern Bhutan. According to one member of the family, the Bhutan Congress agitation was directed more at them than at the Bhutan government, despite the rhetoric used. This, of course, further divided the Nepali Bhu-

least some of the community's grievances. But by the mid-1950s, the Bhutanese authorities had come to realize that repressive measures were insufficient and inappropriate, and that concessions on some points were both justified and expedient. An effort was made by the government to meet Nepali Bhutanese demands on those issues that did not conflict with basic policies. The community was granted representation in the Tshogdu when the National Assembly was first established in 1953–1954, and on proportional terms that were essentially equitable. Bhutanese citizenship was extended to the community in 1959. Although in the view of the authorities this constituted merely formal recognition of an existing status, it did relieve Nepali Bhutanese anxieties. Increasing numbers of Nepali Bhutanese were absorbed into the administration, mostly for assignment in southern Bhutan but occasionally in the capital as well. Members of the community are also now admitted into the army and the police on the same basis as other nationals, and are often stationed in non-Nepali areas.

Settlement by Nepali Bhutanese in areas outside of southern Bhutan, while not specifically forbidden, is in fact still effectively discouraged.[6] But on the other hand, the terms upon which members of this community cultivate land and pay taxes in southern Bhutan are now broadly equivalent to those of other Bhutanese. Thus, while discriminatory policies have not been totally eliminated, the community's economic and political status has been greatly improved over what it was in 1950. This comparatively liberal approach has tended to make Nepali Bhutanese unresponsive to suggestions that political organizations and agitation are required to attain community or regional objectives.

The stance adopted by the Bhutan government on this question is not solely attributable to its perception of the internal situation in southern Bhutan. Indeed, the platform in the politi-

---

tanese community. While there were only a few Newaris in Bhutan, many Nepalis from other ethnic communities held their lands at that time literally on the sufferance of the Pradhan family and were constrained to support it against intracommunity competitors.

6. Please refer to footnote 20 in Chapter 1 on this subject.

cal manifesto of the Bhutan State Congress that aroused the greatest concern in government circles was the call for closer economic and political cooperation with India. The Bhutanese authorities had carefully noted the way in which the Nepali-dominated Sikkim State Congress had made Sikkim's accession to India an integral part of its program in the 1948–1954 period.

When in 1953 the Bhutan Congress leaders called upon the Indian political officer in Sikkim, reportedly to seek Indian support for their projected *satyagraha* campaign, and sent a delegation to the prime minister of Nepal for the same purpose,[7] the determination of the Royal Government to exclude political party activity from Bhutan was intensified. As it turned out the party did not receive support from either source, and it was the Indian government's order barring the Bhutan Congress from using Indian territory as a base of operations that was partly responsible for the failure of the 1954 *satyagraha*. Nevertheless, some Bhutanese continued to suspect that India might adopt a different policy under different sets of circumstances in the future. While the possibility of Indian support for a Bhutan-based political movement has prejudiced the Royal Government against the idea of allowing Nepali-dominated political parties from operating in Bhutan, it also convinced the political elite of the need to integrate the Nepali Bhutanese community into the broader Bhutanese polity on more liberal terms.

After the failure of the 1954 *satyagraha* campaign, the Bhutan State Congress continued to exist as a minuscular party-in-exile with its headquarters at Siliguri in India. But its influence within the Nepali Bhutanese community, limited at best, declined, and by the early 1960s it was a spent force with little apparent capacity for development. In 1969 the Druk Gyalpo granted its few remaining leaders permission to return to Bhutan without prejudice [8] but on the implied condition that they would not indulge in political party activity.

Thus ended Bhutan's first and so far only attempt to func-

7. See *Amrita Bazar Patrika* (Calcutta), March 24, 1953, and *Hindustan Times* (New Delhi), April 17, 1953.
8. *Kuensel*, 3:20 (Oct. 31, 1969).

tion politically along formal party organizational lines. Nor are the prospects for the renewal of such a strategy among the Nepali Bhutanese or other Bhutanese communities very auspicious. This kind of activity is still alien to the Bhutanese political tradition, and in any case most politically conscious Bhutanese have other, more effective, ways of protecting their interests and attaining their objectives.

The government has not formally banned political parties, but it is well understood by the Bhutanese elite that the formation of such organizations at this time is still discouraged. Some high-ranking Bhutanese officials foresee the day when political parties will not only be permitted but will indeed be an essential ingredient in a liberalized, participatory political system. But that is perceived as a relatively distant prospect, feasible only when many more Bhutanese have been educated and when political consciousness among the general populace has reached at least minimum levels. Until then, politics in Bhutan will continue to function along the unstructured, informal factional lines that characterize the polity at present.

Elitist Factionalism—the 1964 Crisis. It has been argued that the nonexistence of political parties or other forms of organized factional activity should not be equated with the nonexistence of politics. What the lack of such organizations does mean is that it is more difficult to identify the largely unstructured and noninstitutionalized forces that underlie political alignments at any particular point. Political factionalism plays a major role in Bhutan's political system, as its recent history clearly indicates. But these factions have generally lacked ideological, class interest, or even social (kinship, locality of origin, and such) motivation, and in most instances would almost seem to be incidental alignments of individuals on a specific issue, or more commonly on an event-by-event basis.

Moreover, these factions have usually operated within the prevailing mode of politics and thus, as is typical of palace politics anywhere, are seldom publicly identified as advocates of particular positions or policies. Their influence is generally applied behind the scenes, and it is often difficult for most Bhutanese (not to mention an outside observer) to identify the line-up of political forces even on major issues under discussion. A capacity for accommodation of divergent views is an integral part of the elitist political system in Bhutan, and it is only under exceptional circumstances that the price of failure in a factional dispute is removal from a position of influence and authority for the losers. In other words, politics in Bhutan is only rarely a winner-take-all proposition.

One of the few instances in modern Bhutanese history in which elitist factionalism surfaced briefly, and with relatively long-term effects, was the crisis in 1964 caused by the assassination of Prime Minister Jigme Dorji. We shall, therefore, analyze this series of events and the cast of characters involved at some length.

On April 5, 1964, Lonchen Jigme Dorji was assassinated at Phuntsholing on the Bhutan-Indian border by a noncommissioned officer in the Royal Bhutan Army. Druk Gyalpo Jigme Dorji Wangchuck was in Switzerland at the time undergoing treatment for the heart attack he had suffered in March 1963, but he returned to Bhutan immediately on hearing the news. On April 14, he ordered the arrest of 41 persons allegedly involved in the assassination conspiracy, including the commander and the quartermaster-general of the army—Brigadier Chabda Namgyal Bahadur (the king's uncle) and Bashu Phugyal, respectively. The quartermaster-general committed suicide in prison on May 8, while the brigadier was tried on May 16 and executed the following day. The Druk Gyalpo reassumed full powers himself, but due to his continuing ill-health, in July delegated responsibility for civil administration to Jigme Dorji's younger brother, Lhendup (who assumed the title of acting Lonchen), and a few months later control over the army to his own half-brother, Namgyal Wangchuck.

In the literature on this crisis (primarily in the Indian press) the factional conflicts involved have been defined in various broad categories—the Wangchucks vs. the Dorjis; the "traditionalists" in the administration and the army vs. the "modernists"; anti-Indian vs. pro-Indian forces; and even the fine hand of the Chinese Communists was detected behind the scene by some Indian sources. But an analysis of the events surrounding the assassination indicates that none of these were, in fact, critical to the conspiracy although all but the last may have played some role.[9] The Wangchucks vs. the Dorjis scenario is probably the one that has received the most attention outside Bhutan, largely because of the nine-year exile abroad of Lhendup Dorji and his once-influential sister, Tashi. Some authoritative Bhutanese sources attribute the split between Lhendup and the Druk Gyalpo to personal rather than political differences. This was not, however, as sometimes alleged, the natural culmination of an old familial rivalry that had its origin in the post-1907 period and reached a final showdown stage in the 1960–1965 period. The facts, according to authoritative accounts in Bhutan, are quite different. There had been no history of antagonism and conflict between the Wangchucks and the Dorjis; indeed, quite the contrary, as the two families had long been mutually supportive in the face of challenges from other Bhutanese elitist elements whenever these surfaced. Lonchen Jigme Dorji's assassination in 1964 was not the consequence, even indirectly, of the expansion of Jigme Dorji's authority as regent during the king's illness and absence from the country, nor of a disagreement over the Lonchen's internal and external policies which, it should be noted, were continued and even expedited after 1964.

Nor was Lhendup Dorji's assumption of the office of acting Lonchen in mid-1964 made over the objections of the Druk Gyalpo or as the consequence of pressure from members of the

9. While I have utilized the available literature in my discussion of this subject, more dependence has been placed upon information obtained through interviews with a wide range of Bhutanese and with some of the more well-informed Indian officials and journalists. There is substantial disagreement between the published sources and what I consider to be the most reliable personal sources, whose accounts correlate better with the actual events and developments thereafter. Since my analysis is based upon an amalgam of information from a wide variety of sources, I will not identify them specifically, particularly since some conversations were "off the record." I was also given access to documents in personal collections that are not part of the government archives. These also, even when quoted, have to remain anonymous as to source.

Dorji family. Indeed, according to one reliable source, Lhen-dup's mother (then the senior member of the Dorji family) spe-cifically advised the king against giving any title to Lhendup, as this might make the internal political situation even more ex-plosive. Nevertheless, Druk Gyalpo Jigme Dorji Wangchuck in-formed the National Assembly in its Fall 1964 session that he intended to appoint Lhendup as Lonchen and Colonel Tanghi as brigadier (i.e., commanding officer of the Bhutan Army). That both these officials sought refuge in Nepal in 1965 was due to certain developments discussed below rather than to the alleged feud between the Dorji and Wangchuck families. It is true that the king advised Lhendup and his sister Tashi to stay out of Bhutan for a time, but it was the National Assembly (that had grudges of its own) that passed a resolution barring their return to the country, a resolution to which the king finally gave his approval.

It is also noteworthy that through all of these traumatic events several members of the Dorji family, including Jigme Dorji's widow and children, continued to reside in Bhutan and were the recipients of various royal favors. Relations between the king and the queen (Lhendup Dorji's older sister) were strained, but this was due to the queen's unhappiness when she learned of the Tibetan mistress kept by the king rather than to any dissatisfaction with the way in which Jigme Dorji's assassins had been treated or with Lhendup's exile abroad. There was no formal dissolution of the royal marriage, however, and a reconciliation was arranged several years later. Obviously, the developments in 1964–1965 placed a tremendous strain on the Bhutanese elitist fabric. But it is inaccurate to analyze Bhu-tanese politics in that period as basically a familial conflict be-tween the Wangchucks and the Dorjis, for the interelite con-flicts and rivalries never fell into such a simple pattern.

Another favorite theme used by foreign observers, that is, to blame the traditionalist/modernist adversary relationships within the political elite, also does not help very much to ex-plain the course of events in the post-1964 period. Some of the army officers convicted of involvement in the assassination of Lonchen Jigme Dorji had been instrumental in the organization and modernization of the army under the program introduced by the prime minister in 1961 and consequently no more warrant identification as "traditionalists" opposed to the Lonchen's reform policy than the two army officers who fled to Nepal with Lhendup in 1965 deserve to be classified as "modernists." In both instances, policy issues were incidental to the roles assumed by these military officers, and factionalism within the army has to be explained on other grounds than support or opposition to the reforms introduced by Jigme Dorji.

It well may be that some tradition-oriented officials in the government and the monastic body, who were opposed to Jigme Dorji's modernization program, also supported the conspirators, but their role in these events was of peripheral importance. It would appear that the motivation of most of the major participants in the conspiracy had little to do with public-policy issues per se, but rather to their perception (or misperception) of the Lonchen as a threat to their power base in a political system beginning to undergo rapid change. The 1964 confrontation, thus, was only to a very limited extent a struggle over policy; far more important was the competition for influence in the decision-making process centered in the palace.

Neither India nor China played a significant role in the 1964 crisis, although India on several occasions had a bit part because of its deep involvement in Bhutan. While there were a number of Bhutanese officials in 1964 who had doubts about the wisdom of Bhutan's broad alignment with India and the opening of the country to a massive external presence, they were by no means united behind any of the contending factions, and the relationship with India was seldom raised as a substantive issue in this period. Nor is there any real evidence that Lhendup Dorji's departure from office in 1965 was due to Indian pressure, as has been alleged, because of New Delhi's concern over his supposed anti-Indian attitude. There was nothing in Lhendup's statements or actions during his short tenure as acting Lonchen that can properly be interpreted as anti-Indian; on the contrary, he had clearly indicated his intention to continue the policies introduced by his brother aligning Bhutan with India. Lhendup's relation with the Indian government deteriorated after he had taken exile in Nepal, and remained strained until after the death of King Jigme Dorji Wangchuck, but this again seemed to be due more to personal than policy factors.

What did happen, then, and why? According to authoritative versions, the primary organizing force behind the assassination of Jigme Dorji was the father of the Druk Gyalpo's influential Tibetan mistress, Yangki. This itinerant family, which had no status or influence in Bhutan prior to Yangki's emergence as the royal mistress in 1961, had become in Bhutan's palace politics an important force to which a number of aspiring officials attached themselves in order to advance their own interests. Here also, there were no strong policy differences between the Yangki faction and Lonchen Jigme Dorji, and it is probable that the two could have coexisted peacefully for an indefinite period. In late 1963, however, Yangki and her father became convinced that the Western doctor the Druk Gyalpo was consulting on Jigme Dorji's recommendation had, in an elaborately contrived assassination plot, induced the king's second heart attack. As Yangki's family was totally dependent upon her relationship to the Druk Gyalpo for its economic and political prosperity, some counteraction seemed necessary.

In early 1964, therefore, Yangki's father related his suspicions to Brigadier Chabda Namgyal Bahadur and, according to the trial records, convinced him that there was a Dorji plot against his nephew, the Druk Gyalpo. The Brigadier then brought a number of his colleagues into the conspiracy in order to provide a stabilizing force in the interim period between the assassination of the Lonchen and the return of the Druk Gyalpo to Bhutan to reassume full authority. The gun used to kill Jigme Dorji was given to the hired assassin by Yangki's father.

Once the deed had been done, the plot began to flounder, primarily because the officials involved had made no plans to seize power. The Druk Gyalpo's immediate return to Bhutan came as a surprse to the conspirators, who were all personally loyal to the ruler and had no intention of overthrowing the monarchy. The Druk Gyalpo had been infuriated by the assassination of his close friend and trusted subordinate. At one point he had even ordered Colonel Tanghi to arrange the "elimination" of Yangki and her father in a motor accident, and it was only through the intercession of the queen and her mother that the order was reversed. Eventually a number of cover-up stories were disseminated to disguise the involvement of the king's mistress in the assassination conspiracy.

In late 1964, the Druk Gyalpo's health deteriorated once again, and he was forced to return to Switzerland for medical treatment without having resolved the political crisis. Lhendup Dorji was functioning as acting prime minister, which led Yangki and her father to suspect that he would use the king's absence from the country to revenge his brother. They attempted to flee into India, but were apprehended and detained at Geylegphug in southern Bhutan. Reports that Yangki had been abused and mistreated while in detention reached the king in Switzerland, allegedly from Indian sources. He immediately sent a strongly worded, if somewhat ambiguous cable to Thimphu which was interpreted by Lhendup Dorji and Brigadier Tanghi as personally threatening. Lhendup Dorji flew to Switzerland to explain these events, but on the advice of Edward St. George, a British confidant of the king, he was denied an interview and was advised to absent himself from Bhutan for six months. When this time period had expired, Lhendup asked if he could return but was told that it was best for him to remain outside the country for some time more. It was at this point that Lhendup went into exile in Nepal and never returned to Bhutan as long as Druk Gyalpo Jigme Dorji Wangchuck was alive. Brigadier Tanghi also fled to Kathmandu but was allowed to return to Bhutan a few years later after a reconciliation with the king.

Yangki and her father, meanwhile, had been released, and she reassumed a prominent position in court circles. The Yangki faction, composed of a random selection of officials from diverse backgrounds, played an important role in Bhutanese politics until the Druk Gyalpo's death in 1972. The four children she bore the Druk Gyalpo were never legitimized, nor were they included in the line of succession to the throne in the ordinance issued by the king in 1969. On his deathbed, how-ever, the king asked the crown prince not to take punitive ac-tion against Yangki or her children, a request to which he agreed. Yangki was allowed to retire to the estates that had been granted to her in the Bumthang area and continued to draw income from the extensive investments made for her in India by the late king. In 1974 she was accused of involvement in the so-called Tibetan conspiracy organized by the Dalai Lama's brother, a scheme which allegedly plotted the assassina-tion of the young king and his replacement on the throne by one of Yangki's male children. She fled the country with her family and settled down in India, while several members of her faction were placed under arrest, tried, and convicted for their involvement in the plot.

The highly personalized character of Bhutanese politics, in which policy or ideological factors play a very minor role, is in-dicated in this account of the country's most serious political crisis in the twentieth century. The kinds of pressures and counterpressures that motivated the late Druk Gyalpo are well illustrated in the document he dictated—countersigned by sev-eral top officials in the Bhutan government—shortly before his death in 1972, in which he stated to the crown prince:

In my life time I have committed a very big blunder by having an af-fair with Yangki. Being young, I stayed with her a few times and before I could keep the affair within limits, not one or two but four children were born, so I could not sever my connection with her. Kesang Wangchuck is completely in the right. She was consecrated with me in the Tashi Ngasol ceremony as my true Queen, and as such children born from her are the legitimate princes and princesses. In the case of Yangki, she is only a girl friend and not a legitimate wife, and as such children born from her cannot be considered royal chil-dren but are to be considered as illegitimate children.

You should never give any Government service and status to Yangki's children. If you grant them status, it will create problems for you. It will be enough if you treat them like other Bhutanese subjects.

I have given them adequate wealth, so they should not face any hardship. In case they do face hardships, may be you will help them.

In case I die, let them stay outside the country for a few years; after

that do as you deem necessary. The reason why I am saying all this is
for your own benefit, Jigme.

What, then, are the lessons to be learned from the events of
1964–1965 with respect to Bhutanese politics other than the
critical importance of personal factors? One lesson would be
how an essentially unstructured factional system places limitations upon the process of political development. There are, to
be sure, several relatively homogeneous political forces in Bhutan with a capacity to influence the decision-making process:
the royal family; the other traditional elite families, including
the Dorjis; the new elite families who have attained this status
through loyal service to the Wangchuck dynasty; the monastic
establishment; the Royal Bhutan Army; the new educated elite
that increasingly dominates the bureaucracy; and the people's
representatives in the National Assembly drawn largely from
village headmen and local landowning interests. But none of
these are integrated institutions in the political sense, nor are
they capable of acting institutionally. Even the royal family, in
which the Druk Gyalpo is conceded the final word, has on occasion been seriously weakened by internal factionalism that
complicated the king's use of his royal prerogatives. Factionalism in Bhutan, thus, is both intrainstitutional and interin-
stitutional. This makes for very complicated politics in which
transinstitutional lines of alignment, pragmatically determined
and usually temporary in duration, are the norm in determin-
ing factional alignments.

What makes the system work at all is the existence of an ultimate source of authority—the Druk Gyalpo—and an arena in
which factional competition can be both exercised and contained—the palace. Factionalism will continue to be highly personalized until political alignments are based on broader, more
rational criteria, such as ideological or group interest con-
gruence rather than personal interests. But this has yet to develop on a significant scale in Bhutan, even among the young
educated elite that appear to share some political values. Given
the almost total political apathy characteristic of Bhutanese society at its base, it is difficult to see how a modern political sys-

tem dependent upon broad-based institutional foundations—political parties, the bureaucracy, the army—would work in Bhutan without a fundamental change in political values and behavior patterns.

Public Policy

Public policy in Bhutan from the establishment of the Wangchuck dynasty to 1952 was simple, straightforward, and internally consistent. The primary objectives were well defined: political centralization, maintenance of the social and economic status quo, and maximum isolation of the country from potentially disruptive extraneous influences. Political centralization involved changed, but it was change in the narrowest sense of the term—the progressive elimination of obstructive and divisive elements within the political elite that might complicate the monarchy's decision-making capacities—rather than change on broader national integrative principles. Bhutan's isolation policy also tended to reinforce this centralization process by virtually excluding dissident forces from soliciting external support against the Wangchuck rulers—which would have been an essential prerequisite to any successful opposition movement.

There are some indications that the first Wangchuck ruler, Ugyen Wangchuck, had given some consideration to alternative political and economic strategies in the years after his ascension to the throne in 1907. Indeed, in 1910 he discussed with British officials the introduction of some development programs that would have undermined the traditional economic structure, and even went so far as to request financial and technical assistance.[10] Whether the Druk Gyalpo was really serious, however, seems doubtful; it is more likely that he was trying to impress the British with his reliability as an ally by seemingly offering to open Bhutan to economic penetration from the south. But he may also have assumed that the British would not be interested, as they were not noted for their generosity to "princely states," particularly those in buffer areas that they preferred to maintain in a state of suspended develop-

10. J. Claude White, *Sikkim and Bhutan* (Delhi, 1971), pp. 232–233.

ment.[11] In any case, no substantial development programs were introduced during the reign of the first two Druk Gyalpos, with or without British assistance. A few schools were opened in the 1930s and 1940s. But these were traditional Buddhist institutions that bore little resemblance to the modern (i.e., Western-style) schools in India, and they were scarcely the agents of change that the contemporary Bhutanese education system has become.

The succession of the third Druk Gyalpo to the throne in 1952 coincided with a significant change in the basic principles of public policy in Bhutan. Initially the shift in policy was limited in scope, but by the 1960s it had become comprehensive enough to affect almost all aspects of life. What induced the Royal Government to adopt a broad range of novel policies? The personality of the new ruler and his partial socialization in the dominant themes of Indian political and economic thought was certainly a key factor. But there were also extraordinary changes occurring in Bhutan's internal and external environment that seemed to make policy innovations unavoidable.

Dramatic developments to both the south and north between 1947 and 1960 signaled the end of Bhutan's insulation from disruptive external influences, in the process making a status quo-oriented public-policy stance inexpedient. Tibet was gradually brought under the effective authority of the Chinese Communists who introduced policies that undermined the traditional theocratic regime in that sister-country and appeared to have dire implications for Bhutan as well. India had introduced a democratic political system that was no less dedicated to the principle of change and development than was China's plan. The pressures from New Delhi and Peking were rarely applied directly, but their competing models of developmental politics were bound to prove increasingly significant to both the political elite and the people of Bhutan.

Some stress in the internal economic and social system, still

11. The British Indian officials had been equally unresponsive to proposals for economic development programs in Nepal, even those emanating from British commercial and industrial firms that were interested in exploiting Nepal's forest and mineral resources.

minor perhaps but persistent, was also becoming evident. Bhutan had never qualified as a wealthy country under any definition of that term, but it had managed to provide its populace with a subsistence existence that was almost prosperous in comparison to that of neighboring states. It had long been a food-surplus area with excess land available for cultivation, and the massive famines that had periodically afflicted its southern neighbor were virtually unknown in Bhutan. But by the 1950s in both southern and eastern Bhutan this was no longer the case, and population pressure upon land resources was becoming a problem in these areas. Bhutan's external-trade structure had also been disrupted to some extent by the Chinese conquest of Tibet, and prospects for the future were not auspicious because of Peking's determination to redirect the Tibetan economy away from the south and toward China. While Bhutan's trade with Tibet had never been impressive in quantitative terms, it had provided the Bhutanese economy with commodities essential to the well-being of the people.

The Royal Government had become convinced of the need to develop new sources of employment and production by 1980 if an economic crisis was to be avoided. Such a change required the acceptance of a developmental strategy. It is probable that the regime could have avoided basic changes in public policy for another decade or two without serious political or economic consequences; but Druk Gyalpo Jigme Dorji Wangchuck was convinced that limited reforms introduced over an extended period under noncrisis conditions were preferable to radical changes that would tear apart the social, economic, and political fabric of Bhutan's traditional system and lead perhaps to national disintegration.

A slow but significant shift in the composition and character of the political elite in Bhutan also contributed to the broad acceptance of a process of guided change. Almost without exception the old elite in Bhutan had been socialized exclusively in the traditional culture—particularly in the palace-centered administrative system. By the 1950s, however, there were a growing number of young Bhutanese educated in India (often in the Christian missionary schools in Darjeeling district) who were being absorbed into the administration. The number of young people may have been relatively few at first, but the group included members of the two key elite families—the Wangchucks and the Dorjis—as well as several civil and military technicians. A modernization ideology had been implicit in their educational experience, and it was only natural for them to accept economic and political development as legitimate objectives of government in the contemporary world.

Also important in the evolution of public policy in Bhutan was the ready availability of foreign assistance for the development of the country's potentially rich resource base. The decision to accept external aid was not an easy one, and was made only after long deliberation and hesitation. But the plan had an obvious appeal to many Bhutanese who saw possibilities for both personal and public gain through the input of foreign economic and technical assistance.

The image of Bhutan as a prosperous, developed society with a diversified economic base was an attractive alternative to its traditional subsistence economy heavily dependent upon the agricultural sector. There was, moreover, the prospect of substantial expansion of government revenues through economic-development programs. This must have been almost irresistible to an administrative system that had to struggle along on extremely limited financial resources. By the mid-1950s, therefore, the debate within the political elite was no longer over whether Bhutan should adopt development-oriented public policies, but rather in what context and at what rate of change. And on these latter points, there were major differences of opinion.

Reform Programs. After his succession to the throne in 1952, the first reform program introduced by the new change-minded Druk Gyalpo Jigme Dorji Wangchuck was directed at a glaring inequity in Bhutan's social and economic structure—a tenancy system that was classically feudal in character. While tenants constituted only a small proportion of the country's population (estimates vary from 700 to 5,000 families), the condition of their servitude was distinctly oppressive. Tenants were not allowed to move from their place of residence or to acquire land of their own (still in reasonably plentiful supply in most areas) for cultivation; nor did they have any rights on the lands they cultivated, although it should also be noted that the short supply of agricultural labor made their replacement difficult and unprofitable for the landowner. Most tenants had served the landowning family to which they were attached for several generations and often provided a variety of services other than those generally associated with land tenancy.[12]

The 1952 land reform program had two aspects: first, tenant and former slave families were given the option to acquire land of their own for cultivation under governmental auspices; and second, a ceiling of 25–30 acres (depending on area and type of land) was established as a guiding principle for landownership. The first part of the program worked reasonably well, and a large proportion of former tenants and former slaves were allocated land and granted some assistance in preparing it for cultivation. The land-ceiling principle, however, was never implemented on any great scale, as the government depended more upon voluntary than on compulsory compliance. The Druk Gyalpo attempted to set a good example by making some of his extensive holdings available for redistribution, but apparently (there are no reliable statistics) few other large landowners followed along. There are, thus, still some fairly large concentrations of landholdings in Bhutan; on the other hand, there is only a small landless labor class, and most Bhutanese families reportedly have access to about as much land as they can cultivate using traditional production techniques.

The most obvious gap in the 1952 land-reform program was the failure to do anything about the onerous *chunidom* (unpaid involuntary labor) system that impinged so heavily upon the

12. According to some reports, on the other hand, there was little in the way of a strictly enforced hierarchical system in the traditional Bhutanese society, and the lines between landlord nd tenant were not as rigid in this respect as in India, Nepal, or even pre-industrial Europe. It was not unusual for such families to intermarry or for sons from tenant families to be adopted into the landlord family. The bitterness and sense of exploitation that characterized this kind of land system elsewhere was not as apparent in Bhutan, and there were reportedly a number of tenant families that opted to retain their traditional relationship even when given the opportunity to become owner-cultivators themselves.

Politics and Public Policy   129

time, energy, and resources of most Bhutanese. At that stage of Bhutan's development, however, there were no economically feasible alternatives available to provide the services obtained under the *chunidom* system, as government revenues were still insufficient to make payment for such labor possible. Moreover, the government's need for *chunidom* labor increased sharply in the early 1960s with the introduction of large-scale road construction projects.

It was only toward the end of that decade, when some of the projects were nearing completion and a system under which labor was imported from outside on a contract basis had been introduced, that the government was in a position to consider major modifications in the *chunidom* system.

The first step in this direction was taken by the Tshogdu in the spring of 1968 when it exempted women from *chunidom* and stipulated that the entire system should be abolished within two years.[13] Subsequent sessions of the Tshogdu formally abolished the conscript labor system, but with certain exceptions (Dzong and monastery repairs, for instance) under which involuntary labor could be exacted from the eligible labor force (Shapto Hurla) but henceforth on a paid basis "to the extent possible." [14] This, in essence, is how the system now works. Bhutanese who are not on the exempt list (and it is now solely the prerogative of the Druk Gyalpo to grant such exemptions) are obliged to contribute labor to public projects at the government's demand, but they are usually paid at least a nominal wage for such services. It was planned, for instance, to use this system to provide most of the labor (probably some 4,000–5,000 workers) for the projected Chhukha hydel project. This would have the dual advantage of avoiding importation of a large number of Nepali laborers from outside as well as expediting the transfer and resettlement of some Bhutanese from the eastern districts that are now beginning to face serious land-shortage problems into land-rich western Bhutan.

Another important agricultural reform program was the change in 1970 from in-kind to cash land taxes. According to

13. *Kuensel,* 2:10 (May 31, 1968).
14. *Ibid.,* 4:10 (May 31, 1970); and 6:48 (July 23, 1972).

authoritative sources (no documentation is available), this change resulted in a drastic reduction in the land tax and virtually eliminated what had become a major source of rural discontent. Under the new program, for instance, a farmer pays approximately Rs. 24 in land tax on an acre of rice land from which he can earn, at 1974 price levels, as much as Rs. 3600. Previously, he may have had to pay as much as one-fourth of his production in in-kind land taxes or other forms of contributions to governmental or monastic institutions.

The new land tax, thus, is strictly nominal in revenue terms, and the Royal Government would seem to have decided against using agriculture as a primary source for the extraction of capital for economic development purposes (like India but unlike China in this respect). Bhutan is in the fortunate position of having alternate sources of capital available—Indian foreign aid now, and substantial revenue from its forest, mineral, and hydel resources in the future—and thus feels it can afford to limit the contribution from the agrarian sector.

Agriculturalists in Bhutan, therefore, have been more beneficiaries than objects of exploitation under the development strategies so far employed, even if compulsory labor obligations are included in the balance sheet. This becomes more evident in the still-small experimental programs directed at modernizing and expanding agricultural production. New seeds, plants, fertilizers, irrigation facilities, and so on have been provided to interested farmers on a limited scale either free of charge or at a nominal price. A few cooperatives have also been established to provide easy credit and marketing facilities for some key agricultural areas. The object is to encourage farmers to introduce new crops and technologies, but placing these services on a self-sustaining basis in the future will probably prove difficult. The results to date, in any case, have not been impressive. Some diversification in land use has been accomplished, primarily through the development of orchards. But most Bhutanese farmers still produce traditional crops using traditional techniques. Neither the government nor the cultivators appear to consider a more rapid rate of change and growth essential, even though Bhutan is now a food-importing country for the first time in its modern history. Apparently such imports are considered a low price to pay when the alternative would be to force a reasonably contented peasantry to accept radical innovations whose benefits are still to be demonstrated.

Educational Reform. The decision to introduce a mass education system was probably the most significant change in public policy proposed by the third Druk Gyalpo in the early years of his reign. A few schools had been established prior to 1952,[15] but it was only thereafter that universal education became the official objective. It is assumed, however, that this will take at least three or four decades to achieve, given the almost total lack of any of the prerequisites for a mass education system (for example, trained teachers) and the limited resources available.

At first the expansion of education had a higher priority than either political or economic development programs in the view of the Druk Gyalpo and his principal advisers. Indeed, development in these other fields was considered dependent upon the emergence of a corps of educated Bhutanese capable of providing the executive and technical skills required. It was felt that political reforms, such as the establishment of the Tshogdu, would have little real impact on the polity until most Bhutanese had become politically "conscious" through exposure to an educational process. And it was apparent that both administrative and technical personnel were needed for economic-development programs if these were not to remain totally dependent upon foreign technicians and consultants. Until 1959, then, the Royal Government was determined to avoid excessive dependency on non-Bhutanese at the cost of postponing the modernization of the economy on the grounds

15. According to one source, some of the more conservative elite families refused to send their children to these new schools, and as a result it was mostly children from poorer families who received an education. This is one of the reasons why a fair proportion of higher officials in the forty- to fifty-year-old category come from nonelite families.

that this would jeopardize the country's independence. "Educate our youth first, and then modernize" was the operating principle.[16]

But the decision in 1960 to inaugurate large-scale economic infrastructure projects—mostly roads and power facilities—modified the top priority previously given to education. However, the attitude of the political elite on this subject did not change, and a substantial proportion of government revenues is still directed to education. The Bhutanization of the administrative system, and in particular of the Development Ministry, has become a key issue in Bhutan's efforts to gain greater economic and political autonomy for itself, and it is understood that this is not feasible until many more Bhutanese have been provided with education through the university level.

A new education policy was introduced in 1975, with "self-sufficiency" in the supply of qualified personnel for key administrative and economic positions as one of its basic objectives. The plan assumes that there will be a long delay in the development of higher educational institutions possessing even minimal standards of quality, and that Bhutanese students will continue to depend upon foreign universities for advanced training in the sciences and social sciences.[17] While India will provide most of the seats for these students, the government hopes to expose a number to diverse educational and political experiences by sending them to third countries.

The emphasis during the next decade will be on developing a few quality high schools on the British public school model. In this way, the government hopes to improve the standard of education for the relatively small number of students who will be sent abroad for advanced training. Mass literacy continues to be an objective, but it is subordinated to the more strongly felt need for a technically qualified educated elite. The primary school system is to be improved, but it is public policy to en-

16. See the interesting and informative interview on this subject with Prime Minister Jigme Dorji in *The New York Times,* May 10, 1956.
17. Under the 1975 education policy, an Ugyen Wangchuck University is to be established by 1978, but there were still some doubts in 1977 about its feasibility and even more about Bhutan's ability to make it a quality institution.

courage only a small proportion of students to advance from this level to the Junior High and High Schools. The emphasis in primary schools is on improving the student's capacity to follow agricultural or craft occupations, and the number prepared for higher education is deliberately being limited. Concern over the situation in neighboring countries where unemployment among the educated is a major source of political and economic dissidence has made it the aim of the Royal Government to contain this problem within reasonable limits while at the same time providing the trained personnel needed for both governmental and private development purposes.

The government faces innumerable problems in its efforts to expand and improve the educational system. Limited financial resources is one of the most serious. Virtually the entire educational budget is dependent upon grants from India, and funds may not be forthcoming on such generous terms in the future. Another problem is the lack of qualified teachers, and dependence is upon India in this respect as well. A Teachers Training Institute has been established, but it will be a decade or more before a majority of the teachers in Bhutan's schools will be native born. The dependence upon Indian teachers and administrators in Bhutanese schools has had several side effects, one of which is the wholesale adoption of a curriculum based upon Indian School Commission formulas and examinations. Some officials question the suitability of the Indian education model for Bhutan, and have sought to mitigate its impact by bringing in a few Westerners—mostly Jesuits from their schools in Darjeeling—as a counterbalance. But a truly distinctive education system is probably infeasible, particularly since most Bhutanese students at the higher level will have to be prepared for entry into the Indian university system.

A problem of a different kind has been the something-less-than-enthusiastic response of the less privileged Bhutanese families to educational opportunities. Only 20 percent of the school-going-age population was in school in 1972, and over half of these were unlikely to go beyond the primary school level. In part this is due to the lack of educational facilities in some localities. But, even given the limited number of schools, it was estimated that the number of students should be more than 60 percent of the six- to fifteen-year-old population. Education for other than religious purposes is a new phenomenon to most Bhutanese. There would appear to be considerable skepticism over the value of an education to the child or his

Table 2. Educational institutions

Institution	Number	Students
Primary (Classes 1–5)	69	6,300
Junior High (Classes 6–8)	12	3,000
Central High (Classes 9–11)	5 *	1,700
Public School (to Class 11) †	2	515
Teachers Training Institute	1	150
Technical School (Kharbandi)	1	200
Rigney Monastery School ‡	1	150

Source: Royal Government of Bhutan, Third Five Year Plan, 1971–1976, (1974).

* Four new Central High Schools were scheduled to be opened during the Third Five Year Plan, but only one had actually commenced operation by 1975.

† The Public Schools cover the entire educational spectrum from Classes 1–11. They have been established to provide a better quality of education to a select group of students than is available in the regular school system in order to prepare them for the Senior Cambridge or equivalent examinations used for entry into college-level institutions. A third Public School is to be opened during the Fourth Five Year Plan (1976–1981).

‡ The Rigney Monastery School was established in the mid-1960s to provide religious and traditional cultural education to some students and to train teachers for Dzongkha language courses. It is planned to establish such schools for each of the eight regional monastic bodies, in the process modernizing to some extent the traditional monastic education system.

family, despite the fact that the government encourages families to keep at least one son in school through matriculation. (Girls constitute only 20 percent of the school-going population, and these are mostly at the primary level.)

The complicated language structure in Bhutan poses yet another problem. Under the 1975 education policy it was agreed that English should continue to be the language of instruction for another ten years, while Dzongkha should be the second language taught in all schools and Nepali a third language "for all those who wish to study it" (mostly in southern Bhutan). Implicit in this policy is the assumption that at some point Dzongkha will replace English as the medium of instruction. Some Bhutanese doubt that this will be possible at any time in the foreseeable future for both technical and political reasons, but it is generally accepted that, in any case, the ten-year period specified in the policy statement is much too short to be practicable. Fortunately for the government, no one objects very strongly to the present policy, and there is thus little incentive to give serious consideration to its modification.

Bhutanese officials are as devoted vocally to the concept of universal education and literacy as their counterparts in other societies and recognize the positive correlation between education and modernization (however the latter term may be defined). But they also tend to be proponents of the possible rather than the ideal, and perceive little value in overeducating a large number of young Bhutanese for occupational opportunities that do not exist now and are unlikely to emerge for at least another generation. An effort is made, therefore, to relate education to economic reality. While it is possible that the Bhutanese have been overly conservative in this direction (after all, a surplus of trained people can be an invaluable resource), their reaction to the chaotic situation in India, where unemployment among the educated has reached massive proportions, can be easily understood and appreciated.

Economic Development Programs. Events both inside and outside Bhutan in the late 1950s have forced the Royal Government to revise its priorities from an emphasis on limited social change to one of rapid economic development. The emergence of a new Indian-educated elite, events in Tibet, and the Indian government's insistence upon economic penetration of Bhutan in the wake of its own dispute with China all contributed to this change in policy. A concern for military strategy of course, was also important to both India and Bhutan. The Indian army considered it essential to develop a logistic capacity for itself in Bhutan through major road construction projects; the Royal Government eventually came to share India's concern that

Bhutan might become the arena for a Sino-Indian confrontation under conditions in which the Chinese had easier access to the political center of the country from the north than the Indians had from the south.

Once the decision had been made to open Bhutan through the construction of roads, the Royal Government felt it necessary to introduce complementary economic-development programs in a wide range of fields. It realized that improvement in communications with the outside world and the infusion of a large number of foreign advisers and technicians would accelerate the penetration of "modernist" values into Bhutanese society, with unpredictable consequences. The government's economic policies, thus, can be viewed as pre-emptive—an effort to introduce change from above before the demand for change from below could become politically explosive.

The immediate impact of the new economic-development programs, however, was probably more negative than positive. The sudden shift from a food-surplus to a food-deficit economy as a result of the introduction of a large force of Nepali laborers and Indian technicians, for instance, had a bad psychological effect, particularly in a period when the acquisition of food supplies from outside had become increasingly difficult and expensive. Developmental policies also led to a shift in labor utilization from agriculture to infrastructure projects with delayed payoff capacities. In contrast to most other Asian societies, Bhutan lacks a large reservoir of unemployed or underemployed labor to divert to such projects. While the long-term impact of these programs is likely to prove advantageous, the immediate consequences reduced agricultural production and aroused widespread resentment among the ordinary Bhutanese whose established lifestyle was disrupted.

The contemporary Bhutanese attitude toward the development strategies adopted in the early 1960s would seem to reflect the country's response to increased vulnerability to economic developments in India. Prior to 1960, what happened to the south was of limited importance to Bhutan, whose social and economic structure was virtually immune to the political and economic crises that periodically engulfed the subcontinent. This is no longer the case, however, and the quantity and direction of Indian aid, the price and availability in India of a wide variety of commodities, and even the political stability and military capability of India are presently of vital importance to Bhutan. This dependency relationship severely restricts the Royal Government's autonomous decision-making capacity on both economic and political issues—not a happy situation for the Bhutanese.

On balance, however, it would appear that most of the political elite support the decision to end Bhutan's economic and political isolation, and indeed view prospects for the future as basically favorable. If all goes as planned, the export of power and forest products from projects already underway will transform Bhutan from a capital-deficit to a capital-surplus economy by the mid-1980s. Bhutan will then no longer be heavily dependent upon the input of foreign capital, largely via foreign aid programs, or even on foreign technical assistance financed externally. The emphasis in the Fourth Five Year Plan on agro-industries and agrarian development also raises the prospect that, through a minimal expansion of the area under cultivation and productivity, Bhutan can once again become a surplus economy in agricultural products. One persistent source of weakness will be Bhutan's continued dependence upon imports of most manufactured commodities in view of the very limited scope of industrial development projected. But it is estimated that the Chhukha hydel project alone will earn enough foreign currency through the sale of power to India (and possibly to Bangladesh) to pay for much of what Bhutan requires.

The successful completion of these projects, however, does not mean that the Royal Government lacks for problems to solve. One of the most persistent, given the nearly total dependence upon governmental initiative and involvement in development, is the virtual absence of an economic planning structure. Bhutan's Third Five Year Plan, scheduled for the 1971–1976 period to coincide with India's Five Year Plan, was really nothing more than a compilation of development pro-

Table 3. Planned expenditures under Third Five Year Plan

Department	Planned expenditure (Rupees: in hundred thousands)
Agriculture	
Production	368.98
Minor irrigation	100.00
Soil conservation	25.00
Animal husbandry	125.00
Forests	160.00
	Total: 778.98
Cooperatives	18.02
Power	248.00
Industries and mining	
Large and medium industries	43.33
Mineral development	3.00
Village and small industries	117.02
	Total: 163.35
Transport and communication	
Roads	691.00
Road transport	69.00
Posts and telegraphs	130.00
Tourism	17.00
	Total: 907.00
Social services	
General education	633.00
Technical education	87.50
Health	286.00
Water supply and sanitation	59.00
Urban development	20.00
	Total: 1,085.50
Miscellaneous	
Publicity	27.00
Statistics	5.00
Development headquarters	100.00
Capital project	200.00
Protection of ancient monuments	15.00
Planning cell in the office of the representative of India	2.15
	Total: 349.15
	Grand Total: 3,550.00

Source: Royal Government of Bhutan, *Third Five Year Plan, 1971–76,* (1974).

jects already underway or projected with Indian financial and technical assistance.[18] As Bhutan's Plan is an Indian concoction, there is little relationship between the programs included and Bhutan's resources and requirements, nor much effort to assess priorities in terms that are relevant to Bhutan.

The Third and Fourth Five Year Plans are only peripherally related to the Royal Government's public policies in various economic fields, reflecting more what India is willing to provide (and is capable of providing) in aid than what Bhutan may require—or prefer. But even if circumstances were less inhibiting, it is doubtful that Bhutan could do much more than project a few vaguely defined objectives for the future. The government in Thimphu lacks anything like the kind of data-gathering and analyzing capacities necessary for a sophisticated and reasonably effective planning process. Indeed, on the basis of existing data, it is not possible to estimate with any sense of confidence Bhutan's gross national product or per capita income. If the economic policy objectives adopted by the Royal Government in 1975 are ever to become anything more than meaningless rhetoric, Bhutan is going to have to correlate its development efforts with something more than India's convenience in mind. This will involve some real economic planning—though not necessarily under the rubric of a five-year plan—which in turn will require a substantial improvement in the bureaucracy's information-base on Bhutan's resources as well as a broad consensus among the elite on development priorities.

Heavy dependence upon governmental administrative institutions has been important for most economic development activities. Lacking qualified managerial personnel for public-sector enterprises, the government policy has been to share these tasks with private entrepreneurs wherever possible. Certain incentives, such as tax exemptions, development rebates, and low taxation rates for new industries, have been adopted as official

18. Royal Government of Bhutan, *Third Five Year Plan, 1971–1976* (Thimphu, Ministry of Development, 1974). The UN technical assistance projects, negotiated after the preparation of the Third Five Year Plan, are not included in the outline of projects in Table 2.

policy in order to encourage private investment in industrial and commercial enterprises that are not, in the words of the economic policy outline, "of strategic importance to the National Economy." These latter fields have not been defined as yet, and in fact most feasible enterprises are probably open to private entrepreneurs on liberal terms.

One complication for the Royal Government, however, is that Bhutanese entrepeneurs are still few in number and lack substantial capital and other resources. They are, thus, heavily dependent upon foreign (mainly Indian) capital sources for any large projects. The government's view on foreign private investment is quite ambivalent. The formal policy is to permit foreign investment in joint stock companies but on the condition that 51 percent of the stock be held by the Bhutan government, which would also retain the option to take over total control of the project if and when it has the managerial capacity available. This is intended to prevent "economic colonialism," in this case Indian economic "neocolonialism." But the likely effect, as understood in Thimphu, is that few foreign entrepreneurs are likely to find Bhutan an attractive area for investment. As a consequence, Bhutan will continue to be heavily dependent upon Indian governmental aid—not exactly an attractive alternative for the Bhutanese who understand very well the political and economic consequences of this policy decision.

The range of choices available to the Bhutanese political elite on this subject, as on most other subjects, is very narrow, but is no less traumatic for that reason. The attitude of the elite toward the whole developmental process has become much more ambivalent in recent years. There is even a tendency for some young bureaucrats who were weaned, educationally speaking, on modernization models and values, to look back nostalgically to the "good old days" and to express a desire to return to the soil—albeit usually to grow apples rather than rice since the former requires much less physical labor. The relevance of development programs for Bhutan is being questioned.

While a return to the old isolationist, subsistence existence might be welcomed psychologically, its infeasibility economically and politically is widely recognized. A condition of interdependence with neighboring economies, primarily India's, is probably unavoidable even though at the present stage of development this constitutes a dependency syndrome that grates on the nationalist sensitivity of many Bhutanese. Among the elite in Bhutan, the result may be an even more exaggerated sense of grievance against the outside world, and an equally strong acceptance of Bhutan's inability to do much about it. A slightly schizophrenic attitude toward the process called modernization may be somewhat less apparent in Bhutan than in much of contemporary Asia. But then Bhutan became involved in developmental activities a decade or two later than most other Asian states.

Whither Bhutan?

From the discussion of the political process and public policy in this chapter it should be clear that the dominant political elite in Bhutan is still very flexible in its attitude toward political systems and their underlying ideologies. Some overriding principles of political behavior have gradually evolved and been accepted as the norm. But pragmatism and a predeliction for gradualism is evident in most cases, and virtually all policy decisions have had an aura of impermanence about them. Changes in direction are frequent, easily contrived and rationalized, but often tentative. Institutions are created to serve a particular set of stated purposes one week, and then either abolished or fundamentally restructured the next.

It is not possible to discuss the future of the monarchical system with any sense of confidence, for statements that Bhutan is moving toward a constitutional monarchy are interspersed with other statements and policies that, implicitly at least, do not conform to this objective. There has been a significant expansion of institutional involvement in the decision-making process, which is no longer the tight-knit exercise it was when it involved only a few key officials. But as yet there has been only minimal participation in politics and very little serious encouragement of popular—as distinct from representative—political institutions. The few representative institutions that have been established (for example, the Tshogdu) are still essentially elitist in composition and operation. Several potentially important political reforms have been introduced, though as yet these have not changed the basic character of the polity. Bhutan may be something less than an absolute monarchy in form, but it still comes close to being one in practice.

Political rhetoric is probably less stultifying in Bhutan than elsewhere in South Asia, due more, one would suspect, to the lack of channels for mass communication (there are no newspapers nor a Bhutanese radio system) than from a sense of propriety on the part of officials. The significant rhetorical exchanges in any case are intraelite, directed at the achievement of a consensus on critical policy issues. The rhetoric tends to be modernist in content, mostly borrowed from the contemporary Indian context in which much of the Bhutanese elite has been intellectually socialized. As might be expected, there is often a degree of incompatibility between this Indian-derived rhetoric and Bhutanese practice, since the former may be irrelevant to the latter. This is probably not very serious as yet, since most of the audience at which the rhetoric is directed are insiders who are more concerned with what is done than said. But unless this gap is reconciled to some extent, the credibility and legitimacy of the regime may be questioned by the next generation who are likely to take the rhetoric more seriously from having been exposed to it since early childhood.

This ambiguity in objectives and performance is also reflected in public policy. Government officials often sound like the Indian Planning Commission in their statements on economic policy—which is perhaps not too surprising since such declarations are usually the products of Indian advisers. But few responsible Bhutanese seem to share the public (as distinct from the private) ideological proclivities of their Indian counterparts. Socialism has not yet become the fetish in Bhutan that it is in India, and Bhutanese do not indulge in that exercise so prevalent in neighboring states of classifying as socialist all policies that are statist (that is, those that expand the powers and capabilities of the state) in content. Egalitarianism is occasionally lauded in Bhutanese public statements, but an egalitarian society is rarely identified as an ideal, perhaps because

Bhutan may already be more egalitarian in practice and social psychology than its neighbors to the north or south. The welfare of the public is usually the proclaimed objective of policy decisions, but this is defined in such broad terms as to encompass a wide variety of alternative policies.

The question raised in the subtitle of this section cannot be answered definitively at this stage of Bhutan's development, even in theoretical terms. The Royal Government has sought to keep alternative paths open, both in politics and in economics. The constraints imposed from outside on their capacity to do this are very inhibiting and may prove decisive over the long run. But there is an element of uncertainty with respect to Bhutan's political future because the trend of developments in the broader region with which the country identifies is subject to sudden and drastic changes. The political and economic environment to which Bhutan must adjust is in a state of rapid transformation and, potentially, disintegration. The most a small, vulnerable society such as Bhutan can do is try to survive by learning to cope. So far, its performance in this respect has been reasonably impressive.

4. Constitutional System and National Political Institutions

Bhutan has no written constitution nor any document that can be reasonably defined as *the* basic organic law. The 1953 royal order establishing the Tshogdu (National Assembly), as amended, is sometimes called a constitution, but it concerns the functions and powers of only one of several important national political institutions—and only in bare outline at that. The other political and bureaucratic institutions exist in a constitutional vacuum, at least in terms of broadly accepted written or unwritten law. In analyzing trends of development, therefore, the highly transitional character of the political system, marked by a proclivity for wholesale experimentation in both institutional and process terms, must be kept in mind.

The political history of modern (that is, post-1907) Bhutan can be divided into two phases in each of which the goals and strategies of the ruling elite were quite different. The first of these covers the period from 1907 to 1952, coinciding with the rule of the first two Druk Gyalpos, during which efforts were made to transform a dispersed, traditional theocratic polity into a highly centralized absolute monarchy. In the period from 1953 to the present, the general movement has been toward a limited and constitutional monarchy in which the throne retains its status as the fulcrum of the political system but shares power and authority with several other political and administrative institutions. The broad terms upon which the royal power is to be shared are still in the process of definition, but the overall trend is clearly apparent. It should be noted, however, that this process of change is so new and largely untested that several alternative paths, including a return to absolute monarchy, are still open to the present political elite. Nor should it be forgotten that Bhutan's political evolution will be strongly influenced by developments in its vastly more powerful neighbors—India with its aspirations toward a democratic socialist society, and China's communist model.

In this chapter I will attempt to analyze the constitutional development of modern Bhutan through the study of several national political institutions—the monarchy, the Tshogdu, the royal advisory councils, and the Council of Ministers. The Drukpa Buddhist monastic establishment, usually classified as a religious institution, will also be discussed in this context. Bhutan's theocratic tradition, the important roles still assigned to the Drukpa church in the contemporary political and governmental system, and its capacity to influence popular attitudes on issues that are essentially political endow the monk body with the status of a national political institution.

The Monarchy

The most important factor to note in any analysis of the monarchy in Bhutan may well be the brevity of its existence, for it was only in 1907 that an hereditary monarchy was for the first time established in the country.[1] Some commentators on Bhutan, usually Indian, have sought to relate the contemporary monarchical system in Bhutan to the principles underlying classical (that is, pre-tenth century) Hindu kingship. But in both conceptual and structural terms, the relationship would seem to be largely nominal.

Some Bhutanese have occasionally referred to the Wangchuck dynasty kings as the successors to the Druk Desi under the Shabdung system, and in this way have traced back the origin of monarchy to 1650 when the latter officer was first appointed by Shabdung Ngawang Namgyal. Following the death of the late King Jigme Dorji Wangchuck in 1972, for instance, the Tshogdu adopted a resolution in which this implication ap-

1. No doubt there were small kingdoms in certain regions of Bhutan prior to the seventeenth century, but none of these ever included anything more than a small proportion of present-day Bhutan.

pears: "Taking into account the fact that Bhutan's long history of Deb Rajas [Druk Desis] and kings has never produced a monarch such as His late Majesty. . . ."[2] It has been argued that the Shabdung political system was in fact dyarchical in structure, with two sovereign powers—the Shabdung in religious affairs and the Druk Desi in temporal affairs. This would seem to be a distortion of the Bhutanese political tradition, for it was the first Shabdung, in his capacity as the sovereign power, who delegated responsibilities on temporal matters to the Druk Desi and on religious matters to the Je Khempo.

The specific circumstances under which the hereditary monarchy was established in 1907 support this hypothesis. The reigning Shabdung died in 1903 and the Druk Desi in 1904. The Je Khempo, who was the Sung trulku of the first Shabdung, succeeded to both titles—in a rather irregular manner. He was disinclined toward involvement in politics, however, and retired to a monastery at the time Ugyen Wangchuck was raised to the throne. But there is no evidence that he surrendered either of his titles prior to his death in 1917 or that the Druk Gyalpo ever laid claim to the Druk Desi title or considered himself to be the successor to anything but the latter's responsibility for the administration of the country.

Nor does there seem to have been any confusion in the minds of the Bhutanese of his time that the first Druk Gyalpo, Ugyen Wangchuck, was creating a new political institution that differed in many respects—the succession system for instance—from anything that Bhutan had known previously. The first problem the Druk Gyalpo faced, therefore, was the one usually subsumed under the rubric "legitimation." No one seriously doubted Ugyen Wangchuck's *capacity* to govern Bhutan; but his *right* to rule was surely questioned by many Bhutanese, both secular and lay.[3]

2. Tshogdu Resolution, 37th Session (Fall 1972), *Kuensel,* 7:6 (Sept. 24, 1972), 2. The use of the term "Deb Raja" in the translation from the Bhutanese is somewhat misleading for a Raja is a king in the Indian political tradition. But when the Bhutanese term Druk Desi is used, there is a very different implication, for a Desi is a regent in the Tibetan/Bhutanese political tradition.
3. Nagendra Singh states that the hereditary kingship was inaugurated in 1907 on an "elective basis" (*Bhutan: A Kingdom in the Himalayas* [New Delhi,

Druk Gyalpo Ugyen Wangchuck would seem to have understood this full well as he set about doing what he could to legitimize this new institution in the eyes of both the elite and the people. He appropriated some of the titles and symbolisms previously associated with the Shabdung, thus maintaining continuity in the outer manifestations of the authority system. He also managed to gain the one essential external political endorsement needed to provide stability, that of the British Government of India, and accomplished this, moreover, without seriously compromising Bhutan's independence. Finally, he managed to persuade virtually the entire civil and religious elite to sign a document indicating acceptance of himself as Druk Gyalpo and recognizing the Wangchuck family as the hereditary dynasty of Bhutan.[4] The signatories to this charter may not all have been acting completely voluntarily, but nevertheless they had made solemn declarations of allegiance to the dynasty of a kind that could not easily be violated by adherents to the traditional Bhutanese value system.

In any case, legitimation under any political system is not achieved so much by the capacity to gain power as it is by the ability to maintain and regularize the use of power over an extended period of time and to have the system broadly accepted. For an hereditary monarchy, in particular, the succession system must be precisely defined and must proceed without serious challenge for dynastic legitimacy to be fully accepted. Bhutan's monarchy has established such a tradition, for three more Druk Gyalpos have since ascended to the throne without incidence and under the prescribed principles of succession. The comparative newness of the monarchy in Bhutan has an important impact on the functioning of this institution, but the legitimacy of the Wangchuck dynasty would now seem to be firmly established.

1972], p. 96). He uses this as a legitimizing device, and also as a connective to the elective Druk Desi system. There is no evidence in available sources, however, that anything even remotely resembling an election was actually used in 1907 in the events that preceded the recognition of Ugyen Wangchuck as Druk Gyalpo.
    4. *Ibid.*, pp. 95–96.

Another major problem the first Druk Gyalpo faced was that of establishing a more centralized system of government over the opposition of an elite that had long been conditioned by an environment that permitted almost total decentralization and limited the efficacy of "national" institutions. Ugyen Wangchuck had managed to outmaneuver or eliminate his principle rivals in the two decades before 1907, but there were still formidable sources of opposition with which he had to contend. These were mostly local or regional in character and, though badly disunited, were still capable of causing considerable trouble. There were, for instance, a number of local elite families, primarily concentrated in western Bhutan which were part of a loyalty combine headed by the former Paro Pönlop Dao Paljor. Although they had all signed the 1907 document accepting an hereditary monarchy, the sincerity of their allegiance to the Wangchucks was certainly open to question.

The first Druk Gyalpo moved deftly to neutralize these potential sources of opposition, indulging them in certain respects while at the same time undermining their support base. The ex-Paro Pönlop's supporters were allowed to retain their offices until his death, after which they were gradually replaced by officials considered more reliable by the central authorities. Even the powerful noble family of Byakar in eastern Bhutan, when caught in a conspiracy against the life of the Druk Gyalpo, was treated very leniently, although the head of the family was exiled to a remote corner of Bhutan, thereby reducing the capacity of the family to indulge in political activity.[5]

Opposition to the Wangchuck dynasty of a different and more subtle character was that of the Drukpa monastic establishment which must not have viewed the termination of the theocratic Shabdung system with any enthusiasm, no matter how nominal its authority may have become. Fortunately for Ugyen Wangchuck, the monastic order lacked strong leadership during the transitional period and was incapable of effec-

5. Ram Rahul, *Modern Bhutan*, p. 54. The fact that the Byakar family is from Bumthang district in eastern Bhutan, which is the traditional stronghold of the Wangchucks, made their involvement in this conspiracy more dangerous than similar opposition movements in western Bhutan.

tive action. The head of the Drukpa establishment, the Je Khempo, was the Sung trulku but a man with little capacity for politics. His two successors as Sung trulku were permitted to reside in Bhutan, but they were in no position to challenge the authority of the Druk Gyalpo even if they had been so inclined for they lacked a support base within the monastic establishment.

A *modus vivendi* achieved between the royal family and the Drukpa monastic establishment proved sufficiently viable and mutually satisfactory to prevent a direct confrontation between these two institutions. The general assumption in Bhutan is that the religious establishment, in accommodating itself to the monarchy, has been progressively excluded from a critical role in the country's polity, particularly in the past two decades.[6] In 1969, for instance, the government abolished the system under which most monastic institutions had collected rent-in-kind from cultivators of certain prescribed lands, substituting in its place a new system under which monasteries and shrines are directly subsidized by the government. The political implications of this kind of dependency relationship are readily apparent. The monastic establishment, however, made no effort to obstruct the reform program which, among other things, substantially reduced the burden on the cultivators, since the land tax paid to the government in currency is much lower than the rent-in-kind formerly paid to the monasteries.

One should not underestimate the potential influence of the religious establishment, however, particularly with respect to those aspects of Bhutan's politics and society that are still considered to be its preserve. The king of Bhutan, in contrast to the ruler of Sikkim prior to 1975, is not directly involved in

6. One example of the relationship between the civil and religious officials was noted by the author during his visit to Bhutan in the fall of 1972. The monastic establishment, which perceives itself as the defender of Bhutan's traditions, had demanded that civil officials wear traditional Bhutanese dress while on duty, and an order to this effect had been issued by the government. On the day in November following the departure of the Central Monk Body from Thimphu for its winter quarters in Punakha, however, several of the younger middle-level officials appeared at the Secretariat in Western dress which, presumably, they continued to wear until the monks return to Thimphu in April.

religious affairs, and in Bhutan this constitutes a serious gap in his authority structure. The Mahayana Buddhist titles used by these respective rulers—Gyalpo in Bhutan and Chogyal in Sikkim—indicate the extent of their authority, for the former connotes only temporal sovereignty and the latter both temporal and religious authority. And, indeed, on his succession to the throne in 1972 Druk Gyalpo Jigme Singye Wangchuck announced publicly that he recognized the authority of the Je Khempo in the sphere of religion and had no intention of making any competing claims.[7] However, this should not disguise the fact that the Druk Gyalpo exercises an effective *indirect* authority over the monastic establishment, even in the conduct of its religious duties.

The Evolution of the Monarchical System. It has already been noted that the first Druk Gyalpo's control over the Bhutanese polity was rather tenuous initially, but that through carefully conceived and implemented policies he had gradually eliminated or neutralized the principal sources of opposition to the hereditary monarchy. His successor, Druk Gyalpo Jigme Wangchuck (1926–1952), was able to build on the solid foundation provided by his father and in the process succeeded in creating a highly centralized system in which the royal powers came as close to absolutism as is possible in a traditional society with a feudal heritage. The regional elites that at one time had held certain district-level offices almost as if by right were now eased out, not always unprotestingly, of course. Virtually all Dzongpöns thereafter were either members of the royal family or servants of the palace who were personally selected by the Druk Gyalpo.

The central government was strictly supervised and controlled by the ruling monarch, and the capacity of the district officers, the monastic order, or the nobility to influence decisions through the consultative institutions that had existed prior to 1907 was greatly diminished. The first Druk Gyalpo established the royal capital at Bumthang in eastern Bhutan, a stronghold of the Wangchuck family well-removed from the

7. *Kuensel*, 7:4 (Sept. 10, 1972).

traditional political centers in western Bhutan. This contributed to the centralizing process, since it strengthened the Druk Gyalpo's control over his main support base and at the same time complicated the task of antiroyalist conspirators in striking at the sources of royal power.[8]

The third Druk Gyalpo of Bhutan, Jigme Dorji Wangchuck, (1952–1972) was the product of a different political socialization process from that of either of this predecessors,[9] and he perceived the role of the monarchy in distinctly different terms. Effective centralization of authority had been the fundamental requirement for Bhutan during the rule of the first two Druk Gyalpos, and had been their primary objective. Since that had now been accomplished, the third Wangchuck ruler concluded that his principal task was to reform and restructure the existing system to allow power and functions to be shared on pragmatic terms with other institutions of government. This was considered essential if the monarchy was to survive in a world that was changing rapidly outside, a world, he believed, that could not long endure unchanged internally.[10]

The new Druk Gyalpo also understood that the monarchy was the only institution in Bhutan that could take the initiative in creating a new governmental structure. The politics of centralization followed by his predecessors had effectively emasculated the traditional elite and, in its place, had created a new elite that was accustomed to a dependence relationship with the palace. Nor had the politicization process that had mobilized large sections of the population in India, Sikkim, and Nepal

8. The transfer of the capital to Thimphu in western Bhutan in the 1950s by the third Druk Gyalpo Jigme Dorji Wangchuck signified in part that the authority of the ruling dynasty was so firmly established that the ruler could safely function in what had previously been the stronghold of the opposition.
9. Part of his education had been in India, and during some of the most critical years of the nationalist movement prior to independence.
10. Reportedly, the head of the Dorji family, Lonchen Jigme Dorji, who was ten years senior to the new king in 1952, was very influential in shaping the Druk Gyalpo's attitudes in the first years of his reign (Nari Rustomji, *Enchanted Frontiers* [London, 1971], pp. 162–163). But the Lonchen's political socialization had taken place largely in India, and he may have been somehwat insensitive in certain respects to some aspects of Bhutan's political culture, a deficiency for which he paid the ultimate price in 1964—assassination.

had any impact as yet upon the people of Bhutan except for a few Nepali Bhutanese on the southern fringe of the country. In introducing structural and procedural reforms, therefore, the Druk Gyalpo could expect broad compliance with his reforms but little enthusiasm for them, at least until a new generation of Bhutanese youth could be educated and absorbed into both the administrative apparatus and the political institutions.

The first important step in the direction of basic structural reform was the royal order of 1953 which called for the establishment of the Tshogdu (National Assembly) composed of representatives from every district in Bhutan, the monastic establishment, and the civil administration. While the Tshogdu has sometimes been compared to the consultative bodies called together on an *ad hoc* basis when critical decisions had to be made under the Shabdung system, it was in fact a novel institution in terms of its composition,[11] the regularity of its sessions, and its role and functions in the broader polity.

Whether the Tshogdu, as established in 1953, can properly be defined as a legislative institution is doubtful. Its functions were primarily consultative and recommendatory, and were in no way binding upon the king or government. Article 18 of the 1953 act, for instance, stated specifically that "all Assembly decisions may be changed either by the Assembly or the king," [12] and in the context of the existing situation this constituted an unchallengeable royal veto power. But the influence of the Tshogdu in the decision-making process should not be underestimated on this account, for there is ample evidence that the king was very sensitive to prevailing sentiment in the Assembly on important issues, and was responsive to their recommendations on most occasions.

Under the 1953 royal order, therefore, it was quite clear that

11. The consultative body under the Shabdung system usually consisted of the top officials of the government and of the Drukpa establishment at both the central and regional level, though it occasionally was expanded to include a broader range of officials during periods of crisis. This is quite different from the Tshogdu which is primarily conceived as a popular representative institution.

12. For the text of the 1953 Act, see *Kuensel*, 6:12 (Nov. 14, 1971), or Nagendra Singh, Appendix XII, pp. 195–197.

the king remained as the sole sovereign authority in Bhutan with the final decision on all legislation. In constitutional terms, this was all changed in the Tshogdu's Fall session in 1968, when Druk Gyalpo Jigme Dorji Wangchuck recommended the following basic amendment to the 1953 "Constitution": "According to Article 18 of the Constitution of the National Assembly, the King was empowered since 1954 to amend any decision arrived at by the National Assembly. Henceforth the King will cease to exercise this power and all decisions of the National Assembly will be treated as final." [13]

The Tshogdu accepted the royal recommendation and passed a resolution, subsequently approved by the king, under which "all decisions of the National Assembly will be treated as final and will not require the approval of the king." The Druk Gyalpo, however, is given the power to personally address the Assembly and request it to reconsider any resolution about which he has "serious misgivings." [14] Given the nature of the relationship still existing between the Druk Gyalpo and the Tshogdu, it is probable that the objections of the palace to any particular resolution would be heeded by the Assembly, and that the king retains what amounts to a *de facto* veto power. But the significance of this reform for the future, when the character of the political system may change substantially, should not be underestimated. Nor is it mere rhetoric that the Druk Gyalpo and the Tshogdu are now officially described as the "dual sovereign powers" in Bhutan, even though the latter institution is not yet capable or ready to use its authority in this ultimate sense.

But even more innovative, indeed unprecedented in monarchical politics, was the Druk Gyalpo's startling recommendation to the Tshogdu in 1968 that all officers of the government, *including the king*, be forced to resign from office if they receive a no-confidence vote in the Tshogdu. The motivations underlying the king's recommendations on this question were eloquently expressed in his statement to the Tshogdu in which he said in part:

13. *Kuensel,* 2:22 (Nov. 30, 1968), 3, Document No. 2.
14. *Ibid.,* pp. 3–4.

During the last Spring Session of the National Assembly, I had expressed my desire to form a government combining the monarchical and democratic systems in order to ensure the stability and solidarity of the country. Our sovereignty may be endangered by the fact that we are placed between two powerful and big countries, although at present we are not faced with external aggression and there is peace within the country as there are no undesirable elements to create disorder. This, therefore, is the time to think of forming a stable government for maintaining the peace and tranquillity of the country in future. With the approach of bad times, the present peace of the country and feeling of the people may change. If the people do not cooperate with the King, it will not be possible for the King alone to protect the people. We have a hereditary monarchy, but the people must also realize their duties and responsibilities. Even if you feel that the system of hereditary monarchy should be abolished, this also should be achieved by proper means, the procedure of which is to be decided. Rebellion will only bring disaster and disgrace to the country accompanied by loss of lives and chaos which will be exploited by outsiders to the detriment of the country. In case of misunderstanding between the King and the people or if the King resorts to repression, the people, instead of rebelling, should convene the National Assembly. . . . I have a feeling that my last speech to the National Assembly was not very clear to all of you. I did not say that the system of hereditary monarchy should be abolished. My intention was to empower the National Assembly to change by peaceful means any King, including myself, who is found unfit to rule the country. I would request you to consider the matter carefully in the best interests of the country, both for the present and future.[15]

This proposal was too radical and uncertain in its consequences for the Tshogdu to approve immediately, and the debate on the issue indicated just how conservative a body the National Assembly is. However, when the king repeated his recommendation on this issue to the Spring 1969 session, the Tshogdu finally approved the resolution with certain modifications. Under this act, the reigning monarch is obligated to abdicate if two-thirds of the Assembly's membership supports a vote of no-confidence on his conduct of office.[16] Furthermore,

15. *Ibid.*, Document No. 1, p. 2.
16. In the Spring 1970 session of the Tshogdu, this rule was modified to specify that the vote on all no-confidence motions must be by secret ballot. It

it was provided that such votes should be taken as a matter of procedure at least once every three years, and that motions of no-confidence could be moved against the king at any time on a petition submitted by one-third of the membership. The Tshgodu's power, however, was limited to removing a particular ruler, not abolishing the monarchy itself, as under the law the next Wangchuck in the line of succession would ascend to the throne automatically on the abdication of his predecessor.

The system for registering confidence in the Druk Gyalpo was abolished by the Tshogdu in its Spring 1973 session, reportedly on its own initiative—which is possible given the very conservative character of this institution. Druk Gyalpo Jigme Singye Wangchuck assented to this change in the rules of the game, noting however that if indeed he should ever lose the confidence of the representatives of the people he would in any case have to abdicate his throne. Thus, this unique experiment in a monarchical polity has been abandoned, but it can be presumed that the concept of monarchical responsibility to the National Assembly has not disappeared in Bhutan.

The basic structural changes introduced by Druk Gyalpo Jigme Dorji Wangchuck were not limited to the Tshogdu. In 1965 he established the Lodoi Tsokde (Royal Advisory Council) which was primarily an appointive body with advisory powers, but which included several representatives elected by the Tshogdu. In 1968, he appointed three ministers and constituted what amounted to the first Council of Ministers in Bhutan. In that same year he recommended to the Tshogdu that all appointments of ministers "be decided by the National Assembly, which will also decide their number and portfolios." [17] The Tshogdu appeared reluctant to assume such power, but finally a system was worked out informally under which the king

---

also clarified the two-thirds-vote provision by stipulating that a quorum for a vote on a no-confidence motion must be two-thirds (100) of the total legal membership of the Tshogdu (150) rather than just two-thirds of the membership in office at any one time (*Ibid.*, 4:10 [May 31, 1970], p. 102). The Druk Gyalpo later repeated his recommendation that a simple majority vote be sufficient to force the abdication of the ruling monarch, but this was again rejected by the Tshogdu.

17. *Ibid.*, 2:22 (Nov. 30, 1968), p. 2.

appoints and the Tshogdu approves ministers. Moreover, the practice has developed under which the ministers report to the Assembly on the functioning of their departments and are subjected to interrogation by that body. While the relationship between the monarchy, the Assembly, and the Council of Ministers cannot yet be described as parliamentary in character, such a system does exist in embryonic form. Whether it will develop along classic parliamentary lines with the power of the king strictly limited and the Council of Ministers elected by and responsible to the representative body is still too early to tell. But it is probably without precedent in the history of monarchies that an absolute ruler has, on his own initiative and without serious overt challenges to his authority, introduced basic structural changes that could eventually transform the entire character of the monarchical polity.

But the farsighted liberal policy of the late Druk Gyalpo, which the present ruler adopted as his own on his accession to the throne, should not obscure the real distribution of power and authority in terms of *real politique* no matter what the legal formulas may be. The Druk Gyalpo is still not only the Head of State but the ruler of the country, and the decision-making process continues to be concentrated in the palace. The Tshogdu has occasionally rejected royal recommendations,[18] or has delayed their implementation, but no one doubts the capacity of the king to persuade the National Assembly to approve any legislation that he considers vital to the country. The ministers may have to report to the Assembly, but their primary responsibility is to the king; in reality it is only on the loss of his confidence that they are in any danger of being removed from office. The monarchy, however, has set the stage for changing the constitutional structure and that is the most it could be expected to do. It is now up to the other institutions and political

18. In the Spring 1969 session of the Tshogdu, for instance, the Druk Gyalpo's recommendation that "freedom of speech" be extended to all Bhutanese citizens was rejected on the grounds that free speech, while good in principle, was premature, given the "backward state of education and political consciousness" (*Ibid.*, 3:11 [June 15, 1969], p. 3).

forces in Bhutan to develop the capacity and the will to use the broad powers—and responsibilities—entrusted to them.

The Tshogdu

The 1953 announcement by Druk Gyalpo Jigme Dorji Wangchuck that a representative body (described as a Royal Advisory Council) would be established to assist in the governance of the country must have caused confusion and some degree of consternation in the ranks of officialdom. Confusion, because a representative body that would include nonofficials was a new concept in Bhutan politics, and there was no immediate indication about how these new participants in the political process were to be selected nor what their powers and functions were to be. Consternation, because new institutions that expand the ranks hold both opportunities and dangers for the established elite, particularly when introduced in the first year of the reign of a new monarch whose authority was close to being absolute but whose philosophy of government was still to be tested.

The 1953 royal order that provided the constitution for the Tshogdu failed to address itself unambiguously to some of the more crucial questions, for it was an open-ended, rather imprecise document in most respects. The constitution consisted of eighteen clauses, but the main provisions can be summarized under the following headings:

1. *Membership.* There are three membership categories, selected separately, in the Tshogdu—the representatives of (a) the official body; (b) the monastic institutions; and (c) the people. The term of office for the last two categories was set at three years.

2 *Qualifications.* Members of the Tshogdu have to be Bhutanese citizens 25 years of age or over, and cannot be convicts or have served a term in prison.

3. *Sessions.* The presiding officer in the Tshogdu, the Speaker, is elected by the body itself. At the king's "royal command," the Speaker can convene emergency sessions of the Tshogdu in addition to the two regular annual sessions held in the Spring and the Fall.

4. *Legislative Powers.* The Tshogdu members are guaranteed complete freedom of speech "in the Assembly" and can discuss and pass resolutions on any subject. All decisions of the Tshogdu require a two-thirds majority under the 1953 constitution, and have to be approved by the king before becoming law.

Adding substance and specificity to this 1953 royal order has been an evolutionary process, and the institution has undergone some vital changes in composition, extent of power, and method of operational procedure since its inauguration.

The size of the Tshogdu was not specified in the 1953 constitution, and there would seem to have been some flexibility on this matter in the first decade of its existence. There were at first about 130 members—10 from the official category, 10 from the monk bodies, and 110 representatives of the people. The membership was increased to 150 in the 1960s with the addition of 20 members from the rapidly expanding government service.

The 1953 document merely stated that the king "will nominate Members of the Royal Advisory Council from Government servants" and did not equate executive office with Tshogdu membership except in this indirect fashion. Later, as it has worked out, the king formally appoints the official representatives to the Tshogdu, but in fact the holders of certain offices are now automatically also members of the Assembly (in this respect, however, it should be remembered that all members of the government hold their offices at the discretion of the king). This group includes the Council of Ministers, the Lodoi Tsokde (Royal Advisory Council), and by common practice several of the district officers and secretaries of the various departments of government. Since their membership in the Tshogdu continues as long as they hold their posts, the three-year term of office provision does not apply to them.

According to the 1953 royal order, the representatives of the Drukpa monastic order were to be selected under a system in which "the monk body will elect its members from the Central Monk Body." Presumably, then, all members of the monk body—that is, members of recognized Drukpa monastic institutions—were enfranchised, but their range of selection for representatives to the Tshogdu was limited to the membership of the Central Monk Body at Thimphu/Punakha. In fact, however, the election system has evolved along quite different lines, in the process providing greater regional representation. Under the electoral procedure now followed, the Central Monk Body elects one member and the eight other major regional monk bodies elect six representatives.[19] The Dorji Lopon (who is a member of the Central Monk Body, the second-in-command to the Je Khempo and usually considered to be the Number Two man in the Drukpa establishment), and the two monk body representatives on the Royal Advisory Council are the other three representatives from the monastic order in the Tshogdu.

The two categories of Tshogdu membership discussed above represented establishment constituencies at the time of the inauguration of the National Assembly. Both groups had long been the active—indeed the only—participants in the traditional consultative institutions under both the Shabdung and the monarchical systems of government. While there have been significant changes in the composition of representation from both groups since 1953, these changes reflect shifts in the constituencies from which the members are drawn—the civil and monastic officialdom.

The third category of Tshogdu membership—the people's representatives—constituted a novel element in the decision-making process at the central level, and one with some unpredictable qualities in 1953. The method of their selection, for instance, was of crucial importance, as this would determine the extent to which the introduction of the Tshogdu constituted a radical departure from the norm in Bhutanese politics. The potential of the Tshogdu as a challenge to the existing order was obvious.

The electoral system as it has evolved has proved only minimally disruptive of Bhutan's pre-1953 polity. While for most of

19. The large regional monk bodies (Paro, Tongsa, Daga, and Wangdiphodrang) each elect one representative, while the other four (Tashigang, Lhuntsi, Mongar, and Shemgang) elect two members.

the country the concepts of direct, secret elections and universal suffrage as incorporated in the 1950 Indian constitutional system were rejected, for southern Bhutan a modified popular electoral system was introduced. In this region, in which Nepali Bhutanese form the large majority of the population, the people's representatives are elected under a system in which each household has one vote, usually cast by the head of the household. In western, central and eastern Bhutan, however, an electoral system based upon the consensual political tradition of Bhutan has been used. The normal procedure is for district-level officials to call a meeting in each constituency to which the headmen (gups) of the villages and selected members of the village community (usually heads of household and other adult males) are invited. When a consensus upon one candidate cannot be achieved through a "sense of the meeting" process, some other method, such as the casting of dice, is used. In 1973, the Lhungye Shuntsog (State Committee) proposed that the popular election system utilized in southern Bhutan be introduced throughout the country, but this was rejected by the Tshogdu—most of whose members had a personal stake in the existing selection process.

Consensus politics in a stable, traditional society are usually elite-dominated politics that provide little scope for popular participation in the decision-making process, and this general rule would seem to apply to Bhutan. The few reports available on the Tshogdu electoral process indicate that constituency election meetings are dominated by the officials and traditional leaders. The consensus on a candidate, if one is reached, is thus a very narrow one among a small body of men, most of whom hold some official rank.

At the operational level, the little evidence that is available indicates that organized factional politics, structured along either vertical or horizontal lines, are not a significant factor in the electoral process. The selection of popular representatives in Bhutan thus differs substantially in form and substance from the panchayat polity in Nepal which also employed a limited franchise system, but one in which the king, the members of the Council of Ministers, and the leadership of the illegal but still functional political parties interfered on a crucial scale in the election of members to the central legislature. This probably reflects the differing stage of development in the politicization of the rural populace—including the rural elite—in the two countries, and the nonexistence in Bhutan of *enduring* political factions based upon ideological, regional, ethnic, familial, or other social or economic factors.

What we have in Bhutan may not be a democratic process in any Western definition of that term, but it is questionable that, given Bhutan's level of political and social development, this seriously affects the Tshogdu's representative character. In a largely nonpoliticized society such as Bhutan where lines of authority are still functional—and respected—a consensus at the top probably also broadly reflects a consensus throughout the society, even at the local or district level. Until Bhutanese society has been transformed, and the concept of broad political participation on factional (that is, party) lines has been generally accepted and operationalized, it is probable that the introduction of a direct election system based on universal franchise would not have much of an impact on the type of local representatives sent to the Assembly.

How representative a body is the Tshogdu in population and regional terms? Assuming the approximate accuracy of the 1969 census figures, the distribution of seats by region at that time was not seriously distorted, although western Bhutan was somewhat over-represented and eastern Bhutan under-represented. Thus, in 1973, western and central Bhutan with 28 percent of the population had about 37 percent of the seats; eastern Bhutan with 57 percent of the population had 48 percent of the seats; and southern Bhutan with 15 percent of the population had that percentage of seats in the Tshogdu. Subsequently, the distribution of Assembly seats among the districts was revised to accord with population figures. This revision was by administrative decree, as there are no hard and fast rules either on the number of Tshogdu members from each electoral district or on constituency boundaries—which can be, and usually are, changed with each election.

The Tshogdu in Operation. The National Assembly is, by gen-

Table 4. National Assembly membership by electoral district

Region	District *	Number of members
Western and central Bhutan	Ha	3
	Paro	7
	Dung	2
	Thimphu	8
	Chapcha	3
	Gasa	3
	Punakha	4
	Wangdiphodrang	7
	Daga	4
Eastern Bhutan	Tongsa	5
	Shemgang	6
	Byakar	4
	Lhuntsi	5
	Shongar	13
	Tashigang	19
Southern Bhutan	Samchi/Chirang	17

* The number of and names for electoral districts do not coincide exactly with those of administrative districts on lists available to the author. The source of the above electoral district list was the Secretariat of the Tshogdu, giving the distribution of seats as of 1973.

eral consensus, strongly conservative, its conservatism matched perhaps only by that of the monastic establishment. With the bulk of its membership reportedly stemming from landowning families that are staunch supporters of the existing order in Bhutan and suspicious of anything new or foreign, it is not surprising that the Tshogdu has been generally resistant to change. For the most part, it has been prepared to accept innovations only under pressure from the palace and/or the civil officialdom, *even* when the intention is to expand the power and status of the Tshogdu itself. This was amply demonstrated by the Tshogdu's cautious and reluctant response to the Druk Gyalpo's proposal in 1968 that the decisions of the Tshogu should no longer require royal approval and that the Assembly should be given the power to remove a king through a no-confidence vote.

Furthermore, as might be expected from a body consisting primarily of local elites representing local interests, the debates during the two short three- to four-week annual sessions tend to focus on local subjects, and national issues are only rarely raised for discussion.[20] This once led Druk Gyalpo Jigme Dorji Wangchuck to comment during a session that the Tshogdu had been established as a consultative body on national affairs, "but of late it is found that the questions raised in the Assembly pertain to private, district and village interests. Matters of national importance are not being raised." He went on to urge the members of the Tshogdu to express their views without any hesitation, no matter how this might displease members of the executive branch of government, even the king. Indeed, he complained that the "love and respect" given to him as Druk Gyalpo prevented the Tshogdu members from "criticizing my actions and blinds them towards my mistakes." Anything the king does, he said, is approved. This is harmful to the welfare of the country, for if the king makes mistakes, these should be "promptly pointed out by the members representing the monks and public." [21]

Whenever it acts on national issues, then, the Tshogdu is usually responding to initiatives from the executive branch of government, and not because it has defined a distinctive position of its own on such questions. There would seem to be two exceptions to this general rule: first, national issues concerning certain aspects of Bhutan's external relations—in particular, its status as a sovereign nation-state; and second, national issues that affect in some way the preservation of Bhutan's traditional culture. In 1967, for instance, when the Indian government proposed an exchange of representatives between the two gov-

20. The king or any of his ministers can propose subjects for discussion to the Speaker, and this is the way in which most issues are brought before the house. Any member of the Tshogdu can propose a private resolution for discussion, but these usually concern minor subjects directly affecting the member's constituency.

21. *Kuensel*, 3:20 (Oct. 31, 1969). Here again may be a situation unique to Bhutan in which the leader of the executive branch of government complains about the *lack of criticism* from the representative body. Druk Gyalpo Jigme Dorji Wangchuck was of the opinion that the failure of the Tshogdu to assert itself institutionally against the monarchy could have long-run harmful effects for Bhutan—and for the dynasty. He was, perhaps, one of the few leaders of a traditional society who understood that most complex concept—that the powers of an institution can be expanded when shared with other political institutions *if* in the process the ability of the government as a whole to function in new capacities is expanded.

ernments, the Tshogdu expressed such strong reservations that implementation of the decision had to be delayed while more acceptable terms were worked out. There were also repeated demands from the Tshogdu in the mid-1960s that the authorities apply for membership in the United Nations, on the grounds that this would constitute international recognition of Bhutan's independence and clarify any confusion abroad about the relationship between Bhutan and India.

With respect to the second exception, members of the Tshogdu have consistently stressed the need to preserve Bhutan's customs and traditions, and reportedly there is near unanimity on this subject. The Druk Gyalpo had to intercede in a Tshogdu debate on one occasion to point out that all of Bhutan's heritage does not deserve preservation and that the imposition of rules and regulations with preservation as the objective could cause unnecessary hardships to minorities—Nepali Bhutanese and Tibetan refugee settlers—who have distinct cultural traditions of their own.[22]

There have been a number of procedural changes in the Tshogdu in recent years that may prove to be of some importance in the future. The 1953 royal order, for instance, had specified a two-thirds majority for the passage of a legislative act or resolution, but this was later changed to a simple majority. Moreover, voting in the Tshogdu had been by show of hands, a procedure that can be intimidating and restrictive, but this was changed to a secret ballot at the suggestion of the Druk Gyalpo in 1968.

There has even been an embryonic committee system, based on regions, introduced in recent years, primarily to deal with economic-development policy questions. These are the government programs that have the most immediate impact on local areas and interests, and the people's representatives in the Tshogdu have come to consider it essential to be fully informed on such subjects. The debates on the annual budget and on the Five Year Plan programs, for instance, are usually the longest and most incisive discussions in the Tshogdu, with the govern-

22. *Ibid.*, 2:22 (Nov. 30, 1968), p. 7.

ment officials responsible for the economic departments subjected to intensive cross-examination on virtually all aspects of
their programs.

One can conclude this analysis of the Tshogdu in operation
by noting that, though perhaps more in spite of itself than
because of any determined and forceful assertion of its rights,
the Assembly is beginning to emerge as a vital cog in the Bhutanese political and governmental structure. On occasion, it has
even demonstrated an independent spirit as well as resentment
over its inferior status to the executive branch of government.
To date, however, it has been the leadership of the Tshogdu
rather than the institution itself which has sought to insist upon
its prerogatives—particularly during the Speakership of Dasho
Shingkar Lam who was elected to that post in 1970.[23] Dasho
Lam was able to use his concurrent status as Speaker, secretary
to the Druk Gyalpo, deputy minister, and member of the
Lhungye Shuntsog to gain for himself an influential voice in
the decision-making process, enhancing not only his prestige
but that of the Assembly as well. Within the Tshogdu, he employed his broad powers unhesitatingly in an effort to transform what has been a rather inchoate institution into a more
effective investigatory and legislative body.

Part of the Tshogdu's weakness as a political institution, however, is the amorphous character of existing factional alignments. Here also the nonexistence of viable and enduring political associations discourages the emergence of long-term
programs and policies with a stable support base within the Assembly. Moreover, under the Tshogdu's haphazard electoral
system, there is limited continuity of membership, and only a
small proportion of the people's representatives in the Assembly at any one point in time would have had a lengthy experience in government. This is a serious handicap in any competition with executive or administrative officials, who, almost by

23. In the contest for the speakership, there are usually three candidates—
one from each category of Tshogdu membership. Despite the large majority of
people's representatives, six of the seven Speakers (1954–1975) have been official representatives, and the other a monk representative, one more indication
of the real power structure within the Tshogdu and the dependent character of
this institution.

definition, are well-experienced and skillful in dealing with complicated political and developmental issues.

Thus, the Tshogdu continues to have some of the characteristics of a novel institutional appendage to a well-oiled political system, mistrusted to some extent by the more established institutions and uncertain of its own status and powers. Druk Gyalpo Jigme Dorji Wangchuck sought to thrust responsibilities upon the Assembly, but its response has been restrained and hesitant. For some time to come it is probable that the initiative in decision-making and policy formation will continue to originate in the palace and affiliated institutions; but it is not unlikely that the Tshogdu will increasingly exhibit the will and capacity to use the broad powers it has been granted and to demand and obtain a greater role for itself as a representative of the people in the political and legislative process.

Royal Advisory Bodies

The first Shabdung, Ngawang Namgyal, established an advisory body, the Lhungye Tsok (State Council) as a regular part of the new political system that he created. This institution continued to function throughout the Shabdung period, and indeed it was a meeting of the Lhungye Tsok, expanded for the occasion to include virtually all higher civil and religious officials, that approved the establishment of an hereditary monarchy in 1907. Nevertheless, the first two Druk Gyalpos in effect suspended the operation of the Lhungye Tsok, seeking its counsel and advice on an *ad hoc* basis when necessary but usually employing the four ministers (Lhengyels)—the Thimphu Dzongpön, the Punakha Dzongpön, the Shung Kalön, and the Shung Drönyer—as an informal advisory body.

As part of his broad-gauge administrative reorganization program, the third Druk Gyalpo revived the concept of a formal consultative institution. The initial step in this direction was the formation of the Lodoi Tsokde (Royal Advisory Council) on an informal basis in the late 1950s and then more formally in 1965. In 1975, this was a ten-member body consisting of a chairman (the Shung Kalön) appointed by the Druk Gyalpo, two representatives of the monk body, five people's representatives, a representative from the Nepali Bhutanese community, and a woman's representative. Except for the Shung Kalön, who serves at the discretion of the Druk Gyalpo, all members of the Lodoi Tsokde serve five-year terms. They are, moreover, members of the Tshogdu in their capacity as Royal Advisers. It is also within the area of competence of the Lodoi Tsokde to check on the implementation of measures that have been approved by the Tshogdu, thus serving in a limited capacity as a supervisory body over the Council of Ministers and the administration.

As is normally the case in Bhutan, the selection of representatives from the monastic and people's constituencies is an internal matter. The Central Monk Body of Thimphu/Punakha and the nine regional monk bodies each prepare separate slates consisting of three candidates; the Tshogdu then elects one monk representative to the Lodoi Tsokde from both slates. The five people's representatives in the Lodoi Tsokde represent regions consisting of two or more districts, but are elected directly by the Tshogdu, acting as a unit, from slates that include the names of three candidates nominated by public leaders in each constituency. The representative from the Nepali Bhutanese community is elected by the people's representatives from southern Bhutan, while the woman's representative is nominated by the king.

Following the establishment of a Council of Ministers in 1968, it was considered necessary to establish a broader-based royal consultative body to advise the king on policy matters and to coordinate the activities of the various organs of government. The Lhungye Shuntsog (State Committee) was created for this purpose, with a membership consisting of the ministers, the Lodoi Tsokde, the Speaker of the Tshogdu, and since 1972 the two sisters of the king who serve as his representatives in the ministries of finance and development. The Lhungye Shuntsog met every Monday, usually with the king in attendance.

The Lhungye Shuntsog was the closest thing to a cabinet in the Bhutanese system, though it lacked several of the essential ingredients of this institution as it exists in classic parliamentary systems. Its primary function was to advise the king on legislation proposed for submission to the Tshogdu for its approval. On minor issues, however, it was not uncommon for the king, in consultation with the Lhungye Shuntsog, to issue an ordinance without obtaining the prior approval of the National Assembly.

By the early 1970s there were complaints that the Lhungye Shuntsog was not a suitable instrument for carrying out the functions for which it was designed. It was too large and unwieldy to serve as an effective consultative body in the decision-making process or as a forum for informed analysis of complex problems. Nor did the Lhungye Shuntsog ever evolve into a coordinating institution capable of resolving conflicts of interests and functions between various governmental departments and institutions. Indeed, its composition—with representatives of the legislative branch in attendance in their role as Royal Advisers—rendered it infeasible for the Lhungye Shuntsog to assume such a role without confusing the division of powers and responsibilities that is implicit in the Bhutanese political system.

Obviously, something new was required, and this need was met by the creation of a Coordination Committee in 1974.[24] This committee is somewhat smaller and more cohesive, consisting primarily of administrative functionaries with executive responsibilities. In 1975, the Coordination Committee was presided over by Ashi Dechen Wangchuck, the sister of the king, who was assigned responsibility for the Development Ministry. The other members were the Home, Finance, Foreign, and Trade and Industries ministers, the secretary-general and secretary of the Development Ministry, the secretaries of the Trade and Industry and the Communication ministries, one representative from the Lodoi Tsokde, and two Indian advisers on economic affairs. The king also attends the sessions

24. The Lhungye Shuntsog has not been formally abolished, but it has ceased to meet since the establishment of the Coordination Committee. Whether it might be revived at some point in the future is unclear, but this seems unlikely.

frequently, and specialists in particular fields may be invited to attend discussions in their fields of expertise.

The Coordination Committee meets every week as a general rule and has been assigned a range of responsibilities much broader than those given to the Lhungye Shuntsog. First, it coordinates departmental activities, resolving conflicts when these arise and eliminating duplication in their operations. Second, the committee is the principal policy-making body in Bhutan, with decisions made on a king-in-council basis in most cases. Third, it has been assigned a major role in the planning process, in particular through its control over the allocation of funds to each department. Control is implemented through the Finance Ministry which was given full authority over the allocation of funds *within* departments as well as *between* departments—a power the ministry lacked previously. Finally, the Coordination Committee has been empowered to draft uniform rules on service conditions for all departments of government, thus eliminating the widely varied terms of employment prevailing in the various ministries for officials at the same rank nominally.

It is widely expected in Bhutan that the Coordination Committee will emerge as the key policy-making institution, and that it will have broad powers of supervision and control over the bureaucracy as well. While the royal writ is still unchallenged—and unchallengeable—under the unwritten constitution now emerging it is highly unusual for the king to ignore the advice presented by the Coordination Committee. If Bhutan continues to move in the direction of a limited constitutional monarchy, it is possible that the Coordination Committee (or some successor institution similarly composed) will gradually assume the role of a cabinet as in a parliamentary system of government.

Council of Ministers

Bhutan took a major step in the direction of a modernized administrative system in 1968 when the Tshogdu, at the request of the Druk Gyalpo, approved the formation of a

Chart 1. Advisory, executive, and administrative institutions

KING

Lodoi Tsokde ———— Coordination Committee

Council of Ministers

Development	Trade and Industry	Finance	Home	Communication	Foreign Affairs
Education	Forests	Revenue and Settlement	Civil Administration	Wireless and Communication	Protocol
Health	Handicrafts	Excise	Police		Passports Visas and Permits
Agriculture	Industries	Customs			Missions Abroad
Animal Husbandry	State Trading Companies	Touring			
Posts and Telegraph		Transport Workshop			
Hydro Projects		Bank of Bhutan and			
Public Works		Guest Houses			
		Surveys			
Information		Account			
Ancient Monasteries and National Library					

Council of Ministers (Lhengyel Tsok). As was typical of the strategy of the third Druk Gyalpo in administrative reforms, this was done in stages with a gradual devolution of powers to the ministers (Lhengyels, today called Lyonpos) over a several-year period. Initially only three ministries were established: Home Affairs; Trade, Commerce, and Industry; and Finance; several of the more important departments of government did not fall under the jurisdiction of the Council of Ministers. By 1973, however, Foreign Affairs and Communication had been added to the list, and there were also three deputy ministers on the Council with more limited responsibilities. Each of the ministries includes a number of departments, most of which are headed by secretaries or assistant secretaries.

While the authority of the Council of Ministers has been extended considerably, there are several important administrative institutions that have not yet been brought under the Council. The Royal Bhutan Army, for instance, is still administered directly from the palace by the Druk Gyalpo; and jurisdiction over the Central Monk Body at Tashichhodzong in Thimphu is still the responsibility of the Je Khempo.

Moreover, the powers of the ministers and their capacity to control the departments under their jurisdiction are limited by several factors. The ministers are responsible to the Druk Gyalpo for the administration of their departments and can be removed at any time at his discretion. Furthermore, the higher red-scarf officers in the departments are appointed by the Druk Gyalpo, although now usually on the recommendation of the departmental minister. The appointment of the two older sisters of the present Druk Gyalpo Jigme Singye Wangchuck, who have served since 1971 as royal representatives in the ministries of development and finance, introduced a precedent whose significance for the future is difficult to determine, for it brings members of the royal family into the Council of Ministers on still-to-be defined terms.

The ministers are also responsible to the Tshogdu which must approve their appointment by a simple majority vote on the recommendation of the Druk Gyalpo. The National Assembly can also force the resignation of any minister by a two-thirds vote of no-confidence. The principle of collective responsibility has not yet been introduced, although the usual practice has been for ministers to support their colleagues in the Tshogdu. The ministers are responsible in a more indirect fashion to the Coordination Committee, which has been given the responsibility to supervise the functioning of the ministries and make recommendations to the Druk Gyalpo on this subject.

While these limitations on the power of the Council of Ministers are important, there is no doubt that the ministers are the most influential officials, other than the Druk Gyalpo, in the government. Their responsibility for the implementation of policy, of course, also provides them with a powerful influence in the decision-making process. While they are responsible to the Druk Gyalpo, he in turn is heavily dependent upon the ministers for effective administration, informed advice upon policies and programs, and for the implementation of policy decisions. It is in recognition of their importance to Bhutan's polity that the members of the Council of Ministers have been granted the honor of wearing orange scarfs, indicative of the highest category of officials next to the wearers of saffron scarfs, which are worn only by the Druk Gyalpo and the Je Khempo.

The Monastic Order

The collapse of the Shabdung system and its replacement by an hereditary monarchy in 1907 constituted a challenge, direct and indirect, to the Drukpa Buddhist establishment. Given the circumstances in which this change occurred, it is not surprising that the monk bodies at both the central and regional levels were reluctant to take up the challenge and preferred to temporize until their own house had again been set in order. The abolition of the Shabdung office deprived the monastic system of the fulcrum upon which it had been balanced for three centuries. While the religious authority of the Shabdung had eroded nearly as badly as his political authority by the beginning of the twentieth century, he was nevertheless essential to the functioning of the Drukpa system. His power to control the monk bodies may have deteriorated, but he was the legitimizing authority upon which all other monastic officials depended for verification of their right to office. A substitute source of legitimation was required, and it took some time for one to emerge that was generally acceptable to everyone involved on both the religious and civil sides.[25]

This did not mean that the monastic order ceased to function during this period, or that it was incapable of exerting a substantial influence on certain kinds of issues. Institutionally, indeed, the system seemed to be little affected by the developments in 1907. All of the monastic officials other than the Shabdung continued to function essentially as they had in the past, and the hierarchy and rules established by the fourth Druk Desi, Gyase Tenzing Rabgye (1680–1694), were retained virtually unchanged.

Under this ancient system, the Je Khempo has full religious authority over all Buddhist institutions, including those that are controlled by sects other than the Drukpa. He is assisted by four high-ranking lamas, all belonging to the Central Monk Body (Gedunpa) at Thimphu/Punakha, who are assigned charge of specific departments of the monastic order. They are:

1. *Dorji Lopon:* the second-ranking monastic official in Bhutan after the Je Khempo; he is responsible for the supervision of monk bodies throughout the country, and also functions as the administrative head of the Central Monk Body at Thimphu/Punakha.

2. *Tshannyi Lopon:* the lama responsible for Buddhist metaphysical studies throughout Bhutan and the head of the "debating society" in the monk bodies.

3. *Yongpi Lopon:* the official who supervises worship ceremonies and also the head of the "reading society" throughout Bhutan.

4. *Dagpi Lopon:* the lama responsibile for grammatical stud-

25. In 1926, at the time of the succession to the throne of the second Druk Gyalpo, the Sung incarnation of the first Shabdung tried to claim sovereign authority for himself but was unsuccessful and was finally forced to "retire" to the monastery at Talo (Nagendra Singh, pp. 141–142).

174 The Politics of Bhutan

ies in the monastic order and also the head of the "writing societies."

The societies headed by the last three monk officials constitute the administrative apparatus within Bhutanese Buddhism, with responsibility over all Buddhist bodies—including non-Drukpa institutions—in Bhutan. The authority of the Central Monk Body is, thus, manifest in a number of ways over all other monk bodies. It is the normal practice, for instance, for lamas belonging to the Central Monk Body to be sent out as heads of the regional monk bodies in other sections of the country, and on their retirement to return to their home base at Thimphu/Punakha.

Part of the crisis faced by the monastic order after 1907 (or, more specifically, after 1917 with the death of the Je Khempo who was in office when the hereditary monarchy was established) concerned the procedure used in selecting a successor when the Je Khempo's office became vacant. Under the first two Druk Gyalpos, it was the normal practice for slips of paper bearing the names of the four top officials of the Central Monk Body to be placed in an urn on an altar; one slip was drawn as "the choice of God" for Je Khempo. The term of office was unspecified and depended upon the Je Khempo, who could serve for the rest of his life if he so desired. This system virtually excluded the civil authorities from any role in the selection of the head of the monastic order.

At the suggestion of the third Druk Gyalpo toward the end of his reign, this selection procedure was changed, and an election system was introduced in which the franchise was restricted to members of the Central Monk Body. While this is not specifically stipulated, under normal conditions the Dorji Lopon (the second-in-command of the Drukpa establishment) will automatically succeed as Je Khempo. If for some reason he should be considered by the monk body to lack the requisite qualifications for the office, one of the other three Lopons, or possibly a former Dorji Lopon who had already retired, would become Je Khempo. The term of office of the Je Khempo under the new system is also reportedly under negotiation. The high officials of the monk body maintain that the old rule still applies, and that the Je Khempo will serve at his own discretion. The civil authorities, however, have reportedly suggested that a three-year term would be more appropriate.[26]

Despite the various problems mentioned above, monastic discipline would appear to have been maintained at a satisfactory standard, both in institutional and personal behavior terms (although stories of misconduct are as common in Bhutan as in any society with large monastic establishments). Recruitment into the system, however, is a persistent problem. Previously young boys had been sent into the monasteries for a variety of reasons—religious devotion; as a path for upper social and economic mobility for nonelite families; and as one way of handling excess population. Only the first really applies today, since the modern education system is a surer road to improved social and economic status and also because, with the new economic development programs, Bhutan faces a severe labor shortage. Druk Gyalpo Jigme Dorji Wangchuck had agreed to maintain the Central Monk Body at 1,000 members, and the prestige of the institution is so high that this is still largely accomplished. Other monk bodies, however, face greater difficulties. The present monk population has been estimated at approximately 5,000, a figure that would be at best the minimum required to maintain existing monasteries and shrines, some of which are badly undermanned. But competition for the services of Bhutanese youth is so intense today, due to government, army, agriculture, and development programs, that an increase in the size of the monastic establishment could come only at the expense of other institutions that would seem to have a higher priority in the eyes of the civil administration.

In addition, the training and education of the young recruits to the monastic system has become complicated in recent years. Until 1959, many young Bhutanese lamas went to Tibet for

26. Limiting the Je Khempo to a three-year term would, of course, also limit his influence over both the civil and religious systems in the country. The old system, under which the Je Khempo held office for life or until his retirement, made this a much more powerful office than what it may now become. On the other hand, the Druk Gyalpo gave the Je Khempo full power to deal with monastic discipline on the same basis as that established by the first Shabdung (*Kuensel*, 7:4 [Sept. 10, 1972]).

their religious education, principally to Dzokchhen monastery in eastern Tibet.[27] With the Chinese suppression of the Tibetan uprising in that year and the stringent restrictions placed upon the functioning of the monastic system subsequently, this channel for training Bhutanese lamas has disappeared. The training function has now been assumed by the monastic college attached to the Central Monk Body at Thimphu/Punakha, while more advanced studies in specific disciplines can be undertaken at a number of the smaller monasteries, such as Tangu in western Bhutan.

The Chinese occupation of Tibet has had other effects upon Bhutan's Buddhist system as well. In the past, a large number of reincarnate lamas (trulkus) now in Bhutanese monasteries have been "discovered" in Tibet, but this is of course no longer possible. In the long run, this may well mean that some Bhutanese trulkus will no longer reappear. This could seriously affect the prestige and influence of the leadership of the Buddhist system, which depends in part upon popular response to the reincarnation process. For the government, however, a more serious problem is the probability that Tibetan reincarnate lamas will now be discovered in Bhutan. If the Chinese regime in Tibet should be liberalized (as it gradually has been since the Cultural Revolution), these trulkus might be invited to their "home" monasteries in Tibet where they would be exposed to Chinese ideological education. In 1969, therefore, the Tshogdu decided that such trulkus would be allowed to leave Bhutan but would have to give up Bhutanese citizenship. They would also be barred from introducing any "new religious practices" and from establishing a monastery or administering any monk body in Bhutan.[28]

27. Ram Rahul, *Modern Bhutan*, p. 95.
28. *Kuensel*, 3:11 (June 15, 1969), 5–6. The ban on the introduction of new religious practices may have been directed at Chinese ideological influences, but was more probably intended to prevent the introduction of Gelugpa sect doctrine by followers of the Dalai Lama. This same regulation barred trulku's of the Gelugpa sect from giving "Manilung or doing preaching of any kind" and also stipulated that such trulkus of Tibetan reincarnate lamas who chose to remain in Bhutan would have to study in the Dzong monasteries and be governed by the rules and regulations of the Drukpa monk body.

Financing the monastic institutions and the expensive worship ceremonies and festivities associated with them is also becoming an increasing problem. Traditionally, religious institutions had depended upon private donations and upon the rents-in-kind received from the cultivation of government lands assigned to particular monasteries or shrines. In its Fall 1968 session, however, the Tshogdu banned the practice under which the district administrator had collected rents-in-kind for the monasteries in their jurisdiction, and substituted an annual subsidy of Rs. 500,000 to the Central Monk Body and the eight regional monk bodies. The Tshogdu also empowered the Finance Ministry to audit the accounts of the monk bodies,[29] and, further, in 1969 it required prior government approval for all soliciting of funds for religious purposes.[30] All these new measures constitute important forms of control over the monastic system, making it heavily dependent upon the government for its financial support. But, in fact, the new measures also hold certain advantages for the monk bodies, for a direct subsidy in currency provides them with more economic flexibility than did the old system under which their main source of income came in the form of agricultural products that were difficult to collect and market. Moreover, under a 1970 Tshogdu resolution, the district and village officials were made responsible for the repair of monasteries and shrines. This had long been a major economic burden for the monasteries and often a source of conflict between religious institutions and the people in their area who previously had to provide such labor free of charge.[31]

Significant insights into the future of government-monk body relations are not possible on the basis of limited observa-

29. *Kuensel*, 2:22 (Nov. 30, 1968), 3–4.
30. *Ibid.*, 3:11 (June 15, 1969), 8. It should not be assumed, however, that the primary motivation behind the introduction of these measures was to enhance the monastic system's dependence on the government. Rather, it formed part of a broader agricultural and tax reform program that would have made the continuance of rents-in-kind to monasteries a gross injustice. But the potential political significance of this economic program is also apparent.
31. *Ibid.*, 4:10 (May 31, 1970), p. 8. The Finance Ministry was instructed to provide funds "to the extent possible" to pay this labor force. Presumably, however, much of this repair labor is "voluntary," but now it is the civil officials who must impose this onerous obligation upon the people.

tion and the even more limited published sources available. Obviously, the civil authorities are now in a position to introduce some changes that might have aroused intense opposition from the monk body two decades ago.[32] But the government remains very sensitive to the opinions and views of monastic officials, who still constitute a potential source of dissidence and opposition in the country. Concessions are continually being made to the religious establishment, usually on issues that are of peripheral importance to the government but central to the social and political philosophy of the lamas. By and large, both sides have done their best to avoid direct confrontations which could seriously weaken both institutions, and a mutually acceptable working relationship would appear to have been achieved on most issues. Whether this will be maintained as the government introduces more modernization programs, however, is still open to question, for these run against the basic instincts and goals of much of the monastic establishment.

32. No statistics on the way in which the monk representatives have voted in the Tshogdu are available to the author, but reportedly they have generally supported most of the economic and social reform programs.

5. Administration
in Bhutan

The Wangchuck dynasty inherited an administrative system notable for its simplicity, both structurally and operationally, and in the first five decades of its rule very little was done to change the bureaucracy's general character. For the average Bhutanese peasant, the change in regimes in 1907 must have passed almost unnoticed. They were perhaps no longer called upon to perform the widely detested militia duties as frequently as had been the case earlier when civil strife had been a common feature of the highly decentralized, conflict-ridden Shabdung political system. But they dealt with the same local and district officials as they had in the past, and on the same limited range of subjects—law and order, involuntary labor, and revenue collection. They may have known that there was now a Druk Gyalpo rather than an incarnate lama to whom they owed ultimate allegiance, but this could not have been a change of any great significance.

For the body of officials, however, the post-1907 developments constituted a major change, which involved a strong shift toward the centralization of political and administrative authority. The powers of the district-level officials continued to be extensive; but these officials were now subjected to a degree of central supervision and control in the exercise of their powers that became increasingly comprehensive as the hereditary monarchy consolidated its position. By the time the second Druk Gyalpo had come to the throne, for example, it was a regular procedure to transfer most district officers periodically, thus denying them the opportunity to build up the local power support bases that had previously guaranteed them a broad degree of autonomy from central control.

This centralization of political authority, however, was not accompanied by a substantial expansion of the central administrative structure. During the reign of the first two Druk Gyalpos, the central secretariat was small enough to be run from a single room in the royal palace at Bumthang—which reportedly contained only a couple of file cases.

There was, indeed, relatively little for the central administration to do except to supervise the activities of the district-level officials. There was no Bhutan army in this period other than the small palace guard. The revenue of the central government—as distinct from the personal revenue of the various members of the royal family—was not sufficient to require elaborate budgeting or auditing procedures. External affairs, which meant primarily relations with British India and the Dalai Lama's regime in Tibet, were managed by the Bhutan agent in India and the Bhutan representative at Lhasa in Tibet.[1] Even trade with the outside world was largely outside the jurisdiction of the central authorities, for most of it was "contracted out" and managed by the Dorjis or members of the royal family.

It was only with the introduction of an ambitious economic and political development program during the rule of the third Druk Gyalpo that an expansion in the size and functions of the central government became essential. Since 1960, a comparatively elaborate central administrative structure has been constructed; it operates out of the new secretariat at Tashichhodzong in Thimphu and is responsible for a wide variety of administrative, developmental, and social welfare functions. Thimphu, in the process, has grown from a small village to a town of 10,000 people, most of whom are connected with the Bhutan civil service.

1. Indeed, it was only in 1972 that a Foreign Ministry was finally established in the Bhutan government, although Bhutan's relations with a growing number of foreign powers had come directly under the control of the palace several years earlier, following the assassination of Prime Minister Jigme Dorji.

The Central Secretariat

Until 1961, the central administration and the palace secretariat were virtually coterminous institutions, for almost all central government officials were posted in the palace and operated under the direct supervision of the Druk Gyalpo. The establishment in 1961 of a separate Development Secretariat, headed by a Secretary-General (Gyelon Chichap), constituted a major administrative innovation in Bhutan. The new Secretariat, moreover, was located at Paro, some 40 miles from Thimphu. While the Druk Gyalpo retained ultimate authority over the Development Secretariat through his representative in that department, until 1964 it was Prime Minister Jigme Dorji who exercised effective control at Paro. This *de facto* delegation of authority to the prime minister was probably attributable to the king's first heart attack in 1958 that disabled him for some time and obliged him to grant Jigme Dorji broad supervisory powers over the entire governmental and political system. The dominance of the prime minister was further indicated in the selection of the first Secretary-General, Tashi Dadul Densapa, who was an experienced Sikkimese official with close ties to the Dorji family.

The establishment of the Development Secretariat did not immediately affect the operation of the regular administrative system at Thimphu which continued to function directly out of the palace. Under this system, the three key officials under the Druk Gyalpo were the royal representative in the Royal Bhutan Army,[2] the Gyaldon (Royal Chief Secretary), and the Gyaltse (Royal Finance Secretary). The Gyaldon's functions were equivalent to those of a Home Minister and included the supervision of both the central and district-level administration. The appointment of the Gyaltse had become necessary only in 1963, as the revenues of the central government had increased and the administrative apparatus for collecting and expending these funds had become more elaborate.

2. A royal representative in the army has been appointed at times when the king himself did not hold what may be classified as the defense portfolio in the Bhutan governmental system.

With the creation of a Council of Ministers in 1968, the role of the palace secretariat was substantially affected. The Gyaldon and the Gyaltse then in office, Dasho Tamji Jagar and Dasho Chogyal, were appointed as Home and Finance Ministers respectively. The later post was abolished within the palace, while the Gyaldon henceforth functioned in a more limited capacity as personal secretary to the Druk Gyalpo. With this innovation the task of running the administration at both the central and district level moved out of the palace and into the new Secretariat at Thimphu. Despite the change, however, the relationship between the top administrative officers of the government and the Druk Gyalpo remained as close as it had been previously. There is still a fairly substantial palace staff whose members function both as intermediaries between the palace and the central secretariat and as the Druk Gyalpo's personal assistants. But perhaps the most important unit in the palace secretariat now is the king's private intelligence service which does not come under the jurisdiction of the Home Ministry but reports directly to the Druk Gyalpo. This provides him with an independent alternative source of information, thus lessening his dependence upon the regular administrative system. Such an agency is probably essential to the functioning of a system in which the ultimate responsibility for decision-making still lies with one man and in circumstances where the objectivity of administrative sources of intelligence cannot be assumed.

The modernization of the administrative system has been a high-priority objective of the Bhutan government since the late 1950s. As Bhutan lacks almost any kind of private institutional infrastructure (with the exception of the monastic system that is in any case at least semipublic), it was realized by the country's change-minded leaders that economic and political development had to be accompanied by administrative reforms that would enhance the government's capacity to initiate and implement new programs. The fact that virtually all of the young educated elite in Bhutan are immediately absorbed into the civil service increases dependence on this institution, for it means that the kinds of tasks that would in such neighboring countries as India and Nepal be turned over to nongovernmental institutions fall by default upon the shoulders of the administration in Bhutan.

Under the first two Druk Gyalpos, the civil service was a compact, tightly-knit group in which most officials came from two sources: members of the royal family, or men, some from non-elite families, who had been brought into the palace for training as young boys. This latter group was selected presumably with the objective of undermining the predominance of traditional elite families in local areas, as it created an administrative cadre whose interests were closely interrelated with those of the Wangchuck dynasty. This strategy was partly modified when the third Druk Gyalpo decided to establish lower-level schools throughout Bhutan and to send a number of young Bhutanese to India for higher education and technical training, after which they were recruited directly into the regular administrative service [3] without any period of training in the palace. But even in the 1970s, several of the highest officials had had most of their political socialization within the palace service; they no longer dominate the administration as they once did, however, as now more and more of the higher officials come from the "India-returned" group with its broadly different background of experience and education.

Regional and Local Administration. There is no separate regional administrative system in Bhutan, for all officials holding posts at the regional level are part of the same service as those posted at the Central Secretariat. This rule does not apply to local (that is, village) administration, however, since these officials are not part of the regular civil service and hold office on an entirely different basis. This is an important factor in Bhutan's polity, for it explains the broad degree of village autonomy that has long been a feature of the country's political system.

The introduction of an hereditary monarchy in the first decade of the twentieth century did not have much of an immedi-

3. The young Bhutanese who have been sent to India for training still come from a broad spectrum of Bhutan society, including poor peasant families. In the future, however, it is likely that children of this new educated elite will enjoy certain advantages in their access to educational facilities and programs.

ate impact on the structure of the regional and local administrative system. The one exception was the change in status of the two supradistrict level officers, the Pönlops of Tongsa and Paro, who had exercised virtually autonomous authority over eastern and western Bhutan, respectively, under the Shabdung system. The Druk Gyalpos preferred to deal directly with the district officers rather than through an intermediate-level official. By the time of the second Druk Gyalpo the Pönlop title had come to be used more as an honorary designation of rank for powerful members of the royal family but had no specific administrative functions or powers attached thereto. For instance, Namgyal Wangchuck, the half-brother of the third Druk Gyalpo, held the title of Paro Pönlop for several years in the 1960s at a time when he had assumed a very active role in the administration because of the king's ill health. And again in 1972, Crown Prince Jigme Singye Wangchuck was given the title Tongsa Pönlop, reportedly in recognition of his right of succession to the throne. This was comparable to the installation of the Crown Prince as Prince of Wales in Great Britain or the coming-of-age ceremony of the Crown Prince in Nepal.[4]

During the reigns of the first two Druk Gyalpos there were eleven Dzongs (districts) in eastern, central and western Bhutan, headed by Dzongpöns (sometimes called Dungpas). Southern Bhutan, which had been the administrative responsibility of the Paro Pönlop, was placed under the jurisdiction of the Dorji family in the early 1890s. For this task, the Dorjis utilized the services of a Nepali family, the Pradhans, who brought in a large number of Nepali migrants into southern Bhutan after 1910 under a contract system. A member of the Pradhan family, the Sipchu Kazi, was assigned responsibility for administration and revenue collection in southern Bhutan.[5]

In the highland areas, there were a number of officials under

4. This, at least, was the explanation given at the time. According to the official publication, *Kuensel*, "each Crown Prince of Bhutan has always been installed as the Tongsa Pönlop signifying his true heritage to the throne" (6:39 [May 21, 1972]). In fact, however, the third Druk Gyalpo held the title of Paro Pönlop prior to his accession to the throne.
5. The Pradhans were a Newari family originally from Kathmandu valley. Earlier a number of Newar families had arranged the importation of a Nepali

the Dzongpön (or Dungpa) who were also part of the government service. The larger Dzongs had a deputy district officer (Dzongtasp). There was also a revenue officer (Nyerchin) in each district whose primary responsibility was to collect the rent-in-kind from cultivators on specified lands; most of these funds were then paid over to various members of the royal family or to religious institutions that held rights to these lands. In addition there were usually two assistant district officers as well as several assistants. The two assistant district officers exercised control over several villages under the jurisdiction of the Dzong. It was also the custom for each village to depute one male to the Dzong headquarters on a regular basis to serve as a channel of communication between the local and district officials.

As representatives of the Druk Gyalpo in the district, the powers of the district officers were comprehensive. They were responsible for law-and-order functions, serving both as the head of the local militia, which was the only police force in Bhutan, and as the judge in the district court. All facets of administration were the district officer's responsibility in his area of jurisdiction, although in the period prior to the introduction of economic development and social welfare programs this was generally not a very strenuous occupation since there were only a few officials with very limited functions and powers under the district officer's supervision.

The village administration was run along what might be characterized as semidemocratic lines; the headmen—called Gups in the highlands and Mandals in southern Bhutan—were elected for three-year terms by the heads of the households in large villages or groups of smaller villages. The hand of the central bureaucracy did not fall very heavily on the village, at least as long as revenue was forthcoming, peace was maintained, and the obligatory labor duties (militia and *chunidom*) were carried out on the traditional terms. Most decisions that were of importance to the villagers were made by the village

---

labor force for work in the tea gardens in Darjeeling district of Bengal as well as for the settlement of much of southern Sikkim by Nepalese.

headman, usually in consultation with the elders of each household. The obligations to the government, such as providing recruits for the militia or for labor at the Dzong, were traditionally divided on an equitable basis among all the families in the village.

On coming to the throne in 1952, the third Druk Gyalpo commenced almost immediately upon a program of political modernization, but it was several years before the administrative system was seriously affected. In 1955, the southern Bhutan administration was strengthened, although this was more a political response to the Nepali Bhutanese agitation that had disturbed this area since 1948 than a step in the direction of basic administrative reorganization. The Sipchu Kazi was replaced by the Lhotsam Chichap (commissioner for southern Bhutan) who was assisted henceforth by two deputy commissioners with rank equivalent to that of a district officer in the highlands.

One of the first important structural changes in district administration was its reorganization in the early 1960s into two subdivisions in southern Bhutan and thirteen Dzongs in the highland areas.[6] This increase in the number of Dzongs in Bhutan was intended to make them more suitable agencies for implementation of the economic development programs that were just being introduced.

Even more basic changes in the district-level administration were introduced in the late 1960s, mostly as a consequence of the reorganization of the central administration. The transfer of the Development Secretariat from Paro to Thimphu in 1967, the formation of a Council of Ministers with broad executive powers in 1968, and the establishment of a separate judiciary in 1968 made structural and functional changes at the regional level necessary. Previously, the district officers had re-

6. In 1969, the title for district officers was changed to Dzongda (and to Ramjam in some areas), symbolizing the change in their status and responsibilities. By 1976, the number of Dzongdas had increased to 17 (Ha, Paro, Thimphu, Wangdiphodrang, Punakha, Tongsa, Byakar, Shemgang, Mongar, Tashigang, Lhuntsi, Lingshi, Gasa, Daga, Phuntsholing, Sarbhang, and Chirang) and the number of Ramjams to eight (Geylegphug, Dagapela, Dung, Chapcha, Sibsu, Kalikhola, Changbari, and Samdrup Jongkhar).

ported directly to the palace, but they come now under the jurisdiction of the Home Minister.[7] The district officers were also deprived of all judicial powers, as a new official, the Thimpön, was constituted as the head of the district court and given responsibility for the maintenance of law and order. There are, moreover, a large number of officials in various departments of the government (mostly under the Ministry of Development) who are now active at the district level. While nominally they are under the jurisdiction of the Dzongda in the district, in fact their lines of responsibility go directly to the head of their department at Thimphu. Thus, much of what is done in the name of the government at the district level no longer is controlled by the district officer. The Dzongpön had been a little lord in his area of jurisdiction in the past; the Dzongda, in contrast, is at best the first among equals in a much-enlarged and more complex administrative system.[8]

Some Problems in Administration

The drastic reorganization of the administration undertaken in Bhutan since 1960 has raised a number of problems, most of which have not yet been resolved. But perhaps the problem least susceptible to quick resolution has little to do with the reorganization program as such but rather to the lack of trained Bhutanese personnel available to the government. In effect, what Bhutan attempted to do was to introduce ambitious economic and social development programs on a scale that was unrealistic in terms of the local administrative and technical resources available. As has been the case in much of the developing world, this has led to a heavy dependence on

7. The Dzongda still has the right to submit reports on confidential matters directly to the Druk Gyalpo, but reportedly this is done only infrequently.
8. In the past the district officer might have had as many as a hundred people, mostly servants, serving under him who received compensation-in-kind. Since the substitution of cash rents for rent-in-kind, however, this situation has changed drastically. Now, in most districts there are only two Home Ministry officers and two clerks, paid entirely in cash salaries, with administrative responsibilities. The Agriculture Department officer in the district, on the other hand, might have a large number of government servants under his supervision.

external advice and technical assistance—which in this instance was almost exclusively Indian.[9]

This may have been unavoidable at the time, for it would have taken two decades to train a sufficient number of Bhutanese to man even a minimal development program, and to the Bhutan authorities in 1960 a delay of that magnitude would have had serious consequences. Having been pushed, with some reluctance, into the decision to modernize Bhutan's economic and political system by developments both to the north and south, the government had no acceptable alternative to a heavy dependence upon India, both financial and technical, given its strongly negative reaction to Chinese policy and action in Tibet and the apparent disinterest of the rest of the world.[10]

There is no doubt that this dependence relationship with India has exacerbated nationalist sentiments. The Bhutanese were already concerned with their country's close relationship with India as a result of the 1949 Indo-Bhutan Treaty in which Bhutan agreed to accept the guidance of India in its foreign relations. There remains, a sensitivity over the country's international image, and some anguish over its relegation to an Indian sphere of influence by much of the rest of the world. The potential for tension between Bhutanese and Indian officials on deputation to Bhutan is further enhanced when the latter may hold the top positions in a department while the former are their immediate subordinates.

It should not be surprising, therefore, that Bhutanization of

9. There is one Japanese agricultural specialist who has played a prominent role in the Agricultural Department; he had been deputed to Bhutan by Japan under the Colombo Plan. There are also a few Western educationists (mostly Jesuits) and technicians employed directly by the Bhutan government. But all other foreign administrators and technicians in Bhutan are Indians, most of whom come under the auspices of the Indian aid program.

10. The disinterest of some countries, including both the United States and the Soviet Union, was in part a reflection of their reluctance to do anything in Bhutan that might complicate relations with India. Even the bringing over of two students for training in engineering in the United States in the mid-1960s, for instance, was approached with considerable caution by the American authorities who finally agreed to the program only after the Indian government had indicated that it had no objections.

the administrative and technical services has become a high-priority goal for most Bhutanese officials, who find both their personal career interests and their nationalist sentiments frustrated by the existing situation. Indeed, what is probably more surprising is that the tension between Bhutanese and Indian officials has been maintained at a reasonably low level and that relations between the two are still quite good. This can be attributed in part to the pragmatic approach adopted by most Bhutanese who realize their own need for more experience, and in part to the generosity of the Indian government in providing slots to Bhutanese for training at Indian institutions that will permit them to acquire the skills and knowledge needed for positions of responsibility. Training has been offered on such a scale that Bhutan cannot always find recruits for the seats available because of inadequacies in its own primary and secondary educational systems. Nevertheless, some Bhutanese would like to see alternative sources of foreign education and training opened to their youth, on the grounds that this would lessen the dependence—or burden—on India and would in some fields provide a better standard of education.

Objections to the utilization of foreign administrators and technicians are common to all developing countries, and the range of complaints on this subject in Bhutan to Indian aid is not particularly unique. It is noted, for instance, that most of the Indian officials serving in Bhutan are deputed there by their Indian administrative and technical services on relatively brief assignments. They come in, knowing virtually nothing about Bhutan's culture, value system, or problems, but are expected to conduct complex programs that require extensive interaction with the ordinary Bhutanese from the time of their arrival. It is only toward the end of their tour of duty that they may have acquired sufficient familiarity with the human environment to function efficiently.

Indian personnel also face some problems in communication, not so much with their Bhutanese colleagues, since they usually have English as a common language, but with the general populace. An agricultural specialist, for instance, may be responsible for the implementation of programs at the district and local level, and it is a severe handicap if he has to communicate with cultivators through interpreters who would usually have only limited technical knowledge about the programs being introduced.[11] The Indian officer's problems are further compounded by the inherent suspicion with which Bhutanese peasants, like peasants elsewhere in the world, interrelate with *any* official, but in particular a foreign official.

These problems are real and inhibit the operation of development programs in Bhutan, but it is generally accepted by the Bhutanese authorities that they have no alternative to continuing to utilize the services of a large number of foreign administrators and technicians for some years to come. And for persuasive political reasons, and their ready availability, most of these foreigners will continue to be Indian. The number of Bhutanese with the requisite training and education has expanded substantially, but it will be some time before complete Bhutanization is possible, at least at the technical level.

There is no reason to view the existing situation in entirely negative terms, for there are some advantages for Bhutan as well as disadvantages. For one thing, it is probable that the Indian officers are more "politically neutral," in the sense of having fewer personal interests to protect on policy issues, than most of their Bhutanese colleagues. It has been useful to have available a body of officials who are less personally involved in decision-making in their area of competence and are usually prepared to carry out whatever instructions are given by the authorities. There is, of course, a potential conflict of interest between their duties as Indians and as officers of the Bhutan government, but this has not yet been a factor of any significance in their operations in Bhutan.

In the traumatic transitional period through which the Bhutan administrative system is passing, the comparative smallness and homogeneity of the Bhutanese official establishment has

11. On the other hand, it well may be that Hindi-speaking Indian officials can communicate more easily with the Nepali-speaking inhabitants of southern Bhutan, where many of the larger development programs are concentrated, than can a Bhutanese official, since Hindi and Nepali are closely related Sanskrit-derived languages.

some distinct advantages, both in the making and the implementation of decisions. The youthfulness of a large proportion
of the official body, even at medium- and high-level posts, and
the similarity in their educational and training background, has
resulted in a broad group consensus on most issues. While
there are still a number of older civil servants reflecting a more
traditional socialization process, there is no well-entrenched
older generation of officials capable of dominating the decision-
making process and frustrating the demands for change and
innovation that are forthcoming from the younger generation
of officials. It may have been correct to speak of a generation
gap in the first decade following Bhutan's decision to embark
on a sustained development program, but the natural law of at-
trition (aided by the "suggested" retirement of some older officials), political developments in the 1964–1968 period, and
the rapid expansion in the ranks of the bureaucracy since 1960
have largely solved this problem. The esprit de corps of the
Bhutanese civil service, so apparent to the outside observer, is
to some extent a reflection of this community of outlook on
basic objectives, even though there are differences of opinion
among the youthful elite on how best to achieve goals.

Another kind of problem that has been chronic in developing countries such as Bhutan is that of the implementation of
programs once a decision has been made. There is all too
frequently a substantial gap between objectives and capability.
So far, however, the implementation record is reasonably good.
There are several reasons for this. Of primary importance perhaps is the fact that virtually all development programs in Bhutan are financed, administered, and staffed largely by the Indian government. If Bhutan had been forced to depend on its
own human and material resources, its deficiencies in all three
areas would have necessitated a much less ambitious program
than it has offered.

The comparative simplicity of the Bhutanese administrative
system has been another advantage, for this has minimized the
impact of institutional obstacles to the implementation of policy
decisions. Students of public administration usually express a
preference for more complex administrative infrastructures

and greater functional diversification than pertain in Bhutan, but it is doubtful whether these would be appropriate for a country at Bhutan's stage of development. To an amazing extent, for instance, orders to subordinates are still communicated orally. This saves time as well as the need for a large (and unavailable) secretarial staff and has not as yet interfered with rapid and effective implementation. The highly centralized and disciplined character of the administrative system, together with the merit-based performance evaluation system utilized in Bhutan, have made civil servants at both the central and district level responsive to directives from above. Bureaucrats have fewer opportunities to sabotage government programs with which they do not agree than is the case in India, with its federal structure of government, or in Nepal where institutional diversification has complicated policy implementation procedures.

The problem in Bhutan, then, is not so much one of getting the administrative services to implement policy as it is a certain degree of confusion in the delegation of authority and responsibility between the various ministries and departments as well as the nonexistence of an administrative chief of staff at a level below the Druk Gyalpo. This is probably most vividly reflected in the continuing efforts to coordinate the activities of the Development Ministry and its various departments with those of the other ministries. This difficulty had its origin in the history of the Development Ministry and dates back to 1961 when the Development Secretariat was set up at Paro. Separated from the regular administration, the ministry continued to function as a parallel institution to the regular bureaucracy even after its transfer to Thimphu in 1967.

By the 1970s, the degree of coordination between the various departments of the Development Ministry and the rest of the Secretariat is less than satisfactory, as the former officials still often react as if they belonged to an autonomous body. In the districts, for instance, the development departments have retained primary responsibility for the implementation of projects on virtually the same terms that existed prior to 1967. The district officer, who represents the Home Ministry and is in theory responsible for everything that goes on in his area of jurisdiction, should be informed about all development projects and should exercise broad supervisory powers over their implementation, but this is not the way the system usually works. Jurisdictional disputes and rivalries occur between ministries, for it is rarely possible to separate development and administrative tasks on a rational basis as these often overlap.

Coordination between departments is further complicated by the fact that the Ministry of Development, though headed by Bhutanese at the higher levels, is still largely an Indian enterprise, while the other ministries are now mostly staffed by Bhutanese. The Indian administrators and technicians deputed to Bhutan have of course their own procedures of administration with which they are familiar and through which they prefer to operate. This confusion also tends to distinguish the Development Ministry from the other departments, which follow a Bhutanese pattern more closely. Attempts are being made to bridge the gap between these different units of administration, but it seems probable that many of the problems of coordination will continue until Bhutanization of the Development Ministry has been achieved on a more extensive scale.

Even within the regular administrative departments, however, there have been problems in defining lines of responsibility and communication. The difficulty is probably most readily perceived at the district level of administration. The district officer is formally a part of the Home Ministry, and reports to that ministry on routine administrative matters. But his reports on financial matters are directed to the Finance Ministry, while those on development programs go to the Development Ministry. He is, in effect, a representative of all three ministries in the district, and the division of his responsibilities is not always easily determined.

All of this might well be of incidental significance if there was a properly constituted and empowered cabinet, headed by a prime minister, with the capacity to define and routinize the spheres of jurisdiction of the various ministries and departments. The creation in 1974 of a Coordination Committee operating at the highest level of government was motivated in part by the perceived need to eliminate duplication of effort and conflict of interest between various departments. But coordination would involve a whole range of programs which might fundamentally change some of the operational rules and procedures within the bureaucracy. How successful the Coordination Committee will be is still to be seen.

Some efforts to institutionalize operating principles within the administration were already underway before the establishment of the Committee. In 1972, for instance, the first civil service rules were introduced, concerning primarily that most important of subjects to bureaucrats—the appointment and promotion system. Previously, the palace had assumed ultimate responsibility for the appointment and promotion of all officials. In 1969 the Home Minister had been entrusted with responsibility for the appointment of lower-level (white scarf) officials throughout the secretariat, but this duty had complicated his relations with other ministers and department heads on several occasions. Under the 1972 civil service rules, therefore, the appointment power was further diversified. "Nongazetted" (that is, white scarf) officers are appointed and promoted by the ministers or department heads concerned without reference to the palace. "Gazetted" (that is, red scarf) officers are appointed by the king, usually in consultation with the head of the particular department. The highest officers of state (that is, orange scarf) are appointed by the Druk Gyalpo with the consent of the Tshogdu.

It was also decided that all appointments and promotions should be made on a merit basis in which the education and work record of each government servant would be given primary consideration. A Service Sub-Committee of the Coordination Committee has been established to standardize both appointment procedures and service conditions. But ministers and department heads continue to appoint and promote officials on their own initiative and without reference to the Council of Ministers, the Coordination Committee, or any other body. Presumably, personal factors frequently play a role in their decisions, and tenure in office is by no means guaranteed to officials at any level of administration, even if they perform their duties satisfactorily. On the other hand, the cadre from which appointments and promotions must be made is still very limited, and there is no great reservoir of educated unemployed upon which to draw. Since recruitment resources are not substantial, at this stage of development at least there is some range of choice for the young educated Bhutanese who is eager to enter the administrative services.

Another persistent problem in Bhutan centers around the effort to introduce modern budgeting practices. It was only in 1971 that a formal budget, allocating funds to the various departments on a regularized basis, was finally introduced. Previously, funds had been dispersed on an "as needed" basis until 1968 by the Gyaltsi Khalowa (Royal Revenue Office) in the palace and thereafter by the Finance Ministry. For the first few years the Finance Ministry controlled the allocation of funds only to the finance, home, communication, trade and industry, and (later) foreign ministries—that is, those ministries and departments which were funded by revenues of the Bhutan government. The much larger Development Ministry budget, funded almost entirely by the Indian government, continued as a separate operation over which the Finance Minister had limited authority. In 1972 it was decided that all departmental budgets should be brought under the Finance Minister, including the departments in the Development Ministry funded through Government of India grants. This was possible since under the system by which aid funds are granted to Bhutan by the Government of India, it is the Indian Planning Commission that determines the total size of the aid grant and the Bhutan government that allocates the funds among the various departments. The 1972 change in allocation procedure merely transferred this responsibility from the Development Ministry to the Finance Ministry.

The fundamental concepts upon which the Bhutanese political system is based, and in particular the principle of tripartite participation involving representatives of the official establishment, the monk body, and the people in the decision-making process at various levels, also complicate the functioning of the administration in some respects. For instance, when an Audit

Department was established in 1969, it was composed of four members representing respectively the Druk Gyalpo, the officials, the monks, and the people.[12] One might surmise that this system was deliberately contrived to introduce extraneous influences with special interests to protect into the administration. There are no indications as yet that special interest groups have become influential, due presumably to the predominate position of the official body vis-à-vis the other institutions at this time. But there can be no certainty that this situation will continue to prevail in the future when such political institutions as the Tshogdu and the monk body may well assume more dynamic roles in the polity.

While there have been serious problems, some still unresolved, the transformation of Bhutan's bureaucracy into an institution capable of undertaking developmental and mobilization tasks far beyond the capacity of its pre-1960 predecessor has proceeded comparatively smoothly. Nevertheless, there is a continuing debate within the bureaucratic elite over the modernization process, as well as doubts about the appropriateness of much that has been introduced in the name of modernity and efficient administration. In particular, there is a growing tendency to question certain Indian administrative principles and procedures that were adopted on a haphazard fashion over the past two decades, and there is now increased interest in alternative developmental models. Bhutanese students are being sent abroad to a number of Asian and Western countries to study organization theory and public administration in a variety of cultures and political systems. Even more important perhaps, some Bhutanese officials are looking inward increasingly to their own traditions to see if these have useful lessons. This does not reflect a growing disenchantment with the concepts of change and development, but rather greater sophistication in their comprehension of the incompatibility of a willy-nilly introduction of alien values and procedures with the maintenance of a distinct Bhutanese cultural identity.

12. *Kuensel*, 3:21 (Nov. 15, 1969).

The Royal Bhutan Army and Police

For most of Bhutan's modern history, its defense requirements were handled in an haphazard fashion, presumably because serious threats to the security of the country from outside were rare occurrences. There was not even an institution that might properly be defined as an army until the mid-1950s. The only semimilitary forces in the country under the Shabdung system were the various private armed units (Zing Gyap), composed of untrained village conscripts fulfilling their obligatory militia duties. These units were maintained by the more important officials at the center and in the districts. There was no officer corps, however, and no military establishment as such. When an international crisis arose and Bhutan was threatened by an external foe, an Arrow Chief (Dapon) was appointed to command all Bhutanese forces, which consisted of the various private units of the officials and some additional militia called to service for the duration. Under this system, Bhutan could put approximately 10,000 men into the field—almost totally untrained, however, and armed only with antiquated weapons.[13]

Several of the British visitors to Bhutan in the eighteenth and nineteenth centuries were witnesses to the periodic civil strife that was a regular feature of the Shabdung system in its final decades. Their remarks on the fighting quality of the Bhutanese soldiery tended to be very disparaging, emphasizing their reluctance to expose themselves to enemy fire and describing these events as playacting scenarios in which the side that managed to mobilize the larger force was automatically conceded the victory. The spirit and the enthusiasm with which the Bhutanese fought the British in the 1865 war, and in particular the fierceness and determination demonstrated in their assaults against an incomparably better-armed foe, came as a surprise. This difference in overt behavior patterns probably has a simple explanation. Being pragmatic people, the Bhutanese were too sensible to expose themselves to bodily harm

13. The Bhutanese have a reputation for being remarkable archers, however, and archery is still the national sport of the country.

while engaged in the mimic war games played by their leaders under well-defined rules. But when Bhutan itself was endangered, the martial qualities of the people came to the fore. Under the hereditary monarchy, there were no immediate changes introduced in either the character or the organizational structure of Bhutan's military force. The Dzongpön in each district continued to have a small militia unit attached to his headquarters which functioned more in a police capacity than as a military force. A Royal Body Guard was organized and posted at the palace, but this was also an untrained force with no regular officer corps. It was only during the Second World War, when neighboring Assam became a battleground between the Japanese and the British, that the Royal Body Guard was given some training and provided with modern small arms. There were also a number of Bhutanese who volunteered for service in the British Indian Army during the war, two of whom were even commissioned as officers, the first Bhutanese that had ever been exposed to modern military training and organization.

The Bhutan Army. With the succession of the third Druk Gyalpo in 1952, a decision was finally made to create a regular military force in Bhutan. Several Bhutanese were sent down to India by the Bhutan authorities for training in the Assam Rifles, a paramilitary force in the Indian Army usually assigned to tribal areas in the rugged mountain areas around the Brahmaputra valley. These men returned to Bhutan on completion of their training, and one of them became Bhutan's first brigadier after the army was organized in the mid-1950s. In 1954, five more Bhutanese were sent to the Indian Officers Training Camp at Dehra Dun, three of whom were commissioned in 1956. They served for approximately eighteen months in Indian Army units before returning to Bhutan. Two of these were deeply involved in the 1964–1965 political crisis in Bhutan, and finally went into temporary exile in Nepal.[14]

14. The press reports from Nepal usually assumed that these two army officers and their three civilian associates were "clients" of Lhendup Dorji who also settled down in Kathmandu at about the same time. There is little evidence indicating that this was the case, however.

In 1955, Bhutan for two reasons undertook the task of organizing the Royal Bhutan Army as a regular military force. First, there was the Chinese invasion of Tibet in 1950–1951, which was followed by the gradual extension of Chinese control along the Tibet-Bhutan border. The outbreak of a major rebellion against the Chinese in Kham (eastern Tibet) in 1954, an event largely unnoticed by the rest of the world but a matter of grave concern to the Bhutanese who were better informed on these developments, strengthened the Bhutan government's resolve to develop the capacity to defend their borders.

The second reason was the obvious inadequacy of the militia even for internal security purposes, much less defense against foreign aggression. The militia's failure to function effectively in the Nepali Bhutanese agitation in southern Bhutan in the 1948–1954 period was obvious. The movement had collapsed largely because of its inability to mobilize the Nepali Bhutanese for political action, but the government could not assume that the results would be the same in any future agitations. An organized, permanent military force might well be needed before too long to maintain the authority of the Bhutan government in this difficult, multiethnic frontier region.

At this point, Bhutan was still adhering to its strict isolationist policy and thus refrained from calling upon India for direct assistance except in the training of a few officers. But the external situation, as perceived by the Bhutanese, grew vastly more ominous in 1959 with the outbreak of a full-scale revolt against Chinese rule in central Tibet, the flight of the Dalai Lama to India, the collapse of the traditional government in Tibet, the serious deterioration in Sino-Indian relations over the Tibetan developments and the China-India border dispute, and the reports that China was laying claim to sizable chunks of Bhutanese territory. It was felt that Bhutan would require substantial foreign assistance, and fast, in the development of its military force if it was too meet the growing threat from across its northern border. India was the only feasible source for such aid, for both political and geopolitical reasons.

A decision to seek—or rather accept—economic aid from India had been made in 1959, following Nehru's visit to Bhutan the previous Fall. But there was apparently a greater degree of reluctance in Thimphu to align openly with the Indian security system in the Himalayas. It was only in 1961 that the Bhutan authorities finally decided that this situation to the north had assumed such threatening proportions that a military alignment with India could no longer be avoided. Bhutan, therefore, approached New Delhi for assistance in training and equipping the Bhutan Army.[15]

India had been pressing Bhutan on this matter for some time and of course responded immediately to Thimphu's request for aid. General Aurora of the Indian Army visited Bhutan in May 1961, and in August 1962 an Indian Military Training Team (IMTRAT) was sent to Bhutan to assist in the organization and operation of the Officer's Training Centre that had been established at Ha Dzong in western Bhutan. For the first few years the Centre produced a number of commissioned officers from its own training program; subsequently, however, it has become a preparatory school for men who are sent to officer training institutions in India.

A major shake-up of the Royal Bhutan Army took place in 1965, following the assassination of Prime Minister Jigme Dorji in which the brigadier (commanding officer) of the army was involved. The political struggle which ensued thereafter culminated in the execution of the brigadier and the flight of two other high army officers to Nepal several months later.[16] The rank of Brigadier (Dozin) was abolished. Lt. Colonel (Maksi Ogma) was the highest rank in the army until 1968 when the Tshogdu, at the request of the Druk Gyalpo, reluctantly re-

15. *Kuensel*, 4:7 (April 15, 1970). All of the Bhutan Army's military equipment has been supplied by India to date. In 1962–1963, however, Prime Minister Jigme Dorji reportedly approached the United States and West Germany for arms aid at a time when Bhutan's needs were great and India's capacity to supply arms was limited by the rapid expansion of the Indian Army following the 1962 war with China. The reply from both countries was that this was an Indian responsibility, and the request was rejected. In 1967 the Bhutanese were reported to have approached the British for arms aid, stating that India provided only outdated Lee-Enfield rifles, while Bhutan required automatic rifles and machine guns, but again they were turned down.

16. *Kuensel*, 2:9 (May 15, 1968): and 2:10 (May 31, 1968).

stored the rank of brigadier; but no officer had been promoted to that rank by 1975.

In 1965 the size of the army was reduced from 9,000 to 4,850, reportedly on the grounds that the larger force had proved to be too heavy a drain on Bhutan's limited human and financial resources. Subsequently, it has been expanded to approximately 6,000 men. Lt. Colonel Lam Dorji was made chief operations officer, but the Druk Gyalpo's half-brother, Namgyal Wangchuck, was given effective command in his capacity as the king's personal representative in the army. In 1968, Druk Gyalpo Jigme Dorji Wangchuck assumed personal control over the "army portfolio," and his successor also retained that post on his accession to the throne in 1972.

While the Royal Bhutan Army is a small force with many organizational and operational problems, it has been entrusted with major responsibilities, some of which it is still poorly equipped to fulfill. Protection of Bhutan's frontiers is an obvious assignment, complicated on occasions since 1960 by small-scale Chinese intrusions in some sections where the border alignments are not too precisely defined or are in dispute.[17] The army also has ultimate responsibility for internal security, given the organizational and training deficiencies of both the police force and the militia. The army has been assigned the task of training the local militia in guerrilla tactics to be used against an invading force, but the officer corps is so overburdened with its regular army duties that it has not been able to devote much time to what it perceives to be peripheral programs.

The development of a technically competent, reliable officer corps has been one of the more persistent problems faced by

17. The construction of border-post accommodations has been a high-priority task for the army since 1960, but the work has been complicated by the underdevelopment of communication in this area and by the small labor force available due to the very sparse population. As late as 1969 the Druk Gyalpo had to postpone the abolition of *chunidom* (obligatory labor) in some key border districts so that a work force could be assembled for the construction of border posts (*Kuensel*, 3:20 [Oct. 31, 1969]).

202 The Politics of Bhutan

the army, and it still faces some deficiencies in this respect.[18] Since the mid-1960s, the training of officers has been entrusted to the Indian Army almost exclusively. Virtually all prospective officers in the Royal Bhutan Army are now sent for training to Indian military institutions. After completing their training, some of the newly commissioned officers serve for a period of time in Indian Army units for experience before returning to Bhutan. But finding officer candidates among the young Bhutanese has not been easy. The very small cadre of young educated Bhutanese eligible for candidacy have shown some reluctance to enter the military service, in part because of the belief that advancement in the civil service, in which there are numerous middle-level openings, tends to be much more rapid than in the army.

Recruitment for the rank and file is perhaps an even greater problem. The Royal Bhutan Army is a conscript force, with Bhutanese males from all communities subject to service for fifteen-year terms at the government's discretion. But in view of Bhutan's severe labor shortage, and the demands from other sections of the government and the economy that have at least equal priority on their services, conscripts are hard to come by and retain. It has been estimated that Bhutan needs only 600 to 700 recruits each year to maintain the army at its stipulated strength, but even this small number is not easily available.[19] Moreover, those who are inducted are sometimes able to obtain exemptions from service on the plea that they are needed at home to take care of domestic affairs. Exemptions reached serious enough proportions that in 1970 the government ordered release from service should be granted only under special circumstances, and that the need for the serviceman's presence at home should be attested by both the village headman and the district officer.[20] This has improved the situation somewhat, but the army is still reportedly slightly understaffed.

18. At one time, several Indian Army officers were deputed to serve with Bhutanese units to compensate for the shortage of Bhutanese officers, according to reports, but it is not clear whether this practice has continued.
19. *Kuensel*, 4:21 (Nov. 15, 1970); and 8:42 (Oct. 21, 1973).
20. *Ibid.*, 3:11 (June 15, 1969).

One does not have to be in Bhutan very long to become aware of the omnipresence of the Indian Army. There are large training units at Thimphu, Ha, Paro, and elsewhere, with support forces attached to the units in numbers that seem more than adequate for the task at hand. DANTAK, the Indian Border Road unit in Bhutan, is primarily an Indian Army operation and working with it are a substantial number of men from the Indian Army Engineering Corps, as well as other construction outfits on work assignments. The roads on which they are working are classified as strategic, and preparations for using them for defensive purposes—such as parking areas for several hundred trucks at various points along the roads—are readily apparent. Obviously the Indian Army does not intend to be caught as inadequately prepared as it was in 1962 to provide logistical support for units engaged in conflict with the invading Chinese should Bhutan be faced with aggression from the north.

There are also recurrent, if unconfirmed, reports of Indian Army units in Bhutan that are not engaged in training or construction programs. There have been reports of joint training operations between Indian units at the brigade level and Bhutan's forces. Whether there is any substance to these reports is still uncertain, and their accuracy has never been acknowledged by official sources in either country. Joint training does not seem unreasonable when consideration is given the nature of the relationship between Bhutan and India, Bhutan's urgent defense requirements, its continuing concern over the Chinese threat from the north, and India's determination never to be humiliated again as it was by the Chinese in 1962.

A substantial foreign military presence in any country usually creates some strains in relations at various levels of contact, and this is of course the case for Bhutan. The Indian officers in Bhutan, both civil and military, are obvious scapegoats for dissatisfied Bhutanese, and it is to be expected that they will be blamed for almost anything that goes wrong. As yet, however, complaints are minimal, and indeed the relationship between the Indian and Bhutanese officer corps is reportedly very good. The Indian Army, which by now is very experienced in operating in difficult mountain terrain, does what it can to limit the ways in which its presence impinges upon the local environment and inhabitants.[21] It also provides social and medical services, still very inadequate in most of Bhutan, wherever it has the facilities. Most Bhutanese would probably prefer to see the external situation develop in such a way that the Indian Army's presence is no longer required, but most of those in responsible positions in Bhutan realize that it may be quite some time before this goal can be safely achieved.

One final question of increasing importance concerns the Royal Bhutan Army as a political institution. In a country such as Bhutan with only the bare skeleton of a modern political and administrative infrastructure, a modern army is potentially *the* decisive political force. The past record of some army officers, moreover, has not encouraged confidence in the reliability of the army as a support base for the Royal Government. Some army officers were involved in the 1964–1965 conspiracies and counterconspiracies that seemed to threaten at one point the very existence of the regime. It has been argued that these officers were acting in their individual rather than their institutional capacities, and that indeed if the army officer corps as an institution had been involved the results would have been quite different. This may well have been the case, but it does not lessen the concern with which the army's potential for political involvement is viewed by the palace, the bureaucracy, and the Tshogdu.

The army today has the appearance of being as depoliticized as any institution of this kind can be, although of course it is impossible for an outside observer to know what is going on behind the scenes. In any case, it is doubtful whether this will continue for very long, given the emergence of a young, educated element in the officer corps, and the enticing (or in some cases, such as Pakistan, foreboding) examples of army involvement in politics elsewhere in Asia. It is reasonable to assume

21. One exception to this general rule is the behavior of Indian Army truck drivers in military convoys who move along at controlled speeds themselves but demonstrate a reluctance to allow a car or jeep going in the same direction to pass—much to the irritation of the Bhutanese drivers and their passengers.

that the army will eventually emerge as one of the key political forces in the country. The real questions, perhaps, are whether the army's officer corps can attain a broad enough consensus on general political goals to cooperate effectively and whether competitive institutional strongpoints can be developed to serve as a counterbalance.

The Bhutan Police. Prior to 1965 there was no formal police force in Bhutan. In each district the local militia, conscripted for temporary duty, carried out whatever police functions were required. The political upheavals in 1964–1965, in which several high army officers were involved, apparently led to the royal order of September 1, 1965, which established a separate police force. The Royal Bhutan Police Training School was inaugurated, and India was requested to send an advisory team to assist in the training and organization of the new force. A number of Bhutanese have also been sent to the National Police Academy and other specialized police institutions in India for training.

The Home Minister is the head of the police force, and all police officials at whatever level of operation are directly responsible to his ministry. The Gakpen, with his headquarters at Phuntsholing, is the official in the Home Ministry who serves as the administrative head of the police, assisted by two Yongzim. Bhutan is divided into three areas—western, eastern, and southern—headed by Dechaps, each of whom has a number of police stations under his jurisdiction. The police detachment at the district level is commanded by a Kepon.

The recruitment of officers into the police force initially proved a difficult task, but the problem was solved when the army was substantially reduced in size in 1965 and a large number of ex-army men were transferred to the police. In recent years, the 900-man police force has provided attractive career opportunities to young Bhutanese, and recruitment is no longer a serious problem. In 1973, for instance, all of the young men undergoing training in the police school had had some education, and in Bhutan this alone would mean that they would have a variety of alternative career opportunities open to them.

The politicizing of the police force has become a question of some concern to the civil authorities, particularly following the alleged involvement of the Bhutanese head of the police force in the 1974 conspiracy against the present Druk Gyalpo. Here again it would seem to have been the case that the official was acting in an individual capacity and had not attempted to subvert the police force as an institution. But this can provide only scant comfort to the authorities who are fully aware of their vulnerability to the kinds of plots in which only a very few officials with institutional power bases are involved.

The Judiciary

The concepts of the separation of powers and an independent judiciary played no role in the system of government under either the Shabdungs or the Druk Gyalpos. On the contrary, government officials at various levels had judicial functions appended to their other responsibilities, and they were expected to carry these out in their capacity as officers of the state. The village headmen (Gups and Mandals) were constituted as the court of original jurisdiction for minor crimes. Appeals from their decisions, and cases involving major crimes (mostly robbery and murder), were heard by the district officer in his capacity as head of the district court. Finally, the Druk Gyalpo served as the highest court of appeal from the decisions of the lower-level courts and also held the sole power to sentence criminals convicted of major crimes.[22]

It was in 1968 that the Bhutan government, then undergoing a major reorganization of its political and administrative institutions, also introduced for the first time the concepts of the separation of powers and an independent judiciary. A High Court (Thimkhang Gongma) was established, consisting in 1975 of six judges: four appointed by the Druk Gyalpo from among Dashos (red-scarf officials), one representative of the Nepali community, and the sixth a people's representative selected by the Tshogdu with the approval of the king.[23] All

22. Nagendra Singh, pp. 109–110.
23. In the original announcement of the establishment of the High Court it was stated that one member representing the monk body would be nominated

6. The Process
of Change

In the mid-1950s the Royal Government of Bhutan embarked upon an ambitious program of guided political, economic, and administrative change at a time when the country possessed few of the institutional or cultural prerequisites usually considered essential to the modernization of a traditional society. By a combination of deliberate choice and historical accident Bhutan accomplished what no other society in southern Asia was able to do during the colonial period—that is, to isolate itself from the wide variety of revolutionary "secular" influences from the West and, more recently, from the "socialist" movement. The Bhutan experience with the development process thus differs in some significant respects from that of most other Asian states. When Bhutan introduced coordinated programs directed toward fundamental change, it was still a traditional society in the narrowest meaning of the term, untainted by the insidious concepts and values of Western origin that have quietly reshaped even those facets of cultures that are often identified as traditional in most other Asian societies.

We find, therefore, that virtually none of the groundwork that usually preceded planned modernization elsewhere had even begun in Bhutan when the third Druk Gyalpo, Jigme Dorji Wangchuck, came to the throne in 1952. Except for a minute proportion of the elite, the social structure, value system, and life style of the Bhutanese did not differ very much from that of their ancestors around 1500 when the Europeans first made their appearance in South Asia. Bhutan's ability to insulate itself over an extended period from the wide variety of political and social forces that dominated the Brahmaputra/Gangetic plains areas to the south must be considered a major accomplishment. Over the past 500 years Bhutan has had to contend with such diverse influences as strongly ethnocentric and expansionist Muslim rulers; a dynamic, traditional Hindu dynasty in Assam; British imperialists and Christian evangelists; assertive Indian nationalists whose concept of *Mahabharat* (Greater India) included all of the subcontinent and some territories beyond; an exotic mixture of dogmatic extremists preaching everything from Hindu fascism to Marxist-Leninist-Maoist brands of terrorism; and finally (and most critically for Bhutan) the democratic ideology that has dominated the Indian political movement since the late nineteenth century.

Given their pervasiveness in immediately adjacent areas, this combination of widely divergent forces should have had a decisive impact upon the Bhutanese culture and polity. The available evidence, however, would seem to indicate that such was not the case, and that Bhutan had successfully resisted penetration. And Bhutan's economy proved equally resilient. By 1950, for instance, some of the agricultural products that Westerners had introduced into South Asia in the seventeenth and eighteenth centuries had been adopted on an extensive scale in the neighboring Himalayan states of Nepal, Sikkim, and even Tibet, but were still unknown in Bhutan. So, too, in the field of education, the Bhutanese had been slow to adopt new plans and had been careful to maintain this vital social function as the exclusive prerogative of the Drukpa Buddhist establishment. A Western-style education system, structured to socialize the educated youth in secular political, social, and economic values, had evolved in neighboring areas in the nineteenth century, but was introduced in Bhutan only a few years before the Royal Government adopted a policy of comprehensive change.

Concepts of modernization and development were as novel and foreboding to most of the literate political elite in Bhutan as they were to the general public. Access to literature on the subject, moreover, was limited. There was not (and is not) a single library in all of Bhutan containing anything more than a few copies of the vast body of literature by Asian and Western pundits that provides elaborate, if often contradictory, developmental models. Bhutanese administrators entrusted with the introduction of programs of change had to devise strategies without the benefit of these guidelines to modernization—except, of course, when these were provided secondhand by Indian advisers.

Nevertheless, the impression one receives in Bhutan is of a comparatively smooth and efficient early-stage transition from a society in which the preservation of traditional institutions and customs was the primary task of government to one in which the process of modernization and change has become integral to the political system. There have been several crisis points over the past two decades but, as argued in Chapter 3, these have been more in the nature of power struggles within the political elite than ideological conflicts over the modernization policy *per se*. A very broad consensus within the elite has emerged on most issues. There is still an ongoing and vigorous debate, but this is not so much over goals as over how best to achieve goals that have been broadly accepted.

The decision-making process within the Royal Government continues to be a very narrow one, involving only a small number of officials in the governmental and religious establishments. It is a highly elitist system, and not much pretense is made that it is anything else. Popular mobilization on a very limited scale for developmental purposes (for example, for road construction) has occurred, but this is not to be confused with popular participation in the governance of the country (as it sometimes is in neighboring states both to the north and south). The elite rules, virtually unencumbered by the need to cater to popular prejudices, preferences, and interests. It is an elite, however, that has certain characteristics which distinguish it from elites in other Asian societies that are similarly in an early transitional stage from traditionalism to modernization. In the remaining sections of this chapter I shall attempt to illustrate this point by analyzing several crucial questions as they apply to Bhutan with special reference to the functioning of narrow elite political systems in which political participation is very restricted.

First, how is elite status attained or, more precisely, what are the operating principles employed by the Bhutanese political system to absorb or reject claimants to elite roles? This may well be the most critical problem faced by societies in which traditional elites are still dominant, and where upward mobility by the rest of the population is severely circumscribed. When traditional elite groups adopt policies of directed change they must either acquire new skills and capacities themselves or absorb recruits from previously excluded social groups that have these skills. Whatever the strategy employed, some changes in the elite selection process is unavoidable. Recruitment on the basis of traditional social criteria such as family, caste, religion, kinship, and so on is no longer sufficient, for that policy tends to create irreconcilable strains between *the society* in its historic setting and *the state* in its pursuit of innovative political and economic goals.

The recruitment and accommodation of new social groups into elite status is a complex and dangerous operation for the existing establishment, but one that is vital to the survival of any change-oriented system. For a country at Bhutan's stage of development, this task is necessarily accomplished through the dominant institutions, the monarchy and the bureaucracy, since alternative political institutions—such as parties, voluntary social, communal, or economic associations, and professional or labor-class organizations—are now virtually nonexistent and, hence, would be unlikely to assume a significant role for some time to come.[1] The focus in this chapter, therefore,

1. It might be argued that the National Assembly as an institution is also beginning to play an important role in the political process. But it is interesting to note that election to the Assembly from a regional constituency has not yet become a channel for advancement to the small clique that dominates the decision-making process. All of the ministers and other heads of department have come from the royal family or the bureaucracy, and no people's representative from the Assembly has yet been absorbed into this critical elite. Moreover, the evidence seems to indicate that it is the official representatives (that is,

will be on the monarchy and the bureaucracy as both elitist and governing institutions.

When Bhutan introduced programs of political and economic change in the late 1950s, there were several factors that permitted the Royal Government to expand the social base of the administrative system at a low cost to the existing elite. Perhaps the most important of these was the absence in Bhutan, in contrast to other South Asian states, of a highly developed and entrenched *national* bureaucracy with a long history, a powerful tradition, and a jealously guarded ascriptive-based recruitment system. With the exception of the Wangchucks and the Dorjis, the other families that could make some claim to elite status were essentially local in character, with at best regional support bases that did not guarantee them access to national political institutions. Indeed, for several decades prior to 1960, the ruling dynasty had recruited aides from nonelite families on a limited scale for positions in the administrative service in the palace and at the district level. This policy had been introduced initially to counter the dominant influence exerted by some competitive traditional elite families at the local level, but it also provided a ready-made process under which the social base of the national administrative system could be expanded. While this did not result in the total exclusion of members of local elite families from the bureaucracy, it did lessen the government's dependence upon their cooperation and support both politically and in the formulation and implementation of policy decisions. Thus, by 1960 some of the top officials in the administration came from nonelite familes that had little or nothing to lose from the introduction of cautious programs of change and modernization.

It is interesting to note the contrast between Bhutan and Nepal on this particular subject. By 1975, after a quarter-century of directed political and economic change, Nepal still had an entrenched bureaucracy dominated by a traditional

---

the bureaucrats) that tend to dominate the National Assembly. Thus, the existence of this representative institution may have complicated decision-making to some extent, but it has not yet modified its fundamental character.

elite in which approximately 90 percent of the higher posts
were held by members of the three communities—the Brah-
mans, Chettris, and Newaris—that have monopolized the administration since the unification of the country in 1769. This is
the critical factor in the functioning of the Nepali polity, for all
programs of development and modernization have had to be
formulated along lines that do not endanger the status and interests of this traditional national elite. Any decisions on policy
issues that run contrary to their interests, even if issued in the
form of royal ordinances, have been vigorously and successfully sabotaged at the implementation stage. The rhetoric used
by these bureaucrats is filled with participatory politics jargon,
but their practice is more often self-serving. As a consequence,
the bureaucracy in Nepal has generally served as an instrument
for the preservation of the political, social, and economic status
quo, and only rarely as an agent of change and growth. The
result has been what Riggs and Eisenstadt have correctly described as "negative development."

Bhutan has had a different recent history in this respect. The
rapidly expanding bureaucracy has been opened to a wide
range of Bhutanese from diverse social backgrounds, and this
is reflected now in the composition of the highest levels of the
administration. Moreover, there is still insufficient coherence
(and a lack of perceived shared interests) within the bureaucracy to allow it to function very effectively as an entity in the
political process.

The third Druk Gyalpo faced some criticism and opposition
from the small coterie of administrators around the palace
when he introduced his modernization programs, but nothing
that was systemic in character or even very persistent. So far,
the "new" bureaucracy has been a reasonably responsive and
effective instrument for the accomplishment of palace-deter-
mined goals, and has yet to develop a capacity or a will for
sabotaging policies and programs inimical to its interests
through its vital role in the implementation process. It is possible, indeed probable, that this new bureaucratic elite in Bhutan will eventually develop many of the traits of the dominant

traditional bureaucratic elite in Nepal and begin to act accordingly.[2] But that is a problem for future generations to cope with; at present the contemporary elite selection process is still relatively open and accessible.

A second question critical to narrow elitist systems such as Bhutan's is concerned with the institutional mechanisms used to determine the allocation of power or, more broadly, the apportionment of participation in the decision-making process. In modernization theory, the principal focus on this issue has been on the strategies used to transform a society from one in which "ascriptive" principles are predominant to a process under which certain acquired skills (usually called merit-based skills) and institutionalized procedures determine the allocation of authority.[3] But once again Bhutan does not seem to fit the norm as observed in most other developing societies. As already noted, it lacked an entrenched ascriptively defined traditional elite, for the bureaucracy was created *de novo* for all intents and purposes in the post-1960 period on what was essentially a merit basis.

The selection procedure was comparatively simple and straightforward, for virtually all appointments at the higher and middle levels of the bureaucracy were made by the king—personally. This may not have been the nonpersonal kind of "institutionalized procedure" that is advocated by most developmental theorists, but in Bhutan it has had some of the desirable consequences of instituionalization in that it has resulted in a bureaucracy in which performance is at least as important

2. It would be reasonably safe to predict, for instance, that most of the small number of students sent abroad for higher education in the next decade (thus qualifying for the top positions in the administration) will come from the new elite families. Indeed, this was already evident on a limited scale by the mid-1970s.
3. This may seem axiomatic, but it is sometimes forgotten that the dichotomy between ascriptive and merit-based systems is not as fundamental as assumed. So-called merit selection systems inevitably contain much that is ascriptive, as indicated in studies of the social origins of successful applicants for elite status in such diverse societies as the United States, Great Britain, the Soviet Union, and Japan. Ascriptive systems, on the other hand, do not exclude merit as one criteria in the selection process, although this may not weigh as much as ascriptive factors.

as ascriptive factors in situations relating to appointments to critical administrative posts and an influential role in the decision-making process.

The substantial expansion of the bureaucracy and the creation of new political institutions have made procedural modifications essential, and the Royal Government has been moving in that direction since 1965. An effort is being made to depersonalize bureaucratic procedures, particularly with respect to appointments and promotions, by having the palace share responsibility in this field with several other political institutions. The National Assembly, for instance, has been assigned a role in the process through its power to approve the appointment or removal of ministers who head the various departments of government. So far, most of the ministers have come directly from the bureaucracy [4] and their appointment to ministerial status placed them at the top of the administrative system. Making them responsible to the Assembly, however, could serve to expand and depersonalize the appointment process to some extent, as, in the future, candidates who have the National Assembly as their constituency are accommodated into the bureaucratic elite.

Institutionalization of the administrative system has also been advanced through the enactment of rules of procedure that are merit-based and very specific in defining the criteria to be used on personnel matters. Indeed, public administration theorists might well consider the Bhutanese regulations as a model for emulation in other developing societies. Reality, however, is more complicated. These rules are largely the product of Indian advisers who merely utilized the principles of public administration expounded in the Western textbooks on this subject, somewhat adjusted to Indian administrative conditions. But in fact, the bureaucracy in Bhutan is still such an intimate body that broad-scale depersonalization of its operations is not feasible, even if it were desirable—which is a debatable ques-

4. The only exceptions to date have been members of the royal family who have been given ministerial status either directly or in slightly disguised forms. In other South Asian states, including Nepal, it is still uncommon for bureaucrats to be appointed to ministerial positions.

tion. Nevertheless, overt nepotism or patron-client relationships are the exception. A young, ambitious bureaucrat
may still require support from above, but in most cases he must
also earn his promotion through a good performance record as
well.

Another aspect of this question concerns the mechanisms developed to involve both political and social institutions and
groups in the decision-making process, thus broadening the
base of political participation. In this respect, Bhutan's recent
record has been mixed, with expansion in participation in some
directions but little change or even some retrogression in others. It has been suggested, for instance, that the decision-making process is more restrictive in the mid-1970s than it was during the last years of the reign of the third Druk Gyalpo. This
change in the rules is usually attributed to the re-emergence of
the Dorji family as a strong influence in the palace at the expense of the ministers, bureaucrats, National Assembly members, and even the Buddhist establishment, all of whom had a
different kind of relationship to the former ruler from that
pertaining today. In the process, it has been argued, decision-
making is more narrowly a palace-courtier enterprise than at
any time since 1965.

Whether this actually is the trend is very difficult for an outside observer to determine. But even if this should be the case,
it would seem probable that this is a temporary, transitional
phase, and one that will prevail only until the youthful ruler
who succeeded to the throne in 1972 at the age of seventeen
has acquired more sophistication and confidence in the exercise
of his high office and greater skill in dealing with the complex,
intricately interwoven political system that was devised by the
third Druk Gyalpo to suit *his* personality and requirements, and
the human resources he then had available and could trust.
Over the long run it would be very difficult to reverse the process under which participation in decision-making was first
thrust upon and then eagerly accepted by an uncertain and
untried bureaucracy and National Assembly. Depriving these
institutions of powers and functions which they have enjoyed
for nearly a decade, while plausible on a short-term basis,

would be likely to inflict permanent damage on the viability of the monarchical system.

Nor can contemporary history elsewhere in the Himalayas be ignored. Recent events in the neighboring principality of Sikkim have strongly impressed all elements of the Bhutanese elite with the dangers involved in internecine conflicts that serve to divide them as a governing force and raise the spectre of internal political instability or even chaos. The delicate balance among the participating factions in the decision-making process is bound to be tentative, shifting, and changing as circumstances seem to require. But the impression one receives in Bhutan is that the overall trend continues to be in the direction of increasing political participation leading to a system that is more broadly representative of the major social units comprising Bhutan's society.

The most encouraging aspect of this trend is the success achieved in introducing programs of political and economic change within the framework of the existing political system. Moreover, to date this has been accomplished without the destructive intraelite conflict that too often has accompanied the change process elsewhere in Asia. While the events of 1964–1965 constituted a systemic as well as a political crisis in Bhutan, and one that was overcome only with considerable difficulty, so far this agitation has occurred only once. The successful accommodation of new groups (such as the leading families in the Nepali community in southern Bhutan) into the elite structure, and their absorption into the existing factional system, has been particularly impressive.

There was the possibility in the early 1960s that the elite would become so fractionalized on policy issues that coordination and cooperation would no longer be possible, and that the regime, in response, would become more rigid and brittle by seeking to suppress rather than accommodate emerging social groups. This would have have hardened the existing divisions within Bhutan society and would have put a premium on the use of violence and force in the place of consensus and compromise. Bhutan might then have reverted to the near-chaos and permanent civil war conditions that characterized its politics in the nineteenth century. The survival of the country, and not just the political system, would have been endangered.

That this did not happen is largely attributable to the determination of most elements in the elite to avoid divisive politics at all cost, an attitude that was still evident in the mid-1970s when dissident members of the Dorji family were accepted back into the political system by their erstwhile opponents on a live-and-let-live basis. The Dorjis, for their part, did not insist upon a purge of those elements that had supported their expulsion from the country a decade earlier. The role of India in encouraging a broad consensual political process has also been an important factor, for New Delhi has generally encouraged and supported Bhutan in its efforts to expand political participation and democratize the political system. Whether developments in India in 1975 will lead to basic changes in that country in the direction of a command (that is, a more authoritarian) system is still uncertain. If this should prove to be the case, then the kinds of pressures placed upon Bhutan by the Indian presence in the country and the ubiquity of Indian attitudinal and ideological influences could eventually have a substantial impact on the political process in Bhutan as well, probably in the long-run in a destabilizing direction.

A third question of potential importance to Bhutan is the viability of the monarchy as the principal agent of change. Bhutan is not unique, of course, in having a "revolutionary" ruler decide to introduce basic reform programs directed at the modernization of a traditional system. Most monarchical polities, both surviving and extinct, went through the same experience at some point in their history. What makes Bhutan somewhat atypical, however, is the virtual nonexistence of competing elite groups ready to undertake this task, and thus the heavy dependence upon a strong-willed and determined monarch for the introduction and implementation of such programs. In most monarchical societies there have been other modernizing agents available: dissident elements within the traditional elite; new elites that are the products of a nontraditional education and socialization system; modernized bureaucratic and military institutions; and the leaders of political organizations, whether extremist (at either end) or middle-of-the-road in their politics. These elite cliques assisted and encouraged the monarch's programs for change, but they were also ready to depose monarchs, or even abolish the monarchical system itself, when this seemed necessary to advance their personal, group, or national interests.[5]

This has not yet been the case in Bhutan, as there have been no institutional competitors to the monarchy and none are evident on the horizon even now. It is not inconceivable that the monarchy could be eliminated through one of the small-scale conspiracies so common to Bhutan's political tradition, but the price paid would likely be high. If this should occur, there is no other institution, group, or individual around that has the capability to rule the country on other than brute-force terms. There are no party organizations, even in an embryonic stage of development, that could provide leadership and legitimacy to a revolutionary regime. The bureaucracy is reasonably competent in administrative tasks, but would probably divide into small cliques and eventually collapse if faced with the responsibilities of governance. Both the military and the police are too new and insecure psychologically to serve, as they have elsewhere, as the bulwark of a new political system. The National Assembly, reflecting localist interests, is inexperienced and indecisive in its approach to national questions and could not be expected to provide the leadership a new system would require. And finally there is the realization at all levels among the elite that neither India nor China could be expected to ignore a condition of political disorder and instability in such a highly strategic buffer area.

Thus, in the mid-1970s there is a broad consensus within the elite on the indispensability of the monarchy, but the question remains whether this institution can continue to serve as effectively as *the* agent of change in the future as it has over the past two decades. In this respect, the record of monarchical polities in the

5. It is interesting to note that the monarchical systems that have been eliminated in the Third World have all been the victims of intraelite coups rather than of popular revolutionary movements. It is the governments that succeed them, sometimes far more radical but always also far more unstable, that are much more vulnerable to mass-based political movements.

twentieth century cannot be very reassuring. Samuel Huntington, in his seminal essay on this subject, has projected a grim
future for the few remaining monarchies, no matter what policies
and strategies they may devise.

These [monarchical] political systems were involved in a fundamental
dilemma. On the one hand, centralization of power in the monarchy
was necessary to promote social, cultural and economic reforms. On
the other hand, this centralization made difficult or impossible the expansion of the power of the traditional polity and the assimilation of
the new groups produced by modernization. The participation of
these groups in politics seemingly could come only at the price of the
monarchy.[6]

The problems faced by change-minded monarchs under this
analysis of the situation are simple but perplexing: if they introduce basic reform programs, they antagonize the traditional
elite; if they do not, the modernizing elite is alienated. Both
forces have the potential to overthrow the monarchical system,
and thus neither can be safely ignored. Huntington concludes:

Whichever course they take, what does seem certain is that the existing
monarchies will lose some or all of whatever capability they have developed for policy innovations under traditional auspices before they
gain any substantial new capability to cope with the problems of political participation produced by their own reforms.[7]

Huntington provides persuasive evidence to support his conclusion that the struggle between a pro-status quo traditional
elite and a pro-change modernizing elite is likely to be fatal to
any monarchical system lacking the western European (and
Japanese?) political-cultural background. It is too early to tell
whether Bhutan will follow this path also or will prove to be an
exception to the general rule, but one might suggest that the
latter possibility is not unreasonable in the Bhutanese context.
It should be noted that the Huntington formula does not apply
in at least one key respect, namely, in Bhutan there is no strong
traditional elite bitterly opposed to programs of change. The
closest approximation to such an institution is the Buddhist establishment, but this is a traditional elite with a difference. So

6. Samuel Huntington, *Political Order in Changing Societies* (New Haven: Yale
University Press, 1968), p. 177.
7. *Ibid.*, p. 191.

far, at least, all but the few basic changes in the political and economic systems in Bhutan that directly intruded upon the religious and cultural prerogatives of the Drukpa sect have been accepted without too much distress. The high lamas may be instinctively conservative, but they bear no resemblance to an aristocratic, landowning class that is usually subsumed under the traditional elite category in Asia, and there is no reason to expect the lamas to react to reform programs as would the landowners.

The *only* politically articulate elite in Bhutan, thus, is the modernizing elite, some of whom, like most of the people's representatives in the National Assembly, may be conservative and cautious modernizers; others, such as the young educated bureaucrats, may prefer to move ahead at a slightly faster pace. But virtually all members of the elite have accepted the palace's position that change and development are essential to Bhutan's survival—as well as to their own.

There is the possibility that at some point in the future the monarchy will fall behind the educated elite in its enthusiasm for modernization. According to one young educated Ethiopian, this is what happened in his country: "Ten years ago," he said, "even five years ago, the Emperor was ahead and leading us. Now it is we, the educated elite, educated by his order, who are leading and the Emperor who lags behind."[8]

But the cultural, political, and economic factors that led the emperor in Ethiopia to reconsider many aspects of his modernization program in the late 1960s do not necessarily apply in Bhutan. There is no reason to assume that the palace will have to surrender the leading role it has played in the modernization of Bhutan to some other elite group, much less to any kind of popular movement. Internal political and cultural factors make continuity and stability both feasible and attractive to most elements in the elite, and to the general populace as well. Whether the outside world is prepared to allow Bhutan to develop at its own pace and according to its own cultural imperatives, however, may prove to be another matter.

8. *Ibid.*, p. 188, quoting *The New York Times*, March 8, 1966.

Glossary

Bhotias: Bhutanese of Tibetan ancestry

Chilas: regional officers under the Shabdung system; title later changed to Pönlop

Chu: river

Chunidom: an unpaid involuntary labor system under which all non-exempted Bhutanese contributed a specified number of hours each year for state-defined projects

Dagpi Lopon: one of the five highest officials in the Drukpa monk body in Bhutan

Dapon: literally "Arrow Chief"; the commander of the Bhutan militia during periods of crisis under the Shabdung system

Dasho: title given to red-scarf (high administrative or judicial) officials

Debai Drönyer: the "treasurer" under the Shabdung system; member of the State Council

Dechap: head of a regional office of the Bhutan police

Dorji Lopon: the second highest official in the Drukpa monk body

Dozin: officer of Brigadier rank in the Bhutan army

Druk Desi: the "Regent of Drukyul"; the head administrative officer under the Shabdung system (1650–1907); called Deb Raja in most Western-language sources

Druk Gyalpo: the "King of Drukyul"; the title given the Wangchuk monarchs since 1907

Drukpa: subbranch of the red-hat Kagyupa Buddhist sect in Tibet; dominant sect in Bhutan

Drukyul: literally the "country of the Drukpas"; traditional name for Bhutan since the seventeenth century

Duars: plains area at the foot of the Bhutan hills

Dungpa: administrative officer at the district level

Dzong: literally "fort," but also used to designate district in Bhutan

Dzongda: title given district officers in the larger districts since 1969

Dzongkha: literally "language of the Dzong"; a Tibetan dialect and also the official language in Bhutan

Dzongpön: district officer

Dzongtasp: deputy district officer

Gakpen: head of the Bhutan police

Gedunpa: the Drukpa Central Monk Body at Thimphu/Punakha

Gelugpa: the yellow-hat Mahayana Buddhist sect led by the Dalai Lama that dominated Tibet politically from the mid-seventeenth century to 1950

Gongzim: translated as "chief chamberlain"; title used by the head of the Dorji family from 1908 to 1958

Gup: village headman in the western and eastern Bhutan highlands

Gyaldon: Royal Chief Secretary

Gyaltse: Royal Finance Secretary

Gyaltsi Khalowa: Royal Revenue Office

Gyelon Chichap: Secretary-General in the Development Ministry

Je Khempo: translated as "Lord Abbot"; the administrative head of the Drukpa monk body in Bhutan

Kepon: head of a district police unit

Kham: eastern Tibet

Khampas: literally the "people of Kham" (eastern Tibet)

Ku trulku: the "body" incarnation of the first Shabdung; incarnation has not appeared since the mid-eighteenth century

Lhengyel: a "Minister" under both the Shabdung and monarchical systems

Lhengyel Tsok: Council of Ministers; established in 1968

Lhotsam Chichap: Commissioner for southern Bhutan (1955–1965)

Lhungye Shuntsog: the "State Committee" formed in 1968 as a superadvisory body to the king

Lhungye Tsok: the "State Council" established by the first Shabdung in the seventeenth century

Lodoi Tsokde: Royal Advisory Council

Lonchen: translated as "Prime Minister"; title used by the head of the Dorji family from 1958 to 1965

Lyonpo: honorary title given members of the Council of Ministers

Maksi Ogma: officer of Lt. Colonel rank in the Bhutan army

Mandal: village headman in southern Bhutan

Nyerchin: district revenue officer

Nyingmapa: the "old sect" in Tibetan Buddhism; active in Bhutan since about the tenth century A.D.

Pönlop: regional governor; Paro and Tongsa were the two most important, but there were several others under the Shabdung system
Ramjam: assistant to the district officer in the larger districts; head administrative officer in the smaller districts
Satyagraha: a nonviolent resistance movement; concept generally associated with Mohandas Gandhi in India
Shabdung: the spiritual and temporal sovereign of Bhutan (1650–1907); called "Dharma Raja" in most Western-language sources
Shapto Hurla: the list of the labor force eligible for work on *chunidom* projects
Shung Drönyer: member of the royal advisory body under the first two Wangchuck kings
Shung Kalön: translated as "Chief Minister"; member of the State Council under the Shabdung system; chairman of the Royal Advisory Council under the Wangchuck dynasty
Sipchu Kazi: the head administrative officer in southern Bhutan until 1955
Sung trulku: the "speech" incarnation of the first Shabdung
Thimkhang: district court
Thimkhang Gongma: the Bhutan High Court
Thimpön: district court judge
Thu trulku: the "mind" incarnation of the first Shabdung; all seven subsequent Shabdungs were of this incarnation
Trulku: incarnate in the Mahayana Buddhist system
Tshannyi Lopon: one of the five highest officials in the Drukpa monk body in Bhutan
Tshogdu: the "National Assembly" established in 1953 by the third Druk Gyalpo
Yongpi Lopon: one of the five highest officials in the Drukpa monk body in Bhutan
Yongzim: assistant administrative officer in the Bhutan police
Zimpön: translated as "Chamberlain"; were the principal aides-de-camp to the Shabdung and the Druk Desi; were also members of the State Council under the Shabdung system
Zing Gyap: traditional militia units in Bhutan

Selected Bibliography

Archival and Press and Periodical Sources

The archival materials on Bhutan in the Indian National Library (New Delhi) and the India Office Library (London) were used extensively, and provided some documentary basis for the historical analysis of modern Bhutan. There are no central Bhutanese archives as yet, but the author was given selective access to documents from various government departments, the files of Bhutanese officials or other public figures, and the manuscript collection in the Bhutan National Library, now in the process of being established.

The only press source in Bhutan is the semi-official *Kuensel*, which is the closest thing to an official gazette in the country. The English-language press and periodicals in India and the press in Nepal were also used extensively, particularly for their coverage of developments during certain crisis periods in Bhutan.

Post-1950 Chinese published sources were also utilized, as translated by the *Survey China Mainland Press* and the *Survey China Mainland Journals* (U.S. Consulate-General, Hong Kong). A number of pre-1950 Chinese publications were also used, the most important of which for Bhutan were:

Chin-Ting-K'uo-er-k'a Chi-Lueh (Official Summary of the Pacification of the Gorkhas), Peking, 1796. 54 plus 4 chuan in 8 volumes.

Ch'ing-Chi-Ch'ou-Tsang-Tsou-Tu (Memorials and Correspondence Concerning the Arrangements of Affairs during the Latter Part of the Ch'ing Dynasty), Peiping: National Academy, 1938. 3 volumes.

Ch'ou-Pan-I-Wu Shih-Mo (Documents Concerning the Management of Foreign Affairs), Peiping: Palace Museum, 1930.

Books and Monographs

Aitchison, Charles Umpherston. *A Collection of Treaties, Engagements, and Sanads Relating to India and Neighbouring Countries.* Calcutta: Govt. of India Central Publication Branch, 1929.

Blagojevie', Moma. *Himalajske Knezevine (Himalayan Principalities)*. Beograd: Sedama Sila, 1966, 62 pp.

Coelho, Vincent Herbert. *Sikkim and Bhutan*. Delhi: Vikas Publications, 1971, 138 pp.

Das, Nirmala. *The Dragon Country: The General History of Bhutan*. Bombay: Orient Longmans, 1974, 99 pp.

Griffith, William. *Journals of Travels in Assam, Burma, Bootan, Aghanistan and the Neighbouring Countries*. Calcutta: Bishop's College Press, 1847.

Haab, Armin. *Bhutan, Fürstenstaat am Götterthron*. (Text by Ninon Vellis and Armin Haab.) Güttersloh: S. Mohn, 1961, 173 pp.

Harris, George L., and others. *U.S. Army Area Handbook for Nepal* (with Sikkim and Bhutan). Washington, D.C.: U.S. Govt. Printing Office, 1964, 448 pp. (Pp. 389–423 are on Bhutan.)

Hunter, William Wilson. *The Imperial Gazetteer of India*. Oxford: Clarendon Press, 1908–1909. (Bhutan is discussed in Volume II of the 2nd ed.)

India, Survey of India Department. *Report on the Explorations in Sikkim, Bhutan and Tibet*. Dehra, Dun: Office of the Trignometrical Branch, Survey of India, 1889, 57 pp.

Karan, Pradyumna. *Bhutan: A Physical and Cultural Geography*. Lexington: Kentucky University Press, 1967, 108 pp.

Karen, Pradyumna, and William M. Jenkins, Jr. *The Himalayan Kingdoms: Bhutan, Sikkim and Nepal*. Lexington: Kentucky University Press, 1967, 144 pp.

Labh, Kapileshwar. *India and Bhutan*. New Delhi: Sindhu Publications, 1974, 275 pp.

Louis, Julien Adrien Hilaire. *The Gates of Tibet: A Bird's Eye View of Independent Sikkim, British Bhootan, and the Dooars, as a Doorga Poojah Trip*. Calcutta: Catholic Orphan Press, 1894, 183 pp.

Mackenzie, Alexander. *A History of the Relation of the Government with the Hill Tribes on the North-East Frontiers of Bengal*. Calcutta: Home Department Press, 1884, 586 pp.

Markham, Clement R. (editor). *Narratives of the Mission of George Bogle to Tibet, and of the Journey of Thomas Manning to Lhasa*. London: Trubner, 1879, 362 pp.

Papers Relating to Bootan: Accounts and Papers, 1865 (Volume 29); and *Further Papers Relating to Bootan: Accounts and Papers, 1866* (Volume 52). London: House of Commons, Government of the United Kingdom, 1865, 1866.

Peissel, Michel. *Lords and Lamas: A Solitary Expedition across the Secret*

Himalayan Kingdom of Bhutan. London: Heinemann, 1970, 180 pp. (English Translation from the French).

Peissel, Michel. *Bhoutan: Royasime d'Asie Inconnu.* Paris: Arthaud, 1971, 225 pp.

Pemberton, R. Boileau. *Report on Bootan, with an Appendix and Maps, 1838.* Calcutta: G. H. Huttman, Bengal Military Orphan Press, 1839. (Reprinted in *Indian Studies: Past and Present,* 2 [July 1961], 665–723; 3 [Oct. 1961], 31–82; and by K. C. Mukhopadhyaya, Calcutta, 1961.)

Political Missions to Bootan, Comprising the Reports of the Hon'able Ashley Eden, 1864, Capt. R. B. Pemberton, 1837, with Dr. W. Griffith's Journal; and the Account by Baboo Kishen Kant Bose. Calcutta: Bengal Secretariat Office, 1865, 206 pp.

Prazauskas, Al'Gimantas. *Bhutan Sikkim.* Moskva: Nanka, 1970, 71 pp.

Rahul, Ram. *The Himalayan Borderland.* Delhi: Vikas Publications, 1970, 157 pp.

Rahul, Ram. *Modern Bhutan.* Delhi: Vikas Publications, 1971, 173 pp.

Rathore, Laxman Singh. *The Changing Bhutan.* New Delhi: Jain Brothers, 1974, 168 pp.

Rennie, David Field. *Bhotan and the Story of the Doar War.* New Delhi: Manjusri Pub. House, 1970, 408 pp. (Bibliotheca Himalayica Series 1, vol. 5; first published, 1866.)

Ronaldshay, Earl of (Lawrence John L. S. Zetland). *Lands of the Thunderbolt: Sikkim, Chumbie, and Bhutan.* London: Constable and Co., 1923, 267 pp.

Rose, Leo E. *Bhutan.* Dobbs Ferry, New York: Oceana Publications, 1974, 31 pp. (Constitutions of the Countries of the World Series.)

Rustomji, Nari. *Enchanted Frontiers: Sikkim, Bhutan and India's Northeastern Borderlands.* Bombay: Oxford University Press, 1971, 333 pp.

Sandberg, Graham. *Bhotan: The Unknown Indian State.* Calcutta: 1897.

Singh, Nagendra. *Bhutan: A Kingdom in the Himalayas; A Study of the Land, Its People and Their Government.* New Delhi: Thompson Press, 1972, 202 pp.

Turner, Samuel. *An Account of an Embassy to the Court of the Teshoo Lama in Tibet; Containing a Narrative of a Journey Through Bhutan and Part of Tibet.* New Delhi: Manjusri Publishing House, 1971, 473 pp. (First published in French in 1800.)

White, J. Claude. *Sikkim and Bhutan: Twenty-one Years on the North-East Frontier, 1887–1908.* Delhi: Vivek, 1971, 331 pp. (First published in 1909.)

Woodman, Dorothy. *Himalayan Frontiers: A Political Review of British,*

Chinese, Indian and Russian Rivalries. New York: Praeger, 1970, 423 pp.

Journal and Press Articles and Papers

Agrawal, K. N. "Indo-Bhutanese Relations," *Political Scientist,* 4 (July–Dec. 1967/Jan.–June 1968), 41–46.

"Anti-Indian Activity by Bhutan Fugitives," *The Hindu Weekly Review,* 13:50 (Dec. 14, 1964), 14.

Australia, Department of External Affairs. "Sikkim and Bhutan," *Current Notes on International Affairs,* 33:12 (Dec. 1962), 5–13.

Bajpai, S. C. "India and Bhutan," *Foreign Affairs Reports,* 13 (Sept. 1964), 141–145.

Bajpai, S. C. "Bhutan: The Himalayan State," *Parliamentary Studies,* 8 (Oct.–Nov. 1964), 14–17.

Banerji, Shibdas. "Bhutan: The Land of the Thunder Dragon," *Amrita Bazar Patrika,* 2:5 (Jan. 11, 1953).

Belfiglio, Valentine J. "India's Economic and Political Relations with Bhutan," *Asian Survey,* 12:8 (Aug. 1972), 676–685.

Bhattacharya, Madhusudhan. "Bhutan in Turmoil," *Mainstream,* 3:16 (Dec. 19, 1964), 8.

"Bhutan and the Chinese," *The Hindu Weekly Review* (July 13, 1964), 5.

"Bhutan and India: Partners in Progress," *Indian and Foreign Review,* 1:3 (Nov. 15, 1963), 18–20.

Bhutan State Congress. "Bhutan's Woes," *Mankind,* 4:7 (Feb. 1960), 43–45.

"Bhutan's Changing Face" (six articles by a "Special Correspondent"), *The Hindustan Times* (June 14, 15, 16, 17, 18, 20, 1960).

"Bhutan's Special Relations with India" (by a "Special Correspondent") *The Hindu Weekly Review* (June 1966), 1–4.

Brinkworth, Ian. "Bhutan, the Unknown Country," *The Geographical Magazine,* 36:6 (Oct. 1963), 320–335.

Deb, A. "Diarchy in Bhutan: the Dharma Raja-Deb Raja System," *Bengal Past and Present,* 91:172 (Pt. II; July–Dec. 1972), 158–165.

Deb, A. "George Bogle's Treaty with Bhutan (1775)," *Bulletin of Tibetology* (Feb. 26, 1971), 5–14.

Deb, A. "Cooch Behar and Bhutan in the Context of Tibetan Trade," *Kailash,* 1:1 (1973), 80–88.

Dev, Murakha. "Isolated Bhutan," *Eastern World,* 15:5 (May 1961), 13–14.

Doig, Desmond. "Changing Face of Bhutan: Roads and Reforms for the Dragon People," *The Statesman* (Aug. 28, 1959), 6.

Doig, Desmond. "Bhutan: Mountain Kingdom between India and Tibet," *National Geographic,* 120 (Sept. 1961), 384–415.

Doig, Desmond. "Report on Bhutan" (three articles), *The Statesman Overseas Weekly* (May 9, 16, and 23, 1964).

Doig, Desmond. "Bhutan Recoups from Political Crisis," *The Statesman* (May 29, 1965).

Field, A. R. "Bhutan, Kham and the Upper Assam Line," *Orbis,* 3 (Summer 1959), 180–192.

Field, A. R. "A Note Concerning Early Anglo-Bhutanese Relations," *East and West,* 13 (Dec. 1962), 340–345.

Gurung, D. B., "Political Problems of Bhutan," *United Asia,* 12:4 (1960), 368–369.

Halder, Hem Chandra. "India's Neighbour: Bhutan," *Modern Review,* 107 (April 1960), 307–311.

Hess, Peter. "Bhutan: The Problems of a Buffer State," *Swiss Review of World Affairs,* 18 (Nov. 1968), 14–17.

"India Bhutan Ties," *Link* (Dec. 20, 1964).

Kakodkar, Avadhuth. "Bhutan and Sikkim" (paper prepared for Himalayan Seminar, Delhi, Dec. 20–23, 1965).

Kapur, B. K. "Sikkim and Bhutan," *Commonwealth Journal,* 5 (Nov. 1962), 275–277.

Karan, Pradyumna. "Bhutan and Sikkim: Himalayan Shangri-la, now darkened by Communist China's shadow, faces up to the 20th century," *Canadian Geographical Journal,* 65 (Dec. 1962), 200–209.

Karan, Pradyumna. "Geopolitical Structure of Bhutan," *India Quarterly,* 19 (July 1963), 203–213.

Krishnamoorthy, K. "Bhutan: Thoughts of Sovereignty," *Far Eastern Economic Review,* 31:7 (Feb. 16, 1961), 295–297.

Labh, Kapileshwar. "The International Status of Bhutan before 1947," *International Studies,* 13:1 (Jan.–March 1974), 75–93.

Levi, Werner. "India's Himalayan Border," *The Contemporary Review* (July 1955), 40–44.

Levi, Werner. "Bhutan and Sikkim: Two Buffer States," *The World Today,* 15 (Dec. 1959), 492–500.

Mathew, K. S. "Bhutan," *The Illustrated Weekly of India,* 64:26 (July 1, 1973), 36–39.

Mehra, P. L. "Sikkim and Bhutan: An Historical Conspectus," *Journal of Indian History,* 46 (April 1968), 89–124.

Morris, C. J. "A Journey in Bhutan," *The Geographical Journal* (1935), 201–215.

Nag, B. C. "Bhutan: A Land in Transition," *Indo-Asian Culture*, 20:1 (Jan. 1971), 30–35.

Pandit, Tooshar. "Behind Bhutan's Throne," *Eastern World*, 18 (Nov. 1964), 7–9.

Parker, E. H. "China, Nepaul, Bhutan, and Sikkim; Their Mutual Relations As Set Forth in Chinese Official Documents," *Journal of the Manchester Oriental Society* (1911), 129–152.

Petech, Luciano. "The Rulers of Bhutan *c.* 1650–1750," *Oriens Extremus*, 19:1–2 (Dec. 1972), 203–213.

Polsky, Anthony. "Bhutan: Palace Politics," *Far Eastern Economic Review*, 69:31 (July 30, 1970), 25–28.

Poulouse, T. T. "Bhutan's External Relations and India," *International and Comparative Law Quarterly*, 20 (Pt. 2; April 1971), 295–312.

Rawlings, E. H. "The Buffer States of Sikkim and Bhutan," *Eastern World*, 16 (Nov. 1962), 12–13.

Rose, Leo E. "Sino-Indian Rivalry and the Himalayan Border States," *Orbis*, 15 (1961), 198–215.

Rose, Leo E. "The Himalayan Border States: 'Buffers' in Transition," *Asian Survey*, 3 (Feb. 1963), 116–121.

Rose, Leo E. "Bhutan's External Relations," *Pacific Affairs*, 47:2 (Summer 1974), 192–208.

White, J. Claude. "Journeys in Bhutan," *Geographical Journal*, 35:1 (Jan. 1910), 18–40.

"Who Inspired Bhutan Coup," *Link* (Dec. 20, 1964).

Index

Library of Congress Cataloging in Publication Data
(For library cataloging purposes only)

Rose, Leo F.
    The politics of Bhutan.

    (South Asian political systems)
    Bibliography: p.
    Includes index.
    1. Bhutan—Politics and government.   I. Title.   II. Series.
DS485.B503R6   320.9′549′8   77-4792
ISBN 0-8014-0909-8